Pseudo-Memoirs

Frontiers of Narrative

SERIES EDITOR

Jesse E. Matz, Kenyon College

Pseudo-Memoirs

Life and Its Imitation in Modern Fiction

ROCHELLE TOBIAS

University of Nebraska Press | Lincoln

Portions of chapter 2 previously appeared as "The Double Fiction in Robert Walser's *Jakob von Gunten*," in *German Quarterly* 79, no. 3 (Summer 2006): 293–307.

Set in Minion Pro by Mikala R. Kolander.

For Ashvin

Contents

Figures

Acknowledgments

A study this long in coming acquires many debts. I cannot begin to thank the many individuals who, in one form or another, have contributed to this project. If I have done them justice, they will see and hear themselves in these pages along with other friends.

I thank my undergraduate and graduate students at Johns Hopkins with whom I have had the privilege of reading literature together over the years and whose insights have always inspired me and challenged my own preconceptions. Many colleagues near and far have discussed various authors with me, read drafts of chapters, and offered invaluable insights. Elke Siegel introduced me to Robert Walser's work almost two decades ago, and I cannot begin to express my gratitude to her for this gift. Naveeda Khan, Kristina Mendicino, and Yi-Ping Ong patiently read through multiple iterations of the introduction and pushed me to clarify the terms of my analysis, to be bolder in my approach, and to be mindful of scholarship. Yi-Ping's encyclopedic knowledge of the novel and its criticism gave my arguments a depth they would not have had; Naveeda's insistence on examples turned purely speculative claims into sharper and more nuanced arguments; Kristina's eye for detail and sensitivity to literary language helped me reconceive key propositions and interpretations. Our meeting of minds in all matters phenomenological has been an extraordinary pleasure. Rüdiger Campe pointed out to me critical passages in *Jakob von Gunten* that reinforced my analysis. I thank him for his generosity of spirit in bolstering a reading, even when it did not match his own interpretation. Marion Picker has been an always insightful, kind, and wise friend whose poetic sensibility colors all my readings.

I have received encouragement, advice, and inspiration from many friends and colleagues on a range of issues from autobiography and story-telling to phenomenology, realism, and idealism: they include Sharon Bisco, Kenneth Calhoon, Márton Dornbach, Eckart Förster,

Samuel Frederick, Jennifer Gosetti-Ferencei, Philippe P. Haensler, Anja Lemke, Michael G. Levine, David Martyn, Jean McGarry, Katrin Pahl, Henry Pickford, Elena Russo, Thomas Schestag, Ann Smock, Sam Spinner, Nicolas de Warren, and Elisabeth Weber. I thank them for the spirited dialogue from which I have learned more than I can possibly convey.

I owe a special debt of gratitude to Bridget Barry for shepherding the manuscript through the review process with an expert hand, and to Heather Stauffer for overseeing the book's production in the most professional and friendly manner. The University of Nebraska Press solicited two perceptive and incisive reviews that guided my revisions and made for a better manuscript. I thank Gerhard Richter for pointing out how to extend the discussion of intentionality beyond a narrow frame and Jan Mieszkowski for illuminating tips on the connection of this study to recent scholarship on form and realism.

An abbreviated version of chapter 2 appeared in *German Quarterly*. I thank the editors of the journal for granting me permission to reprint it. I am also grateful to the estate of W. G. Sebald for permission to reprint three images from the novel *Vertigo* and one from *The Rings of Saturn*. Tucker Smith at the Andrew Wylie Agency in New York handled my permissions request with consummate professionalism and made what could have been a bureaucratic nightmare into a painless episode. I am equally grateful to Jens Tremmel in the Photo and Digitization Department of the German Literary Archive in Marbach am Neckar for finding the images I wanted in Sebald's papers and for arranging for their reproduction quickly and conscientiously. This was no small feat, given that my request came during a pandemic.

My parents never lost faith in this project, and I am grateful to them for that and so much more. Ashvin was the midwife for this book. The delivery could not have happened without him. I dedicate this book to him.

Pseudo-Memoirs

Introduction
Phenomenology and the Truth of Fiction

Je crois me souvenir, je m'invente.

—LOUIS ARAGON, *Le mentir-vrai*

Many have sung the death knell of the novel, none more forcefully than modern novelists themselves, who have questioned the principle of verisimilitude that has defined the genre since its inception. The principle is by no means limited to the novel—Aristotle identified it with literature in general in his *Poetics*—but it has a special relation to a genre that claims to do nothing less than narrate the lives of fictional characters in a fictional universe. A critic as attuned to the history of the genre as Marthe Robert can thus state that the novel is "the only form of art which tries to make us believe that it gives a complete and truthful account of a real person's life."[1] Novels deceive the reader, as Robert would have it, by creating a semblance of life that could be mistaken for historical fact, owing to the prose form of the genre. Prose enables the novel to mask what other genres written in more conspicuously literary forms (especially verse) cannot hide: the artfulness of the novel, its deliberate construction, its method of representation.

While Robert's position may appear naïve, it is in fact consistent with an entire critical tradition that has lauded the novel for its unique capacity to produce a seeming reality. From the early modern theorists of the novel to the structuralists and Russian formalists, the novel has been praised for its power to create a world that strikes the reader as plausible, even if fictional, due to its emphasis on the psychology of the hero. Roland Barthes's suggestion that the novelist fashions a "plausible untruth" fits within this critical tradition, as does Tzvetan Todorov's assertion that the reader of fantastic literature should "consider the world of the characters as a world of living persons."[2] Each of these statements can be traced back to Friedrich von Blanckenburg, who is often hailed as the first theorist of the modern novel in German.[3] In his 1774 treatise *Essay on the Novel*, he declared that every element in the novel is motivated by as well as reflective of the psychology of the hero. As he puts it in an oft-cited statement, the task of the novelist is to portray "possible people of the real world," and his principal means for doing so is by narrating not their outer lives but their "inner history."[4]

This study does not so much take issue with this position as analyze its foundations. It does so by looking at works whose overarching fiction is that they are not fictional at all, but the memoirs of figures who would be forgotten were it not for their account of their storied lives, their recollections of their extraordinary experiences. The fact that many of these figures are simultaneously tricksters points to the novel's origins in the picaresque. But the reverse of this statement is true as well: the novel originates with the picaro, whom, for all his faults, we take at his word because he exposes the deception central to the artist's craft, the sleight of hand that defines the novelist's trade. The picaro is a dissembler who, in spinning yarns, demonstrates the truth of fiction, which is nothing but the act of telling, of narrating stories.[5]

The picaro returns in the twentieth century in what I call the "pseudo-memoir," which encompasses a broad range of texts from fictional diaries to feigned autobiographies and from imaginary notebooks to mock reminiscences. Max Saunders refers to this body of writing as "autobiografictions" to underscore the link between autobiography and fiction in high modernism, otherwise famed for its impersonality.[6] My emphasis in this study is different: I argue that the idea of a life amenable to, if not made for, narration is itself a fiction that pseudo-memoirs bring to the fore in dramatizing the moment of their composition or their genesis as written works. In Rüdiger Campe's terms, they give form to life as they form themselves through the process of self-interrogation and self-theorization.[7] In this manner they draw attention to the act of telling, which is the condition for any tale, but they also do something more, which distinguishes pseudo-memoirs from all other first-person narratives. Pseudo-memoirs reverse the mimetic illusion that art imitates life by asking the reader to believe a manifest fiction or patent illusion: the illusion that their narrator is simultaneously their author, and that his consciousness fuels the work.[8] In other words, they give life to a subject that comes to be in setting out to write an autobiography that does not chronicle the past but instead generates the semblance of one. Pseudo-memoirs are the fiction of fiction-making or the narrative of narrative, and they are arguably as old as the novel itself, as can be seen in the popularity of the genre in the eighteenth century, not only in England (e.g., Daniel Defoe's *Robinson Crusoe*, Jonathan Swift's *Gulliver's Travels*, and Laurence Sterne's *Tristram Shandy*) but also in France and Germany (e.g., Pierre de Marivaux's *La vie de Marianne* and Christian Fürchtegott Gellert's *Das Leben der schwedischen Gräfin von G*).

More important, pseudo-memoirs expose the subjectivity that has enabled the novel's claim to be the most realistic genre, even before the rise of realism in the nineteenth century. As I will discuss, the subjectivity at the root of the novel should not be confused with the inner life of the author: at issue is not the author's intent but the intentionality of consciousness, which is a concept that derives from early twentieth-century psychology and phenomenology. According to Edmund Husserl, the founder of phenomenology, consciousness is always intentional in the sense that it is directed outside itself toward something that transcends it. Yet, as he also underscores, this transcendent horizon does not precede the subject. On the contrary, it is posited with it as the life-world in which the subject always finds itself embedded from the moment it becomes conscious. In other words, from the moment the subject thinks, it finds itself facing a world that has the status of a phenomenon constituted by the subject through its mental acts, or, in Husserl's vocabulary, its *Erlebnisse*. I will treat this matter at greater length in what follows, but for the time being suffice it to say that Husserl was reluctant to judge the existence of the world *apart* from consciousness. One could take his statement "Fiction makes up the vital element of phenomenology" as the epigraph for this study.[9] Pseudo-memoirs reveal how consciousness constructs a world in their double structure as the tale of their own telling or the narrative of their own genesis. In this manner they illuminate the verisimilitude associated with the novel while also challenging this premise.

Double Fictions: The Story of Storytelling

Among the most consistent features of the pseudo-memoir is the protagonist's withdrawal from the world to reflect on his experiences without the distractions of day-to-day affairs. Take, for instance, the opening lines of Thomas Mann's *Confessions of Felix Krull, Confidence Man*, which are paradigmatic for the genre as a whole:

> As I take up my pen at leisure and in complete retirement—in good health, furthermore, though tired, so tired that I shall only be able to proceed by short stages and with frequent pauses for rest—as I take up my pen, then, and entrust my confessions to this patient paper in my own neat and attractive handwriting, I am assailed by a brief misgiving about the educational background I bring to an intellectual enterprise of this kind. But since everything I have to record derives from my own immediate experience, errors, and passions, and since I am therefore in complete command of my material, the doubt can apply only to my tact and propriety of expression, and in my view these are less the product of study than of natural talent and a good home environment.[10]

The excessive length of these sentences should not distract from their aim. To gain the reader's confidence, Krull confides in her in a move that should be expected of any seasoned *Hochstapler* (a cross between a social climber and an imposter), who has learned over the course of his career that the surest way to earn someone's trust is to entrust her with a secret in what would seem like a reciprocal exchange. The key word here is, of course, "seems," as the confidence shared is more often than not a pretense designed to ensnare the unsuspecting individual, who believes what she is told, or at least is willing to suspend her disbelief. Samuel Taylor Coleridge felt compelled to coin the phrase "the willing suspension of disbelief" to describe the stance adopted by readers who accept as true what they know to be a mere "shadow of the imagination"—another phrase we owe to him.[11] In the above-cited passage, Krull relies on the fact that we will take his protests regarding his background and skill at face value for the sake of the work—that is, for the sake of the romp or play that characterizes his text as the parody of a confession. Rarely has a work so plainly shown that the credibility of a novel largely depends on the credit the reader invests in it despite its manifest artifice.

The link between credit and creditworthiness comes up with astonishing frequency in the early modern novel, long considered the first mature expression of the genre. In the introduction that invariably accompanies such novels, a narrator claims to tell a true story based on a treasure trove of documents that he alone has seen. With this boast the narrator asks the reader to take him at his word, and the appeal is invariably framed in economic terms, as if to underscore the transactional nature of trust or belief. Take, for instance, the "Introduction" to Daniel Defoe's *The True and Genuine Account of the Life and Actions of Jonathan Wild* (1725), in which the narrator insists that he is in possession of "authentic and full *vouchers* for the Truth," with which presumably he can repay the reader for her credulity as well as her willingness to finance his labors through the purchase of his publication.[12] (The paltry sum earned in publishing is a consistent theme of the preface and the introduction to *Jonathan Wild*.) As if to underscore the financial metaphor, the narrator reassures the reader that everything reported in the text has been verified, and nothing has been taken at face value or in his vocabulary on "the *Credit* of Common Fame," thereby ensuring that the "Account," itself a financial term, is balanced and that the ledger shows no debts.[13] Lest one think that the issue of credibility and its relation to finance is exclusive to the English tradition, it is worth noting that the supposed author and editor in Christoph Martin Wieland's *Geschichte des Agathon* (1766–67) reminds the reader in the preface to the first edition that he has conducted scrupulous research "because he himself wanted to be certain that he was not *selling* the world any chimeras [*da er selbst gewiß zu sein wünschte, daß er der Welt keine Hirngespenster für Wahrheit verkaufe*]."[14]

All of these motifs find their most cunning expression in Samuel Beckett's *Malone Dies*, itself a pseudo-memoir, which begins with the narrator's pronouncement "I shall soon be quite dead at last in spite of all."[15] The opening paragraph is littered with economic terms. Regarding his impending death, the narrator writes, "I have that feeling, I have had it now for some days, and I *credit* it" (179). And a few sentences later he adds, "Something must have changed. I will not weigh upon *the balance* any more" (179). To maintain this newfound equilibrium, he promises, "I shall *pay* less heed to myself" (179). Finally, he suggests that he does not need to pay attention to himself, as life has already repaid him handsomely:

I shall not watch myself die, that would spoil everything. Have I watched myself live? Have I ever complained? Then why rejoice now? I am content, necessarily, but not to the point of clapping my hands. I was always content, knowing I would be *repaid*. There he is now, my old *debtor*. Shall I then fall on his neck? I shall not answer any more questions. I shall even try not to ask myself any more. While waiting I shall tell myself stories, if I can. They will not be the same kind of stories as hitherto, that is all. They will be neither beautiful nor ugly, they will be calm . . . they will be almost lifeless, like *the teller*. What was that I said? It does not matter. I look forward to their giving me *great satisfaction, some satisfaction. I am satisfied, there, I have enough, I am repaid*, I need nothing more. Let me say before I go any further that I forgive nobody. (179–80, emphasis added)

Malone's staccato delivery could not be more different than Krull's long-winded syntax, and the contrast does not end there. Whereas Krull looks to the reader for an affirmation he cannot furnish for himself, Malone studiously avoids all relationships, as that would trigger a new cycle of debt and repayment and upset the balance—both literal and figurative—he has struggled to attain. He therefore insists, "I am satisfied, I have enough, I am repaid," to signal that he is not indebted to anyone, and no one is indebted to him. He is, as he puts it, "almost lifeless" in the sense that he does not owe his life to anyone, having all but taken the final exit. And yet the modifier "almost" suggests he is not quite done with life, and by extension with the obligations that life inevitably entails. He is still for his remaining days a "teller," which is not only a narrator, but also someone who dispenses cash, a creditor who survives only as long as he is in a relationship with a debtor. This debtor is Malone himself as the first audience for his tales, followed by the reader as his second audience.

Malone tells himself stories to pass the time while he lies in a bed all but immobilized save for his hand, which still has the strength to push a pencil across a page. Sometimes these stories are about "tellers" like himself in the original sense of the term, as someone who reckons or keeps accounts. According to the *Oxford English Dictionary*, the verb "to tell" derives from the Old Frisian *tella*, which means to count or declare; its relation to the German *zählen* can be heard via the Old Saxon *tellian*, which likewise means to say, count, reckon, or relate.[16] So we learn of the boy Sapo who "liked sums, but not the way they were taught. What he liked was the manipulation of concrete numbers. . . . He made a practice, alone and in company, of mental arithmetic" (Beckett, 186–87). It would be hard to miss the reference to Malone in this figure, given his emphasis throughout the text that he would like to take an inventory of everything he possesses before he dies and his anxiety that he will either finish the task too soon, which will necessitate a second count, or start the process too late, which will make the completion of the count impossible. In either case Malone's inventory will come up short. Either he will survive it with the result that his count will still have to account for one, or he will perish during the process with the result that his count will lack its most important member, the one who initiates it. Both possibilities are written into Malone's name, which bears within it the number "one" (Mal-one) and points to his peculiar status as a figure who is both one too many and one too few for his account—that is, his telling understood as his counting and recounting, his *Zählen* and *Erzählen*, his *compte* and *conte*.

The novel *Malone Dies* plays throughout with the relation between counting and recounting encapsulated in the verb "to tell" invoked in the opening paragraph: "While waiting I shall tell myself stories. . . . They will be lifeless, like the teller. What was that I said" (Beckett, 180). The play is at times so intense that it is impossible to say whether a story about a gray hen is not also about numbers given that *hen* (ἕν) is the number one in Greek.[17] My interest, however, is not so much in the problem of telling or narrating as in the problem of the one, which is simultaneously a problem of the subject. The link between the two is particularly stark in English, where the first-person pronoun "I" is also the Roman numeral "I." That "I" is the first word of Beckett's own translation of his novel, originally written in French, seems important in this respect, given that Malone is both inside his own count as the first element and outside it as the enabling condition. But, even if the pronoun "I" and Roman numeral "I" were not orthographically linked, the problem would remain that the first person always exceeds its own account as the one who narrates it.[18] Immanuel Kant himself recognized this problem when distinguishing between the empirical and the transcendental self that guarantees the unity of experience, though it is never given in experience, as this would reduce it to an empirical instance. The one is the Archimedean point from which all narration proceeds—until, that is, it does not, though not because the narrative is complete. All narratives are condemned to unravel, to splinter or fray, as soon as the one who motivates it ceases to be. This is the significance of the final moments of *Malone Dies*, in which Malone babbles incoherently until he falls silent. The sputtering conclusion of the novel reads: "Never there he will never // never anything // there // any more" (Beckett, 288). *Malone Dies* is typical of the genre of the pseudo-memoir in that it reveals the subjectivity that maintains it until its last word, when the fiction and, more specifically, the illusion of life vanishes.

Seen in this light, the dissolution of subjectivity in *Malone Dies* marks the death not only of the narrator but also of a certain novelistic tradition, whose crowning achievement was the realist novel of the nineteenth century, celebrated for its rich depiction of the inner life of its characters and its analysis of social constraints. As I will discuss shortly, what made this mode of representation possible was the idea that everything we perceive is consistent with the requirements of our cognitive faculties, which is a position generally associated with Kant but has its roots in Descartes's rationalization of the universe. Literary realism, one could say, coincides with the conviction that through our faculties we have a purchase on reality. In *The Rise of the Novel*, Ian Watt thus underscores that the novel emerges at roughly the same time as Descartes's philosophy and like the latter places a premium on the individual's access to truth through reason.[19] Once we lose faith in the inherent rationality of the universe, however, we also lose the ability to represent it to ourselves. The real becomes not what we intend but what repeatedly thwarts our intentions and expectations; it emerges as what interrupts our words and undermines our thoughts. The sputtering conclusion of *Malone Dies* is to this extent the most truthful moment in the work, when what either exceeds or falls short of Malone's conceptions finally makes itself heard.

Pseudo-memoirs not only trace the process by which reality is constructed as a subjective phenomenon, but, more important, they trace its demise as the story of a story, the telling of telling, the narrative of a narrative. This doubling or mise en abyme is characteristic of the genre, even if the novels associated with it do not display an obvious split between an internal and an external narrative. The division is implicit to the extent that they are fictional autobiographies or imitations of life-writing, which claims a unique relation to an extratextual reality. As imitations pseudo-memoirs draw on the conventions of autobiographical writing, while at the same time disrupting them. A touchstone for all the readings in this study is, consequently, Philippe Lejeune's structural analysis of autobiography, in which Lejeune advances the theory that the distinguishing feature of autobiography is its status as the one genre in which the author, narrator, and protagonist are identical in *name*.[20] Their identity in name as opposed to personality enables him to claim that the genre can be delineated in purely formal terms without reference to the author's personal history or experience.

For Lejeune, every autobiography involves a pact between the reader and the writer, whose name appears on the title page as the legal author of the text. The presence of the author's name in the front matter functions for Lejeune as a guarantee that the writer will feature in the work as both the narrating and narrated subject—in other words, as the teller of his own tale. Pseudo-memoirs clearly violate this definition of the autobiographical genre. Indeed, we call them fictions precisely because the protagonist does not have the same name as the author, even if he claims to be an author in his own right. (Sebald's fiction will prove to be the exception to this rule, as discussed in chapter 4.) Yet, in their very departure from this model, they reveal it as a distinct convention or form that serves as the foundation not only for an individual's account of his life, but also for accounts of life more generally. Every narrative requires an author who writes it, a narrator who tells it, and a protagonist who acts alone or in concert with others. This is true even when the protagonist is a wholly passive figure or when the role of narrator is occupied by more than one person.

In pseudo-memoirs, however, these fundamental requirements for narrative become fictions themselves. The author, narrator, and protagonist are all invented to produce not a narrative of life but the semblance of such a narrative. This turn whereby the fiction at stake becomes the fiction of fiction-writing or the story of storytelling opens the door for a reconsideration of the terms "semblance" and "life" included implicitly in the two-part name of this genre, "pseudo-memoir." In readings that extend from Thomas Mann's *Felix Krull* and Robert Walser's *Jakob von Gunten* to Thomas Bernhard's *Extinction* and W. G. Sebald's *Vertigo*, this study shows that the fiction or semblance of life gives way to the life of a semblance that can no longer be contained within the narrative framework. Aesthetic forms, however, have the final word to the extent that a life so conceived consists merely in storytelling, in the act of narration.

In the next section I will take up the coincidence of life and semblance in Descartes's philosophy and its implications for the novel before proposing how the novel responds to the skeptical challenge that Descartes believed he had resolved once and for all.

The Cogito and the Novel

"The moment has come," says a confident narrator at the outset of Descartes's *Meditations*, to entertain his greatest doubts: "Today I have discharged my mind from all its cares, and have carved out a space of untroubled leisure. I have withdrawn into seclusion and shall at last be able to devote myself seriously and without encumbrance to the task of destroying all my former opinions."[21] Read in conjunction with Felix Krull's statement that he is picking up his pen "at leisure and in complete retirement" (*Confessions*, 3), it would be hard to overlook the fact that the *Meditations* constitute not only a philosophical treatise but also a pseudo-autobiographical work. The text has all the hallmark features of the genre: the withdrawal of the narrator from the social sphere, his immersion in himself, and, finally, his construction of a world out of his own interiority, which is not just a feature of the *Meditations* but one of its central arguments. One finds the same pattern in Rousseau's *Reveries* (1782), which opens with the pronouncement "I am now alone on earth, no longer having any brother, neighbor, friend, or society other than myself," and this pattern continues into the late twentieth century, as seen in Thomas Bernhard's *Extinction* (1986), which begins as the narrator receives the news that his parents and brother have been killed in a car accident, leaving him the sole male heir.[22] In all of these cases it is evident that in pseudo-memoirs the world must be destroyed to be built anew on a more solid foundation in the self—a self that would appear to be utterly solipsistic if it did not so easily lend itself to communication. Yet, to the extent that the narrating subject communicates itself, it posits a world inhabited by other egos like itself, egos that are in a position to understand the narrator because they too are defined by their inner thought processes.

In her monumental study *The Logic of Literature*, Käte Hamburger indicates that what separates the novel from all other modes of discourse is its ability to represent other minds. Whereas other genres, such as drama, report the words and deeds of other characters, only the novel can convey the inner life of another precisely as another in the third person.[23]

Sentences like "She tried to be sad, so as not to be angry; but it made her angry that she couldn't be sad," from Henry James's *The Wings of the Dove*, or "He didn't know why he was so disappointed, when he spotted the assistant [*Er wußte nicht, warum er so enttäuscht war, als er die Gehilfen erkannte*]," from Franz Kafka's *The Castle*, would be unthinkable in any other context, except in the novel, where it is not only accepted but also expected that the consciousness of others will be narrated and in this manner made available to the reader.[24] As Dorrit Cohn observes in *Transparent Minds*, "The special life-likeness of narrative fiction—as compared to dramatic and cinematic fictions—depends on what writers and readers know least in life: how another mind thinks, another body feels."[25] Seen in this light, the novel would seem to answer the skepticism that Descartes voices in the Second Meditation, when he wonders how he can be sure that the pedestrians he sees from his window are men and not machines engineered to look like them. This question arises as Descartes considers the difference between perceptibility and intelligibility, as demonstrated in the example of a piece of wax, which can appear in different shapes, forms, and sizes, depending on its state as a liquid, solid, or gas. Descartes readily admits that the input of his senses is not reliable, but this is partially his point. Sense perception will never result in certainty since bodies are in a constant state of flux; they shrink, grow, wrinkle, flatten, and swell, to cite some of the changes that the human body undergoes. But the knowledge of a thing's essence is certain, since essence is unchanging over time, and we achieve this certainty whenever we search within ourselves for a thing's unchanging properties, which is to say for that which makes it this entity and not another. We may never be able to prove that the figures we see on the street are human beings— to do so we would have to rely on evidence gathered with our senses— but we can know beyond a shadow of a doubt that all men are thinking things (res cogitans) because we find this definition within ourselves— or, more precisely, in our intellect.

Descartes therefore concludes that in thinking we confirm our own existence as thinking beings in a patently circular argument that lies at the heart of the *Meditations*, long considered the founding work of modern philosophy. But the circle also lies at the heart of the novel, which as the consummately modern genre responds to the same crisis.[26] In much the same manner as Descartes demonstrates his existence in pondering the existence of others, so too the novelist demonstrates his being in narrating the inner lives of others, who do not in fact exist. The portrayal of other minds is central to the novel in that it attests to the subjectivity that motivates it and sustains its representations.

This is true even in third-person fiction, where there is no personal or embodied narrator and possibly no narrator at all, as both Käte Hamburger and Ann Banfield have underscored. For Hamburger, the narrator is not a person but a function of the text; only in fiction can statements be organized around and adopt the perspective of a character narrated in the third person.[27] Ann Banfield extends this argument in *Unspeakable Sentences* by pointing out that in third-person fiction the only self we can speak of is the grammatical subject referenced in any statement.[28] There is no other subject besides the dramatis personae depicted in the text. Yet, as Banfield herself admits, to the extent that the narration represents various instances of mental life, it must issue from a consciousness that never speaks or appears in the work as such but nonetheless makes the work possible: "The true narrating I never intrudes; it structures the intentional object which is the text."[29] The text as an instance of intentionality or an expression of mental life is based in a subjectivity that permeates it as its condition of possibility—in other words, as its transcendental ground.

Michel Foucault provides a helpful illustration of this point in his lengthy preface to his translation of Ludwig Binswanger's *Dream and Existence*, itself an important work in the field of phenomenological psychology. In a telling passage regarding dreams, he writes, "The subject of the dream, the first person of the dream, is the dream itself, the whole dream. *In the dream, everything says, 'I,'* even the things and the animals, even the empty space, even objects distant and strange which populate the phantasmagoria."[30] Every element in the dream says "I," since the dream is powered by a mind that is awake, even if it is oblivious to its immediate, physical surroundings. The same can be said of the novel, whose phenomena all refer to the subjectivity that underlies the work and imbues its every aspect. The circle at the heart of the *Meditations* is of a piece with this mode of representation, in which everything conceived bears witness to the act of conceiving and by extension to the cogito.

Yet even the cogito is treated with a degree of skepticism in Descartes's *Meditations* that will come to haunt the novel as well. As much as the philosopher would like to secure the existence of the ego so he can argue, in turn, that it serves as the basis for the known universe, he is haunted by the method of radical doubt introduced in the First Meditation. A brief summary of this method is useful to elucidate the link between the Cartesian cogito and the consciousness that drives the novel and anchors the fictional space.

At the end of the First Meditation the philosopher vows to doubt everything about which the slightest objection can be raised to arrive at something true, which amounts to saying something he can *know* with absolute certainty. He quickly realizes, however, that "there is nothing of all those things I once thought true, of which it is not legitimate to doubt" (*Meditations*, 16), and this realization extends even to simple mathematical propositions that would at first seem incontrovertible. He cautions that even statements like "two plus three equals five" and "a square has four sides" could be treated with skepticism, given the mind's tendency to err—a tendency that turns each and every thought into a potential error. To account for all these circumstances, he proposes an evil genius that exists for no other reason than to deceive us.

Descartes readily admits that the idea of an evil genius is hypothetical but useful all the same, as it allows him to dismiss everything he once regarded as true as a deception. Relieved of all potentially untrue ideas, he can focus on himself, and here is where his radical doubt turns into radical certainty at his own existence: "I convinced myself that there was nothing at all in the world, no sky, no earth, no minds, no bodies. Did I therefore not also convince myself that I did not exist either? No: certainly I did exist, if I convinced myself of something" (*Meditations*, 18). Descartes continues this reflection by considering how he could be convinced of something erroneous by another: "But there is some deceiver or other, supremely powerful and cunning, who is deliberately deceiving me all the time.—Beyond doubt then, I also exist, if he is deceiving me; and he can deceive me all he likes, but he will never bring it about that I should be nothing as long as I think I am something" (18). When looked at together, these two statements reveal that the philosopher's proof of his existence relies on his ability to act upon himself or, alternatively, to be acted upon by another who is similar to, but more powerful, than himself. As such, it matters little whether he convinces himself that he does not exist, or an evil genius deceives him that he does.

In either case, the fact that he is susceptible to persuasion points to his being as a thinking thing. Put otherwise, his awareness of his thinking verifies his existence.

Husserl's Critique of Descartes

For Edmund Husserl, Descartes's proof of his existence via universal doubt constitutes his most significant contribution to philosophy: it enables him to provide philosophy with a foundation that is evident in itself and that can serve as the basis for all other philosophical pursuits whether theoretical or practical. As Husserl explains in the *Cartesian Meditations*, a series of lectures he delivered in 1929 at the Sorbonne, the *ego cogito* is "apodictic."[31] Technically this means its inexistence is unthinkable, but such a definition with its double negative requires some explanation. The ego attests to itself inasmuch as each and every thought bears witness to the act of thinking, which is the essence of the ego as captured in the formula "I think, therefore I am." The absence of the ego is to this extent inconceivable in that it cannot be thought, since every mental act would reintroduce the very term it seeks to deny or mark as lost. To suggest that the ego does not exist constitutes a contradiction in terms, as this is still a thought, however minimal, that needs an ego to generate it. In finding a ground for philosophy that is not derived from anything else, Descartes earns his reputation as "the founding genius of all modern philosophy"—which is high praise coming from Husserl.[32]

At the same time, he insists that Descartes failed to follow through on this discovery and possibly misconstrued it from the start. A critique running through much of Husserl's writing is that the French philosopher turns early in the *Meditations* from the subject to the object as the basis for experience. This happens most notably in Descartes's Third Meditation, where he proposes that the idea of God cannot originate in him but must come from God, since the idea of an infinite and perfect being requires an equally infinite and perfect cause. Whatever the merits of this argument—which is far more complicated than I have suggested here—one point is clear: Descartes views thought as the representation of a reality independent of cognition—a "formal reality" in his terminology and what Husserl refers to in his own shorthand as "what is in itself [*ein an-sich Seiendes*]."[33] This tendency, according to Husserl, can be found in the first two meditations. What makes them significant all the same is the impetus they give to phenomenology, which as an exploration of consciousness continues the project that Descartes himself abandoned after the Second Meditation, in Husserl's interpretation.

A central tenet of phenomenology from the first volume of *Ideas Pertaining to a Pure Phenomenology* (1913) onward is that the only world we can speak of is the one given in thought. What does not appear to us cannot be said to exist, as we have no relation to it. This, however, does not mean that we each inhabit our own universe; phenomenology is not a form of relativism, even if it questions the legitimacy of the world as an independent sphere. Rather, it aims to elucidate the structure of consciousness itself, and to do so it must first set aside the world assumed in the natural attitude, the so-called objective world. It does so through a process known as the *"epoché,"* which Husserl explains as follows in a passage from *The Crisis of European Sciences* devoted to Cartesian doubt:

> How is it that precisely through the epoché a primal ground of immediate and apodictic self-evidences should be exhibited? The answer is: If I refrain from taking any position on the being or non-being of the world, if I deny myself every ontic validity related to the world, not *every* ontic validity is prohibited for me within this epoché. . . . I am necessary as the one carrying it out. It is precisely herein that I find just the apodictic ground I was seeking, the one which absolutely excludes every possible doubt. (77)

Husserl's technical prose may not do justice to his point, which is in fact elegant in its simplicity. In what is by now a familiar circle, he argues that, in refraining from taking a position regarding the existence of the world, the ego affirms itself not as an object but as a subject—as that which is necessary to withhold judgment. Via this procedure the phenomenologist arrives at a ground that is evident in itself, much like Descartes, who, in doubting everything, discovers (beyond all doubt) the indubitable subject. Yet Husserl is also adamant that his method differs from his predecessor's in one critical respect—critical in that it preserves the radicalism that Descartes introduced and then denied in order to affirm the rationality of the universe. The epoché does not negate the world: it redefines it as a phenomenon that, as the term implies, is not a self-sufficient entity but an appearance that derives its meaning and ontological validity from the consciousness that apprehends it, the mind in which it reveals itself.

It is in this sense that the world is subjectively constituted for Husserl. Every phenomenon bears the trace of the subjectivity that gives rise to it and brings it to the fore precisely as something perceived, remembered, imagined, anticipated, or desired, to name just some of ways in which consciousness constructs its objects. In other words, everything we experience can be classified as something thought, and the primary task of philosophy is to explore the relationship between various mental states and their intentional objects, *cogitatio* and *cogitatum*, noesis and noema.[34] Descartes fails to arrive at this conclusion, according to Husserl, because he never truly abandons the dogmatic idea of a world-in-itself that does not depend on the cogito in any way for its being. Even in his discussion of doubt, he remains wedded to the idea of an objective world, as Husserl notes in what is arguably his most pointed critique of the French philosopher. According to Sieglinde Grimm, the objectification of the world ushered in by the French rationalist contributed in no small part to the treatment of inner states as a function of physiological operations in nineteenth-century realist and naturalist fiction.[35]

Doubt in the *Meditations* never amounts to more than a means toward an end, and its function as a purely heuristic technique is evident in the ego that it exposes.[36] Husserl singles out the following passage in the Second Meditation as particularly significant: "I am therefore, speaking precisely, only a thinking thing [*res cogitans*], that is, a mind, or a soul, or an intellect, or a reason [*mens sive animus sive intellectus*]— words the meaning of which was previously unknown to me. I am there a true thing, and one that truly exists; but what kind of thing? I have said it already: one that thinks" (*Meditations*, 19–20). For Husserl Descartes's characterization of the ego as a thing (*res*) is not accidental. It reveals that he regards the ego not as the foundation of the world but as an element in it—an immaterial element, but an element all the same that can be the object for another ego. This other ego turns out to be God, whom Descartes conceives in almost secular terms as the principle of reason that governs the universe and ensures its intelligibility via scientific inquiry.

In *The Crisis of European Sciences*, Husserl emphasizes that the scientific revolution that began with Galileo did not do away with God but enshrined him instead as the guarantee that the universe could be known by way of rational methods. What Galileo introduced was a split between, on the one hand, physical nature, which is composed of bod-

ies that are sui generis, and, on the other, intelligible nature, which consists of geometrical forms derived from the laws of mathematics.[37] This
split eventually—one might say ineluctably—culminated in the mind-
body distinction associated with Descartes. For this dualistic scheme to
work, however, a third term was needed to negotiate between the two
poles that make up the person. This is where God comes into play in the
Meditations. Husserl asks, "Was God not unavoidable as the principle of
rationality? Does not rational being, even [merely] as nature, in order to
be thinkable at all, presuppose rational theory and a subjectivity which
accomplishes it? Does not nature, then, indeed the world-in-itself, presuppose God as reason existing absolutely" (*Crisis*, 62). The assumption
that God is the hidden cause of nature ensures nature's rationality, even
if the latter remains hidden behind physical bodies that at best approxi-
mate pure geometrical figures. But the assumption also ensures that nature is accessible to us as creatures endowed with a cognitive faculty—or
to quote Descartes, "a mind, or a soul, or an intellect, or a reason." This
is the role of the ego in the *Meditations*: it detects "the natural," if invisible, "light" that shines through all corporeal entities insofar as the ego
is a thing itself, a res cogitans that is not only *in* the world but also *of* it
as the world's intelligible nature.[38]

One might ask what the place of fiction would be in a universe so conceived with God as the transcendental subject that, in thinking, creates
the world as pure intelligibility. What would be the status of an imaginary world that corresponds to neither the physical nor the spiritual
universe? This is not a question Descartes asks, but his philosophy invites it all the same, given its emphasis on the mind's capacity to grasp
the universe in itself apart from all appearances. The question is war-
ranted, moreover, since both the *Meditations* and *Discourse on Method*
dramatize the process of contemplation as fictional narratives. If one assumes that the world is in its essence rational, then fiction would have to
be seen as either a willful delusion, of the sort that I convince myself of
something I know not to be case, or a lapse in judgment, in which I am
deceived by my impressions because I do not examine them sufficiently.
That each of these positions resembles the uncertainty produced by the
evil genius in the Second Meditation is not accidental.

The evil genius is a direct consequence of a philosophy in which the
only measure of truth is God's status as reason. In such a philosophy it is

possible that simple mathematical propositions like "two plus three equals five" could be false, or at least subject to debate, for their truth, it turns out, depends entirely on God's being as rationality itself. Derrida thus argues that Descartes smuggles a form of madness into the *Meditations* with the evil genius that is far more disturbing than the madness explicitly acknowledged in the First Meditation of doubting one's sense impressions.[39] Doubting what is intelligible as opposed to what is perceptible proves to be far more threatening to Descartes's philosophical system, as it calls into question the act of thinking itself, which is the only vehicle the ego has to verify itself. Once Descartes raises the possibility that intelligibility may not be the definition of truth, and that God may be capricious rather than rational, the self-evidence of the formula "I think, therefore I am" suddenly vanishes. It could be the statement of an ego that, in thinking, attests to itself, but it could also be the statement of a character who thinks that, in thinking, he affirms his existence. This dilemma cannot be resolved as long as the ego is conceived as the effect of a foreign cause—be it an evil genius, a benevolent God, or a clever author—and not itself self-generating. Beckett captures this uncertainty with characteristic succinctness in *Company*: "Devised deviser devising it all for company."[40]

In terms of the novel, the uncertainty regarding the rationality of the universe finds its most direct expression in the appeals to the reader characteristic of the early modern novel, whose narrators invariably pose as authors or editors. Take, for instance, the opening lines from the preface to Wieland's *Geschichte des Agathon* (1767), which are typical for not only the early modern German novel but the eighteenth-century novel as a whole: "The editor of the present history sees so little likelihood of being able to convince the audience that what follows is indeed drawn from an old Greek manuscript that he believes it is best to say nothing on this point and to let the reader think what he will."[41] Much like *Felix Krull*, Wieland's *Geschichte des Agathon* begins with a false confession: under the pretext that the reader will never be convinced that what follows is a true story, the narrator manages to claim that the text is based on a historical document. In short, it is a *Geschichte* or *histoire* in both senses of the term. Yet the only authority he can invoke to support this assertion is his statement; the only evidence he can offer is his testimony. His means (i.e., his claim) and his ends (i.e., the proof of his claim) coincide, since the only measure of truth he has at his disposal is finally himself: his word, his person. In a world in which there is no overarching truth and no principle of reason governing all affairs, only the narrator can speak to the truth of his claims in the most circular manner possible, which is by citing himself as an authority.[42]

Yet this tautological structure hardly constitutes proof, as eighteenth-century novelists were well aware. Their reliance on the trope of a "true story" told by "real authors" reveals on the contrary that the subject itself is a fiction. Put otherwise, the self is the effect of a cause it cannot elucidate for itself, for the evil genius calls into question the primacy of reason as a criterion of truth and a path to knowledge. This is the madness Descartes introduces into the *Meditations* in identifying the ego as a thing (*res*) and submitting it to the whims of a benevolent or evil deity that constitutes the sole reality. In such a world it is impossible to distinguish between historical truth and fiction (or *Geschichte* and *Geschichte*), which is why the early modern novel plays so frequently—one might say unrelentingly—with its genre. It will take over a century for the novel to find a new foundation. Georg Lukács will locate it in the transcendental subject that represents the truth of fiction.

Lukács and Transcendental Subjectivity

Lukács wrote *The Theory of the Novel* in 1920 to address what had been a long-standing problem in criticism of the novel. What is the form of a seemingly formless genre like the novel? What distinguishes it from other works? What makes it a quintessentially modern genre unlike, say, drama, which continues to rely on Greek tragedy for its definition? To answer these questions, Lukács considers the evolution of literary forms in classical antiquity from the Homeric epic to Sophoclean tragedy and, finally, Socratic philosophy, which he views as the third great classical genre, as opposed to the lyric. In his taxonomy of genres the lyric is primarily a mood, one he associates with the resignation of the nineteenth century when it becomes increasingly common to abandon the collective sphere and turn inward for fulfillment.

Lukács contends that each genre answers a question that can only be posed after the fact, when a new genre emerges that exposes as problematic what had previously been regarded as self-evident. The novel is the genre of the "problematic individual" who has no home.[43] He finds himself in a world that is not of his own making and has no evident purpose. I will explain Lukács's reasons for this position shortly, but for the time being suffice it to say that every genre represents the "transcendental topography of spirit" (23) characteristic of a certain age. In other words, it reflects the intellectual conditions that give rise to a particular view of the universe and determine the individual's and community's place in it. For the ancient Greeks the idea of a hero who has to make decisions regarding the course of his life is an unimaginable situation, whereas for the novel this is standard fare, since the novel is "the epic of an age in which the extensive totality of life is no longer immediately given and the lived immanence of sense has become a problem, but which is still predisposed toward totality" (47).

According to Lukács, the novel arises at a juncture when the physical world is no longer imbued with meaning, as it had been for the ancient Greeks. In this absence the task falls to the subject to create a sphere in which the disparate elements of life are placed in a meaningful relation. For the Greeks this sphere was given in experience, but for the modern subject it has to be made, and the principal means the subject has for doing so is art, understood literally as producing or making, *poiesis*. Art may not allow the human being to create a world ex nihilo, but it does provide him with the means to reshape and reorganize it and to present a vision of how the world *ought* to be. Only in art does the subject have the occasion to fashion a world that conforms to ideals.

The central thesis of *The Theory of the Novel* is that the genre gives form to life through irony. The Greek epic did not need to do so, as it emerged an age in which everything was already considered to be in its proper place. In keeping with the writings of the early Romantics, and especially Friedrich Schlegel, Lukács defines irony as a twofold process. In the first instance, a protagonist attempts to impress meaning on a world hostile to sense—a world that is diffuse and heterogeneous, since no transcendental purpose is evident in it. This attempt necessarily fails, as the protagonist is not a god endowed with the power to create a world out of whole cloth. His failure, however, is followed by a second act that places subject and object (or protagonist and world) in a relation of mutual dependence.[44]

Here is where the distinction between the portrayal of other minds and the mind's portrayal of itself returns not merely as a characteristic of the novel but as its defining feature. The narrator reflects on the op-position between the subject and object (or protagonist and world) and in so doing absorbs them in a third term. This term is the consciousness that permeates every aspect of the work and is as such the transcendental ground that governs the novel's representations—or, in the vocabulary of narrative theory, the diegetic space. Through reflection the narrator makes the world of the novel whole, as if it were the "extensive totality of life," but which it can never be, since it is produced through the narrator's reflection on himself or, what amounts to the same, through his expres-sion of ideals that exist solely in the intellect. (This dynamic is discussed in greater detail in chapter 3.) Lukács's analysis of the structure of the novel culminates in something of a paradox. The novel's truth is simul-taneously an index of its fictionality: it forges a unity that exists nowhere but in thought and that as a result has no objective validity, though it re-tains its subjective validity as an intellectual or spiritual phenomenon.

The Truth of Fiction

The same insight concerning unity was central to the development of phenomenology. In *Ideas Pertaining to a Pure Phenomenology*, Husserl names as the basis for all scholarly inquiry the following principle: "No conceivable theory can make us err with respect to the principle of all principles: that every originary intuition is a legitimate source of knowl-edge, that everything that is originarily (so to speak in its bodily actual-ity) offered to us in 'intuition' is to be accepted simply as what it is pre-sented as being, but also only within the limits in which it is presented there" (44). Phenomenology begins, as Husserl would have it, with things as they present themselves to us without the mediation of concepts or ideas that would place conditions on experience and in so doing create a gap between subject and object. At the same time—and this caveat is crucial—it recognizes that to speak of things themselves apart from us is an impossible task: it would require us to think of a world in which there is no thought, a world in which nothing appears, as there would be no subject to register anything at all. For this reason, Husserl insists on the epoché, which, as mentioned previously, entails the process of set-ting aside or bracketing the objective world. Only a philosophy that is not distracted by objectivity would be able to explore the world as it re-veals itself and is constituted *in thought*. Such a world would not lose any immediacy; on the contrary, it would gain the immediacy of the subjectivity expressed in it as something thought—or, in Husserl's vocabulary, as an intentional object.

The verisimilitude of the novel likewise depends on the subjectivity that produces it and fuels its every aspect. At first glance this may seem like a revival of authorial intent, but such a critique ignores the difference between intent and intentionality, which is a structure of consciousness. The subjectivity that governs the novel does not belong to the historical author. It belongs to the work as the intentionality that enables it to be interpreted as a representation of inner life, even if interpretations vary wildly. Charles Larmore's contention that "the relation of reader to text is ultimately a relation of the reader to another person," by which he means the author, is mistaken in this regard.[45] The work bears witness not to an individual's thought but to the process of thinking itself, which we ascribe to individuals after the fact in what might be the most routine but also most astonishing act of prosopopoeia, in which we endow anonymous forces with a human face.

Wolfgang Iser's phenomenologically inspired account of reading illuminates how the personification of the author works. Reading, as he sees it, is a dynamic process in which the reader interacts with a text, which consists of definite structures as a meaningful configuration of elements but at the same time retains a level of indeterminacy as a multilayered, if finite, articulation that can never be reduced to a single sense.[46] The indeterminacy and incompleteness of the text creates an opening for the reader's intervention: she sifts through the work and draws connections between elements, producing an assemblage that, on the one hand, is not entirely private but, on the other, is not given in the writing. This assemblage is the intentionality she projects onto the text, as if it were the intentionality of the author instead of the hypothetical subject she fashions to organize the work. Every reading, even the most diffident, posits a hypothetical subject or an "implied author" to narrate the text, since the truth of any work is finally the voice that carries it as if it were a personal communication to the reader. In this vein Schlomith Rimmon-Kenan comments, "Narration both presupposes a narrator and creates him/her in the process of telling,"[47] and Samuel Frederick elaborates on this insight when he remarks that it is voice, not plot, that drives narrative and functions as "the unimpeded energy of narrative in and of itself."[48] Narrator, voice, and implied author, however, are nothing but figures for a subjectivity that does not belong to an individual as his or her psychology but constitutes instead the consciousness that generates and supports any and every imaginary world. This dynamic comes to the fore in pseudo-memoirs, due to their status as the recollection of personae that do not exist anywhere except in the pages of their own narration. The narrator's explanation of his intent in *Tristram Shandy* exemplifies this point: "I have undertaken you see, to write not only my life, but my opinions also; hoping and expecting that your knowledge of my character, and of what kind of a mortal I am, by the one, would give you a better relish for the other."[49]

This study is devoted to teasing out the life of this "I," which as a posited figure draws attention to the self-positing nature of subjectivity. Pseudo-memoirs turn the consciousness that supports them into a phenomenon, which would be a contradiction in terms in any other genre except in fiction, which exhibits what is most secret: inner life, consciousness, or, in Husserl's vocabulary, the stream of lived experience (*Erlebnisstrom*).

Pseudo-Memoirs

A few words are in order regarding the choice of novels discussed in this book, given that it is not a representative sample. As the above-quoted passage from *Tristram Shandy* indicates, the pseudo-memoir has a long history, going back to the eighteenth century at least. Nonetheless this study limits itself to twentieth-century fiction for two reasons. The first is practical: an analysis of all the novels that pose as autobiographies would exceed the scope of a single study and would have to address the difference between fictional autobiographies and fake or fraudulent memoirs, which is not as self-evident as it may seem. How does one distinguish between a travelogue like W. G. Sebald's *The Rings of Saturn*, which supposedly recounts the author's journey by foot on England's North Sea coast, and a memoir like Binjamin Wilkomirski's *Fragments: Memories of a Wartime Childhood*, which recalls people, places, and events later exposed to be fabricated? What makes the first work fictional and the second a fraud? What gives the fiction writer license to dissemble, whereas the memoir writer is held to a higher standard? These are legitimate questions but of little relevance to this monograph, as they focus on the referential dimensions of a work rather than the way the world of reference is constructed. In keeping with this position, this study avoids the distinction between story and discourse, *histoire* and *récit*, *fabula* and *sjuzet* characteristic of structuralist and Russian formalist approaches to narrative, as these distinctions are based on the premise that there is subject matter (a story) that fictional works set out to (re)configure, (re)fashion, and (re)construct (*qua* discourse) as representations of an external object.[50]

A second reason this study limits itself to the twentieth century is that the verisimilitude of the novel was subject to renewed questioning in this period, following the success of the realist novel, which claimed, if not to reproduce reality, to generate a "plausible untruth."[51] The claim to plausibility was based on the assumption that the universe was rational, which by the twentieth century was no longer a tenable position, as is evident in Husserl's critique of Descartes's lapse into dogmatic metaphysics. For the novel this shift in attitudes meant that the omniscience of nineteenth-century fiction could no longer be maintained; it became impossible to accept that a novel could illuminate the minds of others, owing to the transcendental subjectivity at its base. The consequence of this was that, in lieu of third-person novels, first-person narratives emerged that displayed remarkable, if largely unnoticed, parallels to eighteenth-century fiction. A work like Thomas Mann's *Confessions of Felix Krull, Confidence Man*, discussed in chapter 1, owes as much to the Spanish picaresque as it does to Rousseau's *Confessions*; and novels like Robert Walser's *Jakob von Gunten*, discussed in chapter 2, would not be possible without Defoe's *Robinson Crusoe*, which was the first major fictional autobiography in Europe.

The return in twentieth-century German fiction of narrative forms hardly seen since the eighteenth century says as much about the period as it does about the German novel. Thomas Mann once remarked that the novel was not a German genre, in contrast to drama and lyric poetry, which, though they had their origins elsewhere, were taken up by German writers and adapted to fit their new milieu.[52] The comments came in Mann's fiercely and disturbingly nationalistic treatise *Reflections of a Nonpolitical Man*, written during World War I to support the German cause, and at first glance they would seem to distinguish between native and non-native genres, the latter of which, in Mann's view, should be studiously avoided by artists if they want to write works that resonate with the German spirit. Yet, to the extent that Mann was a novelist himself, it would be hard to claim that his comments were meant to denigrate the genre in which he himself had his greatest artistic achievements. The issue, rather, was the German novel itself, which had not undergone the same transformations as the English, French, and Russian novel did when in the nineteenth century they became models of realist representation. In *Mimesis* Erich Auerbach famously criticizes the German realist novel for being hopelessly local and picturesque in comparison with its French counterparts, though he acknowledges in the same breath that life in the German-speaking territories "was much more provincial, much more old-fashioned, much less 'contemporary'" than in cosmopolitan France and hence required a different form of narrative representation, if literature was to satisfy its mimetic function.[53] Auerbach's judgment, however, is surprisingly ahistorical in the sense that it does not account for the theory of the novel that arose with the genre itself in Germany. Friedrich Schlegel's conviction that the novel epitomizes the self-reflexive spirit of the modern age paves the way for the split between the narrating and narrated subject typical of German fiction. Schlegel's prescription that modern literature should present "the producer along with the product" is, in fact, tailor-made for a genre like the pseudo-memoir that narrates its own genesis, or, put otherwise, fictionalizes its own writing.[54]

The only other genre as attentive to its own emergence is autobiography, in which the narrator frequently dramatizes the moment of recollection before launching into a narrative of his earlier years. While pseudo-memoirs are more concerned with the category of fiction and especially the fiction of life than in conveying lived experiences, they nonetheless draw on the conventions of life-writing. For this reason, this study is organized around what Lejeune identifies as the four fundamental requirements for autobiography. Chapter 1, "The Character: Thomas Mann's *Felix Krull*," explores what it means to be a protagonist through a reflection on Mann's celebrated trickster Felix Krull. Early in the novel the narrator reports on his first trip to the theater as a youth in decidedly religious terms as a communal experience that elevates actor and audience alike to a realm of light where they are freed of all material burdens. The episode provides the framework for Krull's subsequent account of his early years as a con artist as he learns the tools of his trade, which are not dissimilar to those of an actor. According to him both actor and con artist create an illusion in which they and their respective audiences can share, relieved of the gravity of existence and invigorated by the aesthetic play. The dynamic extends to the readers of Krull's confessions, who likewise share in the illusion he creates for them as a writer who fashions an image of himself as a once-dazzling beauty. The first two books of Thomas Mann's unfinished novel draw on the theater to elucidate the relationship between the reader and writer as mediated through the character, who represents the aesthetic spectacle. The model is specifically Nietzschean: the Krull we follow as he moves from a lift boy in a hotel to a faux aristocrat is an Apollonian figure, which is to say an illusion marked as an illusion, or a fiction that makes no claim to reality.

Yet, as Friedrich Nietzsche pointed out in *The Birth of Tragedy*, every Apollonian illusion requires a Dionysian ground, and it is this ground that comes to the fore in the straddling third book that does not so much conclude as fizzle out. The line separating Krull, the writer and narrator, from Krull, the character and narrated figure, becomes harder to discern, as Krull turns into every character he meets. In other words, he ceases to be an isolated figure that can be seen and narrated from afar as he turns into the entire fictional world, which is a world of semblance, as registered in the conspicuously doubled names (Loulou, Zouzou, Zaza, Kuckkuck) that dominate in the novel's second half. Krull disappears as an individual character in order to return as the space of the work in a transformation that calls into question the distinction between reality and illusion or being and semblance.

Chapter 2, "The Narrator: Robert Walser's *Jakob von Gunten*," builds on the idea of fiction as a world of appearances, but only to reverse the stakes. If, in *Felix Krull*, the narrator relinquishes his position outside the text that he ostensibly writes, in *Jakob von Gunten* the narrator capitalizes on his position at the edge of the diegetic space, to engineer his escape from his own work—in this case, a diary—as well as from the narrative illusion. According to Jakob he is a pupil in a school for servants, and his stated aim is to become a nobody, "a charming, perfectly spherical zero [*eine reizende, kugelrunde Null*]" that no one notices, which is the perfect comportment for a servant. At the same time, a person that no one notices is everywhere potentially, and the text plays with this paradox to orchestrate Jakob's disappearance from the work and his immersion in a life beyond all semblance. What makes this departure possible is Jakob's dual position: he is not only a narrator or diary-keeper, who tells his own tale, but also the mirror image of another diary keeper, who shares the pronoun "I" with him. In Gérard Genette's terminology he is the homo- and heterodiegetic narrator of the work, which is an impossible proposition as long as one assumes with Émile Benveniste that the "I" is a unique instance of discourse that is wedded to the time and place of its articulation. Yet *Jakob von Gunten* calls this fundamental position of linguistics into question and in so doing provides a fertile ground for reconsidering Lejeune's formalist definition of autobiography and Käte Hamburger's equally formalist account of fiction.

Chapter 3, "The Work: Thomas Bernhard's *Extinction*," considers the excess that accompanies every modern fictional work as a fable of its own production or a narrative of its own creation. This may seem like an odd stance to take with respect to a work whose narrator states that his aim is to extinguish every trace of his birthplace as a result of its Nazi past and continued xenophobia in a memoir entitled *Extinction*. *Extinction* should by this measure be the story not of its production but of its narrative unraveling, its *Zerfall*, which is the German subtitle of the work and means roughly its disintegration or crumbling. Yet such an interpretation assumes that the work we read is the memoir that the narrator wanted to write or that he managed to write before his death, which is registered in the novel's first and final sentences. The text, however, offers another possibility for interpretation, which is more powerful in terms of exposing how literature can undo, unravel, or unwork itself. Here is where the self-reflexive nature of the modern novel first theorized by the German Romantics comes into play.

Extinction tells the story of a work that never comes to pass; it chronicles a wish that is never realized because of the narrator's premature death. The narrator's intended memoir is to this extent extinguished before it starts, and what he takes to the grave with him is finally his birthplace, Wolfsegg, by turning its name into an empty sign. The gesture admittedly comes at a cost: it renders whatever is represented into what the narrator calls "the allegedly factual [*das vermeintlich Tatsächliche*]" and what we might call "fictional." Even fiction, however, is sustained by a voice that it can never capture or reproduce and turn into a represented content. The chapter explores this excess through Lukács's account of transcendental subjectivity in his *Theory of the Novel* and Barthes's concept of the *punctum*.

Chapter 4, "The Author: W.G. Sebald's *Vertigo*," examines what happens when an author becomes a character in his own work and in so doing submits to the vicissitudes of writing and fiction-making. Drawing on Maurice Blanchot's *The Space of Literature*, the chapter argues that fiction and nonfiction, or semblance and life, are no longer distinguishable in modernity, because the author no longer represents a point outside the text. Rather, he is embedded in the work as a written figure that returns from the archive of literature, which is not only the repository of all written works, but also constitutes the world insofar as the world, according to *Vertigo*, is a text. In other words, it is a discursive sphere governed by laws, which, however much an author may seek to articulate them, he can never comprehend or master. Every effort to decipher these laws draws the author deeper into a web, in which the here-and-now becomes indistinguishable from a there-and-then and everything living turns into a ghostly presence. The chapter explores how the narrator, named W. G. Sebald, becomes a doppelgänger for other writers from Stendhal and Casanova to Franz Grillparzer, Franz Kafka, and Hugo von Hofmannsthal. Yet even these historical authors are nothing but faces for the perpetually homeless writer, the Hunter Gracchus in Kafka's similarly entitled tale.

The conclusion takes up the theme of semblance prominent in every chapter from a specifically phenomenological perspective. Departing from Nietzsche's declaration in *The Birth of Tragedy* that existence is only aesthetically justified, the conclusion argues that the phenomena considered in the study can be understood via Husserl's theory of intentionality. Felix Krull serves as the quintessential intended object—that is, an appearance with no claim to being—as soon as he abandons his position as a memoirist and becomes instead each and every character in the third book, which is to say a figure that is a double without any reference to an original. Jakob von Gunten, by contrast, is the quintessential intending subject, who constantly depicts what turns out to be a mere appearance to engineer his escape into a world beyond all semblance. The narrator of Bernhard's *Extinction* is unable to begin his memoir, which is intended to extinguish all trace of his past, so he produces instead a memoir that extinguishes the possibility of this project by literally and figuratively robbing him of breath. The narrator and supposed author of Sebald's *Vertigo* suffers a similar fate, but what disappears with him is not the possibility of a work but of authorship itself, as the writer is transformed into a character in his own text. He is exposed as written figure, dictated by an invisible hand (an evil genius, perhaps), which is at once the Cartesian nightmare of an irrational world and the truth of fiction as the expression of a subjectivity that is not the possession of any one person.

1 The Character
Thomas Mann's *Felix Krull*

What would happen if a character in a novel were to renounce his claim to existence? What if he told us he was merely an invented figure? Would we continue to read the novel with the same interest we had when we cast all doubt aside and took the fiction for the truth for no other reason than that it gave us pleasure to do so? Would we be inclined to follow the adventures of a hero who so proudly proclaimed he was not like us? Would we be able to lose ourselves in a fictional world, if the fiction itself foregrounds that it is nothing but a "shadow of the imagination"?[1]

These are basic—and nonetheless pressing—questions in that they underscore that fiction requires the faith or trust of the reader that a seeming life can tell us something about living. This faith exceeds that encapsulated in the phrase "the suspension of disbelief" that is invariably invoked to describe a reader who has the luxury of believing what her better judgment tells her is false. Belief in fiction is not necessarily a temporary condition, nor does it have to imply a lapse in judgment, as if we exercised our critical faculties only when skeptical about phenomena. Rather, we believe stories we know to be untrue because we accept that illusion is an integral part of life insofar as human beings not only act but also imitate actions. Thinkers as varied as Aristotle and Johann Huizinga have repeatedly pointed out that imitation is not only how we learn, but how we interact with others as social beings who participate in all manner of collective life as much for our enjoyment as our survival.[2]

Aristotle's definition of epic and dramatic literature as "the imitation of men in action" has set the standard for some time not only for what literature is but also life insofar as life is the supposed subject of literature.[3] According to this definition, life is the sphere in which people engage in actions of various kinds, from tilling the soil to arguing over the

31

price of goods, and from building houses to discussing the foundations of knowledge. Hannah Arendt does not so much dispute as expand on this position in *The Human Condition* when she claims that in drama actors imitate not actions but the playing or acting that constitutes existence.[4] Our life unfolds in the sphere in which we show ourselves to others through speech and action, which are fundamentally different than labor and work, the two other pursuits identified by Arendt as characteristic of our existence. We labor to secure the basic conditions for our survival, and we work to ensure our comfort by manufacturing tools and instruments that extend our body so we can accomplish more than our immediate objectives. Speech and action are different in that what motivates them is neither need nor utility. We speak and act to disclose ourselves to others who, like us, are unique individuals with distinct pasts and particular prospects for the future.[5] This is what separates the human being from all other creatures, according to Arendt. We appear to each other not simply as something (say, a member of the species), but also as someone, whose life can never be exchanged with that of another. Speech and action communicate this "intangible" uniqueness, as Arendt puts it, and in so doing create a space in which we are equal but distinct individuals, which, for the political philosopher, is the hallmark of being human.[6]

Arendt places particular emphasis on the community that speech and action foster insofar as they are always directed at someone who can speak and act on her own or in response to others. What Arendt does not account for, however, is the possibility that someone may speak to disavow all community on the grounds that she is nothing but an appearance and has no "living essence," which, according to Arendt, is what our words and deeds always express.[7] This is the situation sketched at the beginning of this chapter; it also arises in the third book of Thomas Mann's unfinished novel *Confessions of Felix Krull, Confidence Man*. In this pseudo-memoir the narrator retreats from the reader's sight, as he assumes the identity of another to such a degree that he can no longer be distinguished from the role he feigns, plays, or acts in his own narrative. Arendt would no doubt argue that the narrator can lose himself in this manner because he is "made" as a work of art, whereas a living person is never "made," only born, parented but never manufactured.[8] The distinction, however, is not entirely convincing if we accept with Arendt that literature as the "imitation of men in action" says something about life and the ways in which we appear to each other in our uniqueness. If literature reveals how we disclose ourselves to each other in our public life, then it matters little whether its figures are self-producing or the products of an invisible hand. In either case they reveal a fundamental aspect of our social life—namely, that we interact with each other on the public stage as appearances, or, to recall Thomas Hobbes's term, "personae." In the *Leviathan*, he writes, "The word person is Latin, instead whereof the Greeks have prosopon, which signifies the face, as persona in Latin signifies the disguise, or outward appearance of a man, counterfeited on the stage."[9] We interact with each other in our public roles in disguise. We are each to this degree confidence men.

As the title of Mann's novel indicates, Felix Krull is also a confidence man, and he earns his living impersonating others who are usually—but not exclusively—types he imagines. He only appears to this degree hidden behind a mask: the mask of another's appearance, another's speech and actions. This is what he tells the reader, at least, in the confessions he writes at the age of forty, when he has aleady left the world stage because of failing health and fading beauty. He takes the reader into his confidence as he recounts his journey up the social ladder from a mere lift boy at a hotel like Kafka's Karl Roßmann to a European aristocrat. Krull insists that the position he attains is his natural right as an individual "cut from the finest cloth [*aus dem feinsten Holze geschnitzt*]," to cite one of his favorite expressions (*Bekenntnisse, 273*). Indeed his insistence that he is an aristocrat by nature, if not by birth, lends his confessions the air of a confidence man's last ploy—that is, an attempt on the part of the narrator to convince the reader that he is something he is not. Yet it is questionable whether Krull is anything apart from his performances, if he has another life, or whether living in this novel is not simply the process of appearing to be unique and of disclosing what one does not possess.

Thomas Mann worked on *Felix Krull* throughout his life. As early as 1906, he wrote two entries in his notebooks that formed the basis for key chapters in the second and third books of the novel.[10] In 1910 he began to work on the project in earnest before abandoning it to devote himself to "Death in Venice," which he completed in 1912. He then returned to *Felix Krull* and by late 1913 finished both the first book of the novel as well as the conscription episode in the second. A hiatus of some forty years followed. In 1943 Mann considered returning to the novel, but decided that it was outdated in its emphasis on the tension between the artist and bourgeois society. Indeed, with war raging in Europe and the questions that National Socialism raised about German culture, Mann had more pressing concerns, such as the legacy of Friedrich Nietzsche, Richard Wagner, and Arthur Schopenhauer, whom he had named as his intellectual forebears in his controversial 1918 essay collection *Reflections of a Non-Political Man* and whose works were now invoked in the service of a genocidal politics and ethnonationalism.[11] In this World War I volume, Mann defended Germany as a unique culture that was compelled to defend itself against the homogenizing forces of Western civilization. The volume would cast a cloud over Mann's reputation throughout his life, even as he made explicit statements condemning fascism and urging the development of democratic institutions in Germany. Between 1943 and 1947 he worked on the novel *Doktor Faustus*, which presents an allegory for Germany's demise in the figure of the composer Andreas Leverkühn, who is modeled after Nietzsche and himself represents the consummate Dionysian artist that Nietzsche praised in *The Birth of Tragedy*. In 1951 Mann resumed work on *Felix Krull* and by 1954 drafted the third book. Throughout this period he was plagued by the fear that the novel was frivolous and, as such, unbecoming for an author of his advanced years. At the same time he mentioned in at least two letters, including one to Theodor W. Adorno, that the novel had taken a "Faustian" turn.[12] Unable to complete the project, Mann published the first three books with the subtitle "Der Memoiren erster Teil" (Part 1 of the Memoirs) in 1954.[13] He died the following year at the age of eighty.

Frivolity and Faust—these two terms are not usually associated with each other, and yet it is their conjunction that makes *Felix Krull* more than a picaresque novel, as its immediate literary precedents would suggest. According to Hans Wysling, Thomas Mann read Georges Manolescu's popular two-volume autobiography shortly after its publication in 1905.[14] The skill of this hotel thief in simulating mental illness no doubt influenced Mann as he wrote the first and second books of the novel, in which Krull successfully displays the symptoms of fever, migraines, and epilepsy. Yet the other precedent for *Felix Krull* that Mann acknowledged was Goethe's *Dichtung und Wahrheit*, which served as a model for this novel not only in its construction of a mythical version of the self, but also in the questions it raised about the truth of literature, *die Wahrheit der Dichtung.* It is no accident that, when Krull meets the Marquis de Venosta and Venosta proposes that they trade places, Krull has a ticket to see Gounod's *Faust* in his pocket, which had been his original destination that evening.[15] The passage into the world of spectacle occurs under the sign of Faust, and the stay there ends with the emergence of the Faustian mothers in the form of the dark and sensuous Maria Pia.

This chapter argues that the text's principal concern is not the relation of literature to reality. It does not contend with the issue of what is real or feigned, even if Krull sometimes refers to his performances in this fashion, for even when he does so, it is invariably to underscore that he is as he appears, or, put otherwise, that he embodies what he shows. These and similar comments point to the Nietzschean dimensions of the text as an exploration not of the imitation of reality but of the reality of imitation, which is to say the truth particular to fiction. It is as the supposed confessions of a confidence man that Mann's novel shows the invented nature of any character and, one might say, of character itself as an illusion.

The Faustian turn of the text is a continuation of the exploration of art in *Doktor Faustus* as the sphere where truth appears, or, in Heideggerian parlance, "happens."[16] In *Doktor Faustus* truth sounds at the end of the novel in what would seem to be a literal expression of what Nietzsche called "primordial pain" in the following remark on the Dionysian artist in *The Birth of Tragedy*: "The Dionysian musician is, without any images, himself pure primordial pain [*Urschmerz*] and its primoridial re-echoing [*Urwiederklang*]."[17] When Andreas Leverkühn sets out to play his magnum opus, *Dr. Fausti Weheklag*, he produces only a dissonant chord and then a wail that is simultaneously the text's comment on an art that has sought to divest itself of all images: "At the same time he opened his mouth as if to sing, but from between his lips there emerged only a wail [*ein Klagelaut*] that still rings in my ears. Bending over the instrument, he spread his arms wide as if to embrace it and suddenly, as if pushed, fell sideways from his chair to the floor."[18] While Krull would appear to be the opposite of this Dionysian artist in almost every respect, he takes a decided turn toward the demonic in book 3 as he abandons his dual role as narrator and protagonist. The restraint that in the first two books had singled him out as the consummate Apollonian artist gives way to an excess that can only be described as Dionysian, because it destroys the boundaries that made Krull recognizable as an artist in the first place. Krull becomes an image that is infinitely mutable, or, in his vocabuarly, a *Gleichnis* (fiction, simile, or analogy) that extends beyond the confines of this unfinished—and possibly unfinishable—work, owing to the perpetual metamorphosis of its protagonist.

Birth

The beginning of *Felix Krull* is doubled, like so much else in the text. In the first chapter Krull introduces himself as the supposed author of this confessional work, which he writes not only "at leisure" but also "in complete retirement" (*Confessions*, 3) owing to his failing health. In the second chapter he introduces himself again as a character beginning with his birth, which he claims to remember with surprising vividness: "Frequent reflection on this subject, moreover, inclines me to the belief that this reluctance to exchange the darkness of the womb for the light of day is connected with my extraordinary gift and passion for sleep, a characteristic of mine from infancy" (8).

What Krull resists at birth is not only the encounter with light but also with himself, which would come about were he to leave the maternal womb, where he had not yet experienced being divided from anything else.[19] In "On Narcissism" Sigmund Freud argues that the persistence of this memory and fantasy leads to narcissism in later life, and his analysis of this pathology has influenced the reception of Mann's novel. Bernhard F. Malkmus, for instance, writes, "In *Felix Krull*, the regressive element of self-affection is conflated with a panerotic embrace of the world. Felix presents his environment as an obliging servant who never ceases to tend to his narcissistic desires, and he is more than willing to return these favors."[20] It is this autoerotic tendency that explains in part Krull's unusual gift as a child to sleep for hours on end and to lose himself in "dreamless forgetfulness" (*Confessions*, 8). Sleep represents not an entrance into but a respite from dreams, which preoccupy him most the day, if one takes him at his word. In this vein he recounts that as a boy he imagined he was a prince named Karl and "clung to this fantasy [*Träumerei*] all day long" (*Confessions*, 10; *Bekenntnisse*, 272). One could object that fantasies are not the same as dreams, which surface at night when consciousness sleeps, but this is not a distinction that Krull accepts for reasons that become apparent when he comments on his current situation. At the age of forty, Krull is no longer able to sleep as he once did.

Indeed, he becomes an insomniac when he can no longer enchant audiences with his grace and beauty: "It is only now that my capacity for sleep is impaired so that I am in a sense a stranger to it" (*Confessions*, 9). Unable to see himself in the eyes of others any longer, he is forced to take up the pen. His insomnia drives him to write his memoirs, in which he can still dream of himself as a figure of unparalleled charm and beauty.

Part of this fantasized life is his birth, which Krull takes ownership of by claiming to remember it in some detail. Much like Tristram Shandy in what is arguably the model for all pseudo-memoirs, Krull narrates his birth as if it were an event that, as a newborn, he had already anticipated he would record decades later. Seen in this light, the description has a twofold purpose. First, it enables Krull to give birth to himself as a character who will always bask in the light of sun. Second, it allows him to harken back to a time when he was still shrouded in darkness, unknown to the world and even to himself. It is from this unconscious state that he ushers himself into being as a radiant, if not godlike, creature encountered only in dreams. The same structure will inform his discussion of his Christian name, which follows closely on the heels of his birth.

Baptism

Krull introduces his name to deny his actual parentage in favor of another, which is more suited to his image of himself as a natural aristocrat rather than a commoner:

Often enough I heard from my parents' lips that I was a Sunday child, and although I was brought up to reject every form of superstition, I have always thought there was a secret significance in that fact taken in connection with my Christian name of Felix (for so I was called, after my godfather Schimmelpreester), and my physical fineness and attractiveness. Yes, I have always believed myself favored of fortune and of Heaven, and I may say that, on the whole, experience has borne me out. Indeed, it has been peculiarly characteristic of my career that whatever misfortunes and sufferings it may have contained have always seemed an exception to the natural order, a cloud, as it were, through which the sun of my native luck continued to shine [*daß alles, was an Leiden und Qual vorgekommen, als etwas Fremdes und von der Vorsehung ur-*

sprünglich nicht Gewolltes erscheint, durch das meine wahre und ei-
gentliche Bestimmung immerfort gleichsam sonnig hindurchschim-
mert]. (Confessions, 9; Bekenntnisse, 271)

Krull does not hesitate to declare that his name is emblematic of his
being. Throughout the passage he emphasizes that good fortune—the
Latin root of the name "Felix"—has characterized his life, and that any
misfortune he suffered was a mere accident that his true nature overcame. Chief among these accidents was the biological family into which
he was born and from which he distances himself by highlighting that
he is named after his godfather, Schimmelpreester, who often painted
him in his youth. Even his godfather, however, is not so much a model for him as a figure he invents to claim that his identity has nothing
to do with his biological family. The one function of his parents in this
passage is to declare that he is not of their kind: "Often enough I heard
from my parents' lips that I was a Sunday child." Taken figuratively "a
Sunday child" would mean that he is a youth blessed by providence,
but a more literal interpretation would suggest that he is a child of the
sun, perhaps even a descendent of Apollo. If the latter possibility carries more weight, it is because Krull himself underscores that throughout his life his true nature has always shone through adversity like the
sun through a cloud.

This is how Krull baptizes himself Felix. He takes his given name
and turns it into an emblem for his fate, so that his "native luck" can
overcome all adversity. The curiosity of this statement is that what Krull
calls his "native luck" is the calling he has chosen for himself as the
person who functions in this passage as a priest, both christening himself as well as washing away the taint of his biological origins. Krull is
truly and properly Felix, a fortunate creature, only in a world of semblance in which a given name can become a providential sign because
the narrating subject opts to see it in this fashion. Krull would seem
to recognize the stakes of this operation when he states that the "sun
of [his] native luck continue[s] to shine." His felicitous nature shim-
mers like the sun because it is pure *Schein* in both senses of the term,
as the shining of the sun and as an illusion.[21] In turning something as
arbitrary as his given name into his essence, Krull sets himself up as
character who is all surface, with no hidden depths. The reward for

this transformation is pleasure at the sight of a character who can surmount any obstacle because he is literally "Felix," a lucky creature. It is a pleasure shared by the reader and narrator alike, since the delight in semblance is always reciprocal, as Krull discovers when he goes to the theater with his father.

Communion

The trip to the theater falls in Krull's fourteenth year, which would be a trivial detail if Krull did not make so much of it in his prologue to the episode. His ostensible purpose in mentioning his age is to demonstrate the liberties he has taken in representing his childhood up to this point. A writer, he tells us, should not adhere anxiously to chronology when it does not suit his purpose. But the age of fourteen is significant in another context. Originally the sacrament of the Eucharist was celebrated only when a child had reached the age where he could distinguish between the communion wafer and ordinary bread. Krull likewise emphasizes the maturity necessary to appreciate the theater. He attends it for the first time as "[his] physical and mental development . . . was well advanced and [his] receptivity to impressions of a certain kind much greater than ordinary" (*Confessions*, 23). At this age of discretion he is introduced to the mysteries of the stage, which he does not hesitate to describe in quasi-mystical terms:

> Never before except in church had I seen so many people gathered together in a large and stately auditorium; and this theatre with its impressive seating-arrangements and its elevated stage where privileged personages, brilliantly costumed and accompanied by music, went through their dialogues and dances, their songs and routines— certainly all this was in my eyes a temple of pleasure [*eine Kirche des Vergnügens*], where men in need of edification gathered in darkness and gazed upward open-mouthed into a realm of brightness and perfection [*eine Sphäre der Klarheit und Vollendung*]where they beheld the ideals of their hearts. (*Confessions*, 24, translation modified; *Bekenntnisse*, 287)

One has all the trappings of a church here: the cathedral ceilings, the altar at the front, and the regally costumed figures who perform songs and dances and recite a preordained text. The only missing element is the incense, but Krull more than makes up for this deficit by pointing out the effect of the performance on the audience. What he calls a "realm of brightness and perfection [*eine Sphäre der Klarheit und der Vollendung*]" provides an occasion for the audience's transfiguration. For the duration of the performance, the audience members are transported to a realm of light, even if they remain seated in the dark. What they see before them is not an objective phenomenon but the "ideals of their hearts." Theater is the place where viewers experience "the realization of all their own secret dreams of beauty, grace, and perfection" (*Confessions*, 29). This is the mystery of the theater, the miracle performed there night after night. And, consistent with the miracles of the Church, the theater concludes with the sharing of something that Krull names with surprising direct-ness, given his otherwise overblown diction. Summing up the accom-plishments of the main actor, he states, "Yes, that was it. Müller-Rosé dispensed the joy of life [*Lebensfreude*]" (*Confessions*, 26; *Bekenntnisse*, 289). "Joy of life" is the Eucharist of the "temple of pleasure." It trans-forms and transfigures young and old alike to such a degree that, when "Müller-Rosé left the stage, shoulders slumped and vitality seemed to go out of the audience" (*Confessions*, 26, translation modified).

It is tempting to assume that this description of the theater is tongue-in-cheek due to the extravagance of Krull's rhetoric, which is consistent with the overall tone of the novel as a romp or parody. At the same time, the commentary is dead earnest in its exploration of the pleasure of illu-sion or spectacle. This may seem like an odd position to take in light of Krull's disillusionment later in the chapter, when he meets Müller-Rosé in his dressing room. Whatever glory the actor radiated from the stage is replaced with a sight that Krull finds repugnant, although his dis-gust does not dampen his rhetoric; if anything, it makes it more florid. He remarks with perverse relish that Müller-Rosé's upper body is cov-ered with particularly grotesque pimples: "They were horrible pustules, red-rimmed, suppurating, some of them even bleeding" (*Confessions*, 28). More important, stripped of his makeup and costume, the actor no longer seems human in Krull's eyes. He refers to him as "this repulsive worm [*dieser unappetitlicher Erdenwurm*]" (*Confessions*, 29; *Bekenntnisse*, 294) and compares him to "one of those repellent little creatures that have the power of glowing phosphorescently at night [*eines jener eklen Weichtierchen, die, wenn ihre abendliche Stunde kommt, märchenhaft zu glühen befähigt sind]"* (*Confessions*, 29; *Bekenntnisse*, 294). In short, he is not a man, but a dissembler of one, which is a curious position inasmuch as it identifies being human with a mere performance. Müller-Rosé is a human being only when he appears masked on the stage. In the flesh he is nothing but "stench and innards [*Gekrös' nur und Gestank*]" (*Bekenntnisse*, 633), to recall a nursery rhyme that causes Krull some aggravation in the third book.

This is not coincidental. Throughout the episode Krull underscores that the theater elevates actor and spectator in equal measure. Müller-Rosé leaves behind the shell of his body to become a gallant hero who is impeccable in every respect, as the audience leaves behind its cares and worries to participate in a dreamlike realm where they are not burdened by the weight of existence. Krull therefore concludes that the theater is a reciprocal venture in which the audience and the actor satisfy each other's desires, thereby creating the spectacle on stage. This would seem to be the impetus behind the rhetorical question Krull poses at the end of the chapter: "And if he [the actor] bestows on them [the audience] the joy of life and they satiate him with applause for doing so, is not that a mutual fulfillment, a meeting and marriage of his yearning and theirs?" (*Confessions*, 30). For all the flourish of Krull's phrasing, his question is marked by a curious understatement. He reduces theater to a commercial transaction in which the actor is paid with applause for the joy he disseminates. The mundane nature of this exchange is designed to contain a more dangerous potential in the theater that is not far removed from the world of insects and earthworms.

At first Krull would seem to adopt the position that theater edifies actor and audience alike, so that each can appear human for the first time. The audience is relieved of the burdens of daily life, as the actor is relieved of the burden of his blemished body. Krull emphasizes this aspect of the theater from the actor's perspective. After meeting Müller-Rosé, he calls him "a charmer [*ein Herzensdieb*]" (*Confessions*, 29; *Bekenntnisse*, 294), which is consistent with the myth of the artist as a thief that his godfather told him in his youth. All artists are thieves to the extent that they take from others what they do not possess themselves to produce something that would seem to be of greater value. Müller-Rosé steals the dreams of his audience to transform himself into a figure that is not tarnished by any blemish. But the same could also be said of the audi-

ence that takes Müller-Rosé's appearance onstage as an occasion to realize its dreams and fantasies.

This is where the dangerous potential of theater emerges for Krull. At
first he tries to treat it as an epistemological problem, albeit with limited success:

> But the grown-up people in the audience, who on the whole must
> know about life, and who yet were so frightfully eager to be de-
> ceived, must they not have been aware of the deception? Or did
> they privately not take the deception for deception [*Oder achteten
> sie in stillschweigendem Einverständnis den Betrug nicht für Betrug*]?
> And that is quite possible. For when you come to think of it, which
> is the real shape of the glowworm: the insignificant little creature
> crawling about on the palm of your hand, or the poetic spark that
> swims through the summer night. Who would presume to say?
> (*Confessions*, 29–30, translation modified; *Bekenntnisse*, 294)

The example Krull chooses is no doubt self-serving. It is in his interest to maintain that the firefly is most itself when it appears as a "poetic spark" at night, since this ensures that he, too, is most himself when
he appears as a radiant figure in his own writing. Yet the allusion to the
animal kingdom comes back to haunt Krull in his exploration of the
magic of the stage and, by extension, the magic of semblance. Already,
when he looked at the audience, what he saw was not a collection of be-
atific faces but a swarm lost in self-forgetfulness and intent on its own
destruction: "Yes, this whole shadowy assembly was like an enormous
swarm of nocturnal insects, silently, blindly, and blissfully rushing into
a blazing fire" (*Confessions*, 27). Lest one think that this is a chance image, Krull refers to it again: "Recall the picture you saw before: the giant
swarm of poor moths and gnats, rushing silently and madly into the enticing flame" (30). What enables the theatrical spectacle to come about is
the willingness of the audience and the actor to abandon themselves to
their dreams. Yet, in abandoning themselves, they lose sight of the performance that had enchanted them; they become a swarm that throws
itself into the fire ignited on the stage, a Dionysian mass that transforms
the Apollonian "realm of brightness and perfection" (34) into a space
devoid of light and emptied of all discernible figures. Krull attempts to
contain this thought in an analogy, but the analogy of a swarm can only

be seen if the reader shuts her eyes and looks at the darkness in front of her, her blindness serving as (a) vision.

Apollo and Dionysus

In *The Birth of Tragedy*, Nietzsche insists that the Apollonian and Dionysian drives are opposing forces in nature; to suggest otherwise would be false. Yet what becomes a more vexing question as the work progresses is whether the arts associated with each of these tendencies can be characterized as strictly Dionysian or Apollonian. At first the distinction would seem to be self-evident: Apollo as the god of the sun presides over the arts that triumph in the production of the beautiful semblance, *der schöne Schein*, which we encounter, among other places, in our dreams at night. Dionysus, by contrast, as the god of festivals and of wine, is the father of those arts that dissolve the boundaries between individuals and unite them in a flowing whole, such as music or the dithyramb. Nietzsche sums up the Apollonian and Dionysian drives under the headings of dream (*Traum*) and intoxication (*Rausch*). The former as a visual phenomenon consists in clarity and light, whereas the latter as an acoustic phenomenon consists in movement, energy, and exuberance.

Were this the extent of the opposition between the two drives, it would not be difficult to separate them from each other. The distinction, however, is troubled from the start by what could be considered the metaphysical mission of art as the expression of the truth of existence. This added dimension makes it all but impossible to conceive of an art that is purely Apollonian or Dionysian, since the two drives have a common origin. Every static image is a figuration of the universal ground of being as, conversely, every articulation of this ground is a particular work that adheres to the dictates of form, no matter how dynamic it may seem. What distinguishes various art forms, then, is not the drive that motivates them but the balance between opposing tendencies. Apollo needs Dionysus, as Nietzsche himself admits, but Dionysus also needs Apollo, if he is not to throw himself headlong into the "enticing flame" and to devour his own image.

Nietzsche first locates the Apollonian tendency in the world of dreams, which he argues is the basis for all the fine arts, as well as the epic and some forms of lyric poetry. His analysis begins with dreams rather than, say, cultural artifacts, for two equally important reasons. First, the presence in dreams of a formative drive indicates that the Apollonian tendency arises in nature, not in our conscious or waking faculties. (Later he will suggest that we bear nature within ourselves, even if we are unaware of it.) Second, the implicit contrast between dreams and waking reality provides Nietzsche with an occasion to introduce the notion of semblance (*Schein*) that will dominate the remainder of his discussion. He is quick to point out that, however real a dream may seem, we never lose sight of the fact that it is a semblance: "But even when this dream reality is most intense, we still have, glimmering through it, the sensation that it is *mere appearance* [*Schein*]" (*Birth*, 34, emphasis in original). This sensation does not reflect the intrusion of reality into our dreams but is a feature of appearance itself, which always draws attention to itself as an appearance. It foregrounds its immateriality to set itself apart from all the other elements as a perfectly defined form, a beautiful appearance, an aesthetic phenomenon.

Nietzsche borrows Schopenhauer's concept of the "principium individuationis" to denote the limit that the dream imposes on itself. In his variation on this concept, Apollo represents the most conspicuous manifestation of this principle as "the 'shining one,' the deity of light," who makes all things visible in his radiance. Yet what he opposes is not the empirical world or waking reality, as one might expect. This, too, will come to rank as a mere illusion for Nietzsche. Rather, Apollo is separated from the ground of being that he at the same time represents in his very image, which forms a "middle world" between Titanic chaos and human frailty:

> The Greek knew and felt the terror and horror of existence. That he might endure this terror at all, he has to interpose between himself and life the radiant dream-birth of the Olympians. That overwhelming dismay in the face of the titanic powers of nature . . . was again and again overcome by the Greek with the aid of the Olympian *middle world* [*Mittelwelt*] of art; or at any rate it was veiled and withdrawn from sight. It was in order to be able to live that the Greeks had to create these gods from a most profound need. Perhaps we may picture the process to ourselves somewhat as follows: out of the original Titanic divine order of terror, the Olympian divine order of joy gradually evolved through the Apollonian impulse toward beauty, just as roses burst from thorny bushes. (*Birth*, 42–43; *Geburt*, 30)

The seemingly trite simile at the conclusion of this passage is telling inasmuch as it indicates that the "middle world" of the Olympian gods grows out of the "titanic powers of nature" just as "roses burst from thorny bushes." Even if the Olympian gods would seem to be opposed to this subterranean current, they remain connected to it as the projection of this ground in a beautiful image or blossom. It is precisely this image that *mediates* or *intervenes* between the "terror and horror of existence" and humans as mortal beings. Nietzsche refers to the gods as a reflection of the individual and asserts that their chief purpose is to allow mortals to see themselves transformed into divine beings. Mortals triumph over the forces of nature that would otherwise engulf them through the image of the gods, which they create as a beautiful semblance or a work of art: "This is the sphere of beauty in which [the Greeks] saw their mirror images, the Olympians" (*Birth*, 44).

The relation of the Greeks to their gods resembles that of the audience to the actor in *Felix Krull*. Just as the Greeks see themselves elevated and transformed in their gods, so, too, the spectators see the "ideals of their heart" realized in the actor on stage. It is not only the actor, however, who functions as an image; the audience does so as well, if one takes Nietzsche's words to heart regarding the empirical world we normally assume to be a given reality. As part of an extended thought experiment, Nietzsche proposes:

If, for the moment, we do not consider the question of our own "reality," if we conceive of our empirical existence, and of that of the world in general, as a continuously manifested representation of the primal unity [*Vorstellung des Ur-Einen*], we shall then have to look upon the dream as a *mere appearance of mere appearance* [*Schein des Scheins*], hence as a still higher appeasement of the primordial desire for mere appearance. (*Birth*, 45; *Geburt*, 33, emphasis in original)

According to this thought experiment, the empirical world is an illusion generated by the "primal unity" of existence, which Nietzsche elaborates on elsewhere in the chapter as "primal pain" and "as that which is eternally suffering and contradictory [*das Ewig-Leidende und Widerspuchsvolle*]" (*Geburt*, 32, my translation). This unity is never apparent in itself, since in itself it is nothing but the unity of all opposing forces or contradictions. Whenever the ground of being appears, then, it does so veiled—specifically, as one of the manifold forms contained within it as basis for all existence. According to Nietzsche both we and the world we inhabit constitute this veil. Put otherwise, we are the reflection of the primal unity which appears in infinitely many forms, each of which is distinct but which all share a common origin. It is in this spirit that he declares that we are an appearance and that our dreams as well as our artworks constitute "*a mere appearance of mere appearance* [*Schein des Scheins*]." Where the necessity for this double appearance comes from remains a question for Nietzsche. He would seem to provide a partial answer when he remarks that the ground of being needs "the rapturous vision, the pleasurable illusion, for its continuous redemption" (*Birth*, 45). Yet the explanation only goes so far, since it does not clarify what redemption through illusion would be.

I would argue that the answer lies in the manner in which the primal unity, *das Ur-Eine*, appears according to Nietzsche—namely, as a multitude of phenomena that are not self-generating and consequently not self-sustaining. To unify this manifold, a second appearance is needed that embraces all phenomena so that they may reflect their ground, which is, again, the unity of opposites. This is the redemption of nature in aesthetics referred to in the quoted passage above. Nature can appear as a whole and as something glorious and divine only through a second appearance that subjects the wild stirrings of nature to the *principium individuationes*. Nature's enchantment with its own image stands in direct proportion to our own delight, since the image of nature is simultaneously an image of ourselves as semblances. The split between the human being and nature is overcome in the "mere appearance of mere appearance," which mirrors both its human producer and its primordial source and unites them in a single aesthetic phenomenon. For this reason, Nietzsche famously declares, "It is only as an *aesthetic phenomenon* that existence and the world are eternally *justified*" (*Birth*, 52, emphasis in original). Inasmuch as we as well as the world are mere appearances of a hidden ground, we can be true to the nature of our being only if we reproduce it in a further image, a work of art. In so doing we reestablish a relation with our foundation, from which we had been divided, as nothing but an illusion that expresses but does not contain its own source.

The three-part scheme sketched here typifies the epic for Nietzsche, which as a genre is to be understood as "the complete triumph of Apollonian illusion" (*Birth*, 43, translation modified). Yet, in insisting on the completeness of this victory, Nietzsche also betrays a doubt that stems from his uncertainty about whether an illusion or appearance will be recognized as such, which is the condition for the triumph of Apollonian measure (*Maß*) over Dionysian excess (*Übermaß*). For Nietzsche what maintains the distinction between the two is self-knowledge, which is an unexpected claim. According to him self-knowledge is inextricably linked to our ability to recognize a dream as a dream, since this recognition derives from our awareness of our own constraints. The opposite of self-knowledge is, consequently, self-forgetfulness, which Nietzsche usually associates with the Dionysian drive, although in one important instance he identifies it with the epic. This occurs when he criticizes Euripides for his use of affect on stage, which he opposes to the "epic absorption in mere appearance [*jenem epischen Verlorensein im Scheine*]" (*Birth*, 83; *Geburt*, 72) in a comment that is as surprising as it is illuminating. Euripides has to invoke dramatic sentiment because what his work lacks is the Dionysian excess and intoxication that can be found even in the naïve art of Homer.

The awareness of this excess informs Krull's image of the theater audience as a swarm of moths that flies into the flame of the spectacle that it sees before it. The audience abandons itself to the illusion onstage in a moment of self-forgetfulness that dissolves all boundaries between individual members. Krull will likewise dissolve or evaporate in book 3 as he becomes every character he meets.

Nietzsche's analysis of lyric poetry and tragedy illuminates Krull's departure as a character from his own text in that Nietzsche treats both the poet and the tragic chorus not as spectators but as participants in the artwork. The poet and the chorus lose themselves in the aesthetic phenomenon and in so doing introduce something into the work that is not aesthetic in the most literal sense: it never *appears* undisguised or naked. In a passage that turns on the verb "to appear," Nietzsche argues that the unaesthetic element of art is the will:

If, therefore, we may regard lyric poetry as the imitative fulguration of music in images and concepts, we should now ask: "As what does music *appear* in the mirror of images and concepts?" It *ap-*

pears as will, taking the term in Schopenhauer's sense, i.e., as the opposite of the aesthetic, purely contemplative, and passive frame of mind [*als Gegensatz der ästhetischen, rein beschaulichen willenlosen Stimmung*]. (*Birth*, 55; *Geburt* 43, emphasis in original)

The passage is based on the assumption that music is a copy, an "Abbild" (*Geburt*, 37), of the primal unity, which is a peculiar statement, given that music is usually considered the one form of art that does not rely on images. Nietzsche would not dispute this position; if anything, he plays on it, to argue that music is, on the one hand, a distinct image of the primal unity and, on the other hand, consistent with its source. It is continuous with the being that it reproduces and represents, which is why it is the only truly Dionysian art mentioned in the text.[22]

Consistent with the three-part scheme discussed earlier, Nietzsche proposes in this passage that the unity of being gives rise to music, which, in turn, gives rise to lyric poetry. Of key importance is that lyric poetry is the appearance, if not the translation, of music into metaphors and concepts. Poetry expresses the essence of this Dionysian art in another medium, with its own vocabulary and laws of syntax. It is in this context that Nietzsche claims that music *appears* as the will in lyric poetry, which brings to the fore the ground of being otherwise excluded from aesthetics, as it can never be a phenomenon. Poetry makes evident what is foreign to appearance: it represents the unrepresentable by exposing the limits of semblance (*Schein*) and in so doing creating a space for a unity that is not contained in metaphors and concepts but undergirds both as their foundation.

This seemingly abstract scheme returns with ever greater persistence in Nietzsche's analysis of tragedy. He argues that tragedy originally consisted of a chorus composed of satyrs that, as patently mythical creatures, could not be confused with nature itself: "For this chorus the Greek built up the scaffolding of a fictitious *natural state* and on it placed fictitious *natural beings*" (*Birth*, 58). As the genre developed, however, the chorus came to face a second element: the tragic spectacle, which Nietzsche characterizes as a vision of Dionysus because it expresses the myth that binds the community, as Dionysus expresses the oneness of everything. Once the spectacle is introduced, the function of the chorus changes. It now lives in and through characters to such a degree that it can no longer be said to look at them from afar but instead to inhabit them: "This process of the tragic chorus is the *dramatic* proto-phenomenon [*Urphänomen*]: to see oneself transformed before one's own eyes and to begin to act *as if* one had actually entered in another body, another character" (*Birth*, 64; *Geburt*, 52, emphasis added). What Nietzsche presents here under the guise of the conditional (i.e., the "as if" formulation) becomes a fact a few sentences later: "Here we have the surrender of individuality and a way of entering into another character [*Einkehr in eine fremde Natur*]" (*Birth*, 64; *Geburt*, 52). Inasmuch as the chorus and, by extension, the audience abandon themselves to live in the tragic mythos on the stage, they experience the enchantment that for Nietzsche can come about only as discrete forms are dissolved and absorbed in the ground of being. He thus concludes that the essence of tragedy is "the shattering of the individual and his fusion with primal being [*sein Einswerden mit dem Ursein*]" (*Birth*, 65; *Geburt*, 53).[23] That this dissolution still occurs within the bounds of representation or art is what makes tragedy "the Apollonian embodiment of Dionysian insights and effects" (*Birth*, 65). In tragedy the audience becomes the artwork itself, which is a dynamic process rather than a static image, something living as opposed to something dead.

The idea of the human being as an artwork (i.e., something crafted or made) could not be further from Arendt's notion of how we disclose ourselves to each other in our individuality. Although we make ourselves known through our appearance and, more specifically, through our words and deeds, these remain mere tools to demonstrate our uniqueness. That Nietzsche places little stock in the notion of uniqueness is evident from the absence of any discussion of this concept in his work. But the deeper reason lies in his skepticism about whether what singles out the human being is, in fact, humanness. Nietzsche's remark in "On Truth and Lies in an Extra-Moral Sense" that truth is "a mobile troop of metaphors, metonymies, anthropomorphisms, in short, a collection of human relations" is worth recalling in this context.[24] If truth is nothing but a "troop of metaphors" marshaled for whatever purpose, then the idea of the human being is equally metaphoric, as Professor Kuckuck implies in his lengthy monologue in the third book of *Felix Krull* on evolution and the chain of being. In a lecture worthy of Nietzsche that touches upon everything from the history of the cosmos to the origins of life, Kuckuck proposes a secret correspondence between all living forms in nature that turns each thing into a metaphor for the other in a potentially never-ending cycle. The correspondence between elements bears witness to nature or, in Nietzsche's vocabulary, the "primal unity" of all forms. To what degree the philosopher serves as the inspiration for Kuckuck can perhaps be gleaned from the professor's ostentatiously fictional name, which recalls Nietzsche's quip in "On Truth and Lies" that the truths of philosophy and science derive from "Wolken*kuckuck*sheim," which literally means a cloud-cuckoo-home and is roughly equivalent to a phrase like "castles in the air."[25]

In *The Birth of Tragedy*, however, it is the work of art in general and tragedy and lyric poetry in particular that display the human being's embeddedness in nature as opposed to its preeminence over it: "If we add to this terror [at the splintering of form] the blissful ecstasy that wells from the innermost depths of man, indeed of nature, at this collapse of the *principium individuationis*, we steal a glimpse into the nature of the *Dionysian*, which is brought home to us most intimately by the analogy of intoxication" (*Birth*, 36, emphasis in original). According to this passage, not only nature delights in the overthrow of individual forms but also the human being, as if the two were one and the same in spite of their different appearance. And, indeed, when read carefully, the passage could suggest that mortals and nature would be one, were it not for their division into forms, which occurs whenever they appear as finite entities. Nietzsche accordingly identifies nature as the human being's innermost ground, and the consequences of this insight are far-reaching. In themselves human beings are boundless; one could even say they suffer under the yoke of form, since in their essence they are not human but pure being—in a word, Dionysus.

Tragedy is the genre in which humans glimpse the "essence of the Dionysian" that is simultaneously their own essence. Both are on display in the Satyr chorus, which is an image not only of nature but also of the audience's innermost being. In this spirit Nietzsche asserts that the chorus is the "mirror image in which the Dionysian man contemplates himself" and reiterates a few sentences later, "The satyr chorus is, first of all, a vision of the Dionysian mass of spectators, just as the world of the stage, in turn, is a vision of this satyr chorus" (*Birth*, 63). Yet, in elaborating on this relation, Nietzsche puts the accent elsewhere. Both the audience and the chorus impersonate each other; both participate in the spectacle to such a degree that the spectacle comes to life as something given. The self-reflection of the Dionysian masses is best exemplified by the actor "who, being truly talented, sees the role he is supposed to play quite palpably before his eyes" (63). The prerequisite for good acting is the capacity to dream because it enables one to inhabit the vision before oneself—or, in Krull's vocabulary, to live in a *Gleichnis*. The chorus is, on the one hand, the dream projected by the masses and, on the other, the place from which they speak, and what they speak is their jubilation at the sight of a god who is nothing but a transfigured reflection of themselves. Lyric poetry and tragedy are unique among the arts in that they allow every participant to be "poet, actor, and spectator" (52) at once. When the individual assumes all three roles, he rises above his "human, all too human" appearance and becomes one with nature, which for Nietzsche is simultaneously to become the god Dionysus. The philosopher could not be more categorical on this point. The intoxicated spectator "feels [himself] a god" (37) when in the grip of art.

Doubles

Krull's account of the theater in the first book of Mann's novel is no less Nietzschean. According to him we lose ourselves in the theatrical spectacle and in so doing achieve a purely aesthetic existence that fills us with a zest for life otherwise lacking in our daily experience. One could object that this stance reflects Krull's desire and not our own wish and therefore should be approached with the caution expected of any critical reader. Yet to be skeptical about Krull's performance is to mistake the nature of this work; it assumes that we could differentiate between who Krull is and what he says about himself, even though the novel hints at every turn that he is an invented figure drawn more from lore and convention than any supposed experience. That is to say that, even in his capacity as a narrator and an author, Krull is marked as a fictional creation, as Eric Downing points out in noting his "clumsy, kitschy, convention-ridden clauses or sentences that fail to conceal their artifice or their ambitions."[26] Krull is a product of "self-artefaction," as Downing puts it, at several levels: within the space of his own narrative as a character who routinely deceives the people he meets to advance his own ends, and as a narrator-cum-author who repeatedly performs for his audience (ie., the readers) to enact his (and their) fantasy. True to the genre of the pseudo-memoir, the novel fictionalizes the writing process to call into question the originality of any writing that relies on narrative convention.

The artifice of Krull's performance as a writer is evident in his depiction of his birth. He is brought into the world by a Dr. Mecum, whose name is an abbreviated version of the Latin phrase *vada mecum*, which literally means "go with me" but more customarily refers to the handbooks used by professionals and, especially, doctors. Likewise the name of the aged female author with whom Krull has his most significant sexual adventure is taken explicitly from myth. The author Diane Houpflé is modeled after the Roman goddess Diana famed for her lust as well as her status as a protowriter who immortalizes her lover Orion by turning him into a constellation. (Houpflé promises to do the same to Krull in her books.) Lastly, all the doubled names in the third book (e.g., Kuckuck, Zaza, Zouzou, and Loulou) indicate that what is at stake in the text is not a representation of reality, but the representation of representation: the self-concious adoption of elements associated with the realist novel to generate its air of verisimilitude. To say Krull skews reality to depict himself in the most flattering light is to place stock in the idea that Krull is something besides a narrator—namely, a character with a past apart from his representations. But this is arguably the supreme deception of the text: to believe that Krull has a past to recount, even if he exaggerates it to aggrandize himself. He himself intimates that the text should be read in another way, in a comment whose self-referential implications are unmistakable: "Thus I masqueraded in both capacities [as a man of means and as an elevator operator, RT] and the undisguised reality between the two appearances, the real I [*das Ich-selber-sein*], could not be identified because it actually did not exist" (*Confessions*, 230; *Bekenntnisse*, 498). Krull is a confidence man not only as a character, but also as the narrator and ostensible author of the text. He paints a picture of himself we can either accept in the name of pleasure or reject in the name of truth.

In other words, he is a double in his role as narrator, which explains the preoccupation with doubles throughout the text, which is a feature not only of this work but of every pseudo-memoir in which we witness the narrator-author crafting his own image. The issue of doubles is broached explicitly in book 2, when Krull and his mother move to Frankfurt to embark on a new life following his father's suicide and the liquidation of the family's assets. Since Frankfurt is primarily a transit station in Krull's life, he spends his time roaming the streets of the city, where one evening he spots a brother and sister on a balcony: "Onto [the balcony] stepped one afternoon—it was so simple that I apologize—two young people, as young as myself, obviously a brother and sister, possibly twins—they looked very much alike—a young man and a young woman [*Herrlein und Fräulein*] moving out together into the wintry weather" (*Confessions*, 79–80; *Bekenntnisse*, 345). Of singular importance for Krull is that the siblings are not of the same sex, since as male and female versions of each other they mirror his own sexual indeterminacy. He recalls that, in his youth "[his] hair was silken soft, as it seldom is in the male sex" (*Confessions*, 11), and later he will tell us that, while the women of Frankfurt ignore him because of his impoverished dress, the men are drawn to him because he looks like neither a man nor a woman but "some extraordinary being in between [*etwas Wunderbares dazwischen*]" (*Confessions*, 108; *Bekenntnisse*, 374). The siblings on the balcony evoke this wondrous in-between as mirror images of each other whose identity is heightened by their gender difference.

Krull is quick to point out that neither sibling alone would enchant him: "The beauty here lay in the duality [*im Doppelten*], in the charming doubleness [*in der lieblichen Zweiheit*], and it seems more than doubtful that the appearance of the youth alone on the balcony would have inflamed me in the slightest, apart perhaps from the pearl in his shirt, I am almost equally sure that the image of the girl alone, without her fraternal complement, would never have lapped my spirit in such sweet dreams" (*Confessions*, 81; *Bekenntnisse*, 346). In emphasizing the charm of these two precisely as twins, Krull draws attention to the peculiar nature of doubles, which are neither independent figures nor a unity. Indeed he indicates as much when he meets his own double Rosza in the next chapter, who as a muscular trapeze artist is herself sexually indeterminate: "We were not alone and even less were we as two" (*Confessions*, 113). If the twins are more than one but less than two, it is because of an element they share, which becomes apparent in their pairing. Krull speaks of this common element in the loftiest of terms, "Dreams of love, dreams I adored because they duplicated, I would like to say, an original unity and indeterminacy and to this extent were all of a piece [*das heißt doch erst: ganzen Sinnes waren*]" (*Bekenntnisse*, 346, my translation), but his effusiveness is a smokescreen for something else. What excites Krull is not the idea of the androgynous origin of the species first proposed by Plato in the *Symposium*, but a union that he as an artist brings about and which constitutes a "middle world," much like the Olympian pantheon did for Nietzsche. In this context he confesses, "And yet verbal communication is not my element; my truest interest does not lie there. It lies rather in the extreme, silent regions of human intercourse—that one, first of all, where strangeness and social rootlessness still maintain a free, primordial condition and glances meet and marry irresponsibly in dreamlike wantonness" (*Confessions*, 83).

While it may be tempting at one level to read Krull's admission regarding his verbal gifts as false modesty, at another level the statement is illuminating regarding the structure of the work as a whole. Words may not be Krull's métier, but human relationships are, inasmuch as they transpire in the space between individuals where they cede their identity to relate to each other. Krull's "interest" lies in the secret regions of human relations precisely because he is himself an *inter-esse*, an intermediary being, in his role as a character who reflects simultaneously the desires of the narrator-author and the reading audience. In other words, he is as much a product of the narrator as he is of the reader of the text, who can choose to see in him either a self-congratulatory trickster or an artist who discovers that "to live in a fiction [*im Gleichnis*], spells true freedom" (*Confessions*, 105, translation modifed; *Bekenntnisse*, 372).

Common Interests

Krull entertains the possibility that a mutual interest can be a mutual deception in his encounter with the writer Diane Houpflé in the final episode of the second book. Krull had previously glimpsed Mme Houpflé at the German-French border, where the two happened to stand next to each other in the customs office. In this scene we see that not only a small jewelry case belonging to Houpflé slips into Krull's bag but an idea slips into his head in keeping with the logic of a felix culpa. It is the idea that he could be the object of someone's fantasy. When Krull sees the writer again at the hotel, he assumes she is preoccuppied with him, which later proves to be, if not untrue, overstated: "She has been carrying me featureless [*gestaltlos*] in her thoughts ever since the moment . . . she had discovered that the jewel case was missing" (*Confessions*, 151; *Bekenntnisse*, 420). Lest one think that this idea is nothing but a passing fancy, Krull repeats it later while waiting for Houpflé to board his elevator: "I was waiting for her who bore me, featureless in her mind and whom I bore most distinctly in mine [*Auf sie wartete ich, die ich bildhaft—und die mich bildlos— im Sinne trug*]" (*Confessions*, 167; *Bekenntnisse*, 435).

However mistaken Krull's fantasy is, it is important as the only instance in the novel in which he imagines himself to be invisible in another's eyes. "Bildlos," without an image, he can be larger than life, a mysterious stranger who preoccupies Houpflé, although she cannot identify him in any fashion. That this fantasy eventually comes true has less to do with Krull than Houpflé, who convinces Krull to indulge her fantasy for the sake of a common interest. As Eckhard Heftrich has suggested, Houpflé is a figure for the author Thomas Mann in more than one sense.[27] She is, first and foremost, a fiction writer who promises to immortalize Krull in her texts, as Mann immortalized the blond Adonis named Tadzio in "Death in Venice": "Yet, when the grave covers us, me and you too, Armand, *tu vivras dan mes vers et dans mes beaux romans*, every one of which—never breathe this to the world!—has been kissed by your lips" (*Confessions*, 181). More important, she seems to derive more pleasure from articulating her fantasies than in acting them out. So frequent are her comments during the episode that Krull can stop her only by reasserting his role as narrator: "Never was there a more articulate woman! . . . It was her habit to put everything into words" (173). Lastly, she speaks intermittently about her husband, or, in German her "Mann," in what is perhaps a veiled reference to the name of the author of the text. Heftrich reads her statement "My husband [*Mein Mann*] can do nothing . . . at least with me" (*Confessions*, 177; *Bekenntnisse*, 446) in this vein as an oblique allusion on the part of Mann to his sexual difficulties with his wife, Katia.[28]

Whatever the autobiographical reference, the scene attests to the power of fantasy to join two beings who have nothing in common save an interest in seeing their respective fantasies fulfilled. Krull confesses to Houpflé that he stole her jewelry case in keeping with his fantasy of being a "Herzensdieb" (*Bekenntnisse*, 294) which, according to his godfather, is the true nature of an artist. If this is Krull's attempt to dictate the scene, however, it takes an unexpected turn when Houpflé assumes the role of creator and director. She takes Krull's fantasy of being a thief and embeds it in her own narrative: "I am lying in bed with a thief! *C'est*

une humiliation merveilleuse, tout à fait excitante, un rêve d'humiliation!
Not only a domestic—a common, ordinary thief" (*Confessions*, 179). She
then demands that Krull steal from her again, this time under the cover of darkness: "I will not see you. I will only listen to the parquet soft-
ly creaking under your thief's tread" (180). The conditions she places on
Krull ironically ensure the fulfillment of his fantasy of being anonymous:
"I was waiting for her who bore me, featureless in her mind and whom
I bore most distinctly in mine [*Auf sie wartete ich, die ich bildhaft—und
die mich bildlos—im Sinne trug*]" (*Confessions*, 167; *Bekenntnisse*, 435). He
gets to steal from a woman who cannot see him and who in her blindness presumably imagines him to be a Greek god of unparalleled beauty and vitality. Houpflé, however, has a hand in the situation to the extent that she orchestrates it to achieve her own end: "Secretly [*verstohlen*]
I'll watch you steal [*stehlen*]" (179; 448). She sneaks a peek at Krull as he
sneaks around in the dark in the mistaken belief that he cannot be seen
by anyone. What joins the two, then, is a mutual interest and a mutual deception. Krull sees himself, however mistakenly, deified in another
person's eyes, as Houpflé sees herself, however mistakenly, humiliated
at the hands of a common rascal. Both take in the same measure as they
give, since both are artists who engineer the fulfillment of their own desires through the other's fantasies.

Rebirth

The episode with Houpflé will prove to be unique in the novel in that
the writer will be the only figure who seduces Krull as he seduces her.
In wanting to have something taken from her, she herself becomes a
"Herzensdieb": she steals Krull's innocence by inviting him to steal from
her as the object of her dreams. In all of Krull's previous encounters, he
did not have to face anyone who could take anything from him, since all
his previous interlocutors mistook the image he presented for his true person. What enables Houpflé to gain the upper hand is that she has no interest in knowing Krull, only in fantasizing about him, and this suits his
purposes as much as hers, because in both cases he gets to be the imagined object. An entirely new situation arises in book 3, when Krull comes
face to face with his fantasy: himself as a nobleman of considerable means.

At first glance the Marquis de Venosta would hardly seem to be Krull's
double. He is outgoing and careless, whereas Krull is disciplined and

reserved. Yet the two share a surprising number of biographical features that call into question whether the Marquis is in fact anything other than Krull's projection. In book 1 Krull emphasized that he was of both French and German ancestry; indeed, his father's most memorable feature is that he peppers his German with French phrases. The Marquis's mother, we later learn, is German, which is why the son is fluent in German and French, in a curious doubling of Krull's language skills. In addition the Marquis cannot speak of his parents without uttering "mes pauvres parents," as Krull in the first book refers repeatedly to his father as "mein armer Vater." That Krull and the Marquis intersect in terms of family background would suggest that Krull grew up in the wrong household—or, more forcefully, that he was the child meant to be in the Marquis's place.

The Marquis raises this point explicitly when he jokes with his mistress that she would be equally attracted to Krull, were he the one in a dinner jacket and the Marquis in a waiter's suit. Of note is that Krull interprets this comment as a mere reiteration of what he had already thought: "How strange that he should have put into words the thought-experiment of my leisure moments, my silent game of exchanging roles" (*Confessions*, 228, translation modifed). This pattern will continue throughout Krull's encounters with Venosta. The Marquis will always repeat what Krull had secretly conceived, raising the question if he is anything more than a double for Krull even before they exchange identities. Krull broaches the subject of his double life on the evening he was supposed to attend a performance of Gounod's *Faust* but instead runs into the Marquis, who proposes that they trade places. While dressing in the room he rents to store his fine clothes, Krull asks himself, "This amounted, as one can see, to a kind of dual existence, whose charm lay in the ambiguity as to which figure was the real I and which the masquerade" (*Confessions*, 230). While Krull ponders his identity in terms of the opposition between reality and masquerade, the matter is more complicated than this, for Krull is nothing but a mask. He leads a double life not because he occupies two roles, but because his life is that of a double or semblance. The external features linking the Marquis and Krull reveal just that. However much Krull would like to believe that the Marquis mirrors him because he is "cut from the finest cloth," the similarity between the two suggests a more disturbing possibility: it implies that the two reflect each other because they are both personae, masks, fictional characters who exist only in their appearance and have no being in themselves.

The encounter between Krull and the Marquis is too staged in this respect to be taken at face value. Krull would have us believe that it is a sheer coincidence that he meets Venosta, whose place he then takes in life, thereby fulfilling his lifelong dream of being a nobleman and confirming his belief that he is a natural aristocrat. But this dream is itself enclosed within another: the narrator dreams of himself as a character who dreams of joining the ranks of Europe's aristocrats. To the extent that the youthful Krull achieves this ambition, he leads a dreamlife. He is, in this respect, the dream of a dream, or the vision of a purely aesthetic existence, which explains why the narrator frequently interrupts the narrative to highlight how he has crafted his own narrative. Krull as a character, a narrated figure, is the mask that the narrator dons as the ultimate trickster who presents himself to us in the guise of another (i.e., his imaginary self or persona). But there may be no alternative to such a posture, such a swindle or confidence act, since the moment one presents oneself, one assumes a public face, a mask. As long as Krull and the Marquis face each other, the relation of the narrator Krull to the character Krull can still be discerned; in Nietzsche's terminology the line dermacating the semblance as semblance is still evident. As soon as Krull becomes the Marquis de Venosta, however, the distinction is lost. The narrator dissolves into his character inasmuch as his character dissolves into another narrated figure (i.e., Venosta), thereby forfeiting any relation to the outside. The final chapters of book 3 following Krull and Venosta's identity swap represent the unhinging of fiction from any outside. Krull's life henceforth unfolds in a direction that he cannot determine in advance, since he no longer occupies a place inside and outside the diegetic space as both a narrator and a character. The destiny he crafts for himself in christening himself Felix dissolves as the narrator and character merge into one.

The Dionysian turn in the text is given a preamble in the form of a lengthy discourse on the genesis of the universe. Krull's passage into a fantastical space in which he can no longer see himself from a position outside coincides with his journey to Lisbon, Europe's frontier, from the continent's heart in Paris. Krull's confinement in a train makes the whole trip appear as a passage through the birth canal (which is a trope we will see again in chapter 2 in the discussion of Robert Walser's *Jakob von Gunten*). In this second birth, however, Krull does not sleep, oblivious to everything around him. This time he sleeps only in fits and starts and is haunted by dreams of the natural world in the absence of humans. The immediate cause for these dreams is his dinner conversation with the paleontologist Kuckuck. But, one could say, this lecture is preceded by a growing tendency on Krull's part to regard himself as something more animal than human. Of note is that he compares himself to a snake that molts its skin: "It was the change and renewal of my worn-out self, the fact that I had been able to put off the old Adam and slip on a new one that gave me such a sense of fulfillment and happiness" (*Confessions*, 258). Krull's allusions to Adam and the serpent are not incidental. His genesis as Venosta will occur under the direction of a Creator. Kuckuck will serve this function, as Krull loses control of his own confession.

Krull becomes Venosta not when he introduces himself as the Marquis, but when Kuckuck reiterates his name and provides him with details on his family that the Marquis had failed to mention in Paris. Henceforth Krull will seldom speak in his own name in the text. Most of the final chapters of the novel consist of reported dialogue, and even the interior monologues with few exceptions represent the perspective of the Marquis in his newfound situation.[29] That Kuckuck plays a particular role in this transformation is evident from his introduction in the text. Krull invents the term "starry" or "starlike eyes," *Sternenaugen* (*Confessions*, 259; *Bekenntnisse*, 530), to describe his otherwordly appearance: "'The light in his eyes' [*Augenstern*] is a common expression, but it refers to something purely physical; it by no means connotes the description that forced itself upon me; something specifically moral has to be involved for bright eyes to be star-like eyes [*Sternenaugen*]" (260; 530).

Krull's insistence that Kuckuck's "star-like eyes" represent something moral is out of character for him, given that does not concern himself with ethical matters elsewhere in the text. Yet, to the extent that he opposes the moral universe to the physical world, he would seem to be evoking Kant, whose comparison of the "moral law within" to the "starry heavens above" resonates with the moral dimensions of Kuckuck's starry eyes. The cosmological topic of his lecture also associates him with this sphere, although in his account this sphere is all but bereft of morality, because the human being does not stand at the center of it. Nietzsche articulated this position already when in the *Genealogy of Morals* he claimed that life is essentially amoral and, as such, alien to Christianity. But this was also Nietzsche's transvaluation of all values, his reversal of conventional morality which favors what is supposedly immutable over anything precious and fleeting. Kuckuck is similarly critical of any notion of permanence, observing and admiring instead nature's continual transformations, its inexhaustible capacity to reinvent itself. Indeed he would seem to embody this transformative potential to the extent that the stars of his eyes (*Augensternen*) have become the eyes of the stars (*Sternenaugen*) that greet Krull as he becomes Venosta.

The mystery surrounding Kuckuck is not limited to his eyes. Although Krull is the first to extend a greeting, the scientist would seem to be awaiting him when he enters the dining car in his first public appearance as the Marquis. Krull immediately notes, "[His eyes] remained fixed on me as I sat down, and only very slowly was the accompanying expression of earnest attentiveness replaced by an assenting, or shall I say, approving smile" (*Confessions*, 260). Kuckuck in short solicits the encounter with Krull. He even makes the accomplished confidence man uneasy by following his every movement, as if evaluating how well he performs in his role as a nobleman. That his expression is approving, if not bemused, would suggest his general pleasure at the sight. What disconcerts Krull is that he cannot see himself performing as he did before. As the text moves increasingly toward the form of reported speech, Krull no longer has the luxury of seeing himself perform in front of an audience that deserves, as it were, to be duped. Whether it is the physician who treats him as a boy or the military doctor who examines him in the conscription scene, all deserve to be deceived because of their misplaced confidence that they cannot be fooled by any masquerade. Krull outwits them all, and we are there to applaud his work, since we are ultimately the intended audience for his performance, which may be limited to the pages of his confessions.

We observe Krull's artistry, and, to the extent that we recognize the "deception for deception," we are filled with the "joy of life," to recall Krull's earlier characterization of the theater. The reward of his performance is accordingly twofold. Our capacity to regard the deception as a deception invigorates us as it elevates Krull to the status of an artist, who can make anything *appear* to be true. The only requirement for this reward is that a narrator be present to report to us what the protagonist does from a spatial and temporal distance. Hence Krull stresses from the start that he is writing his memoirs after having retired from active life. His voice is the outside in the text, the supposedly objective reference point for everything he utters. Yet as soon as Krull assumes the identity of Venosta, he can no longer narrate his life from afar, since it has become the life of another outside his control—indeed, outside his outside. It takes an otherworldly character with a doubled name to recognize this fact. Kuckuck temporarily takes over the narrative function when he delivers a lengthy monologue on the origins of the universe that contains within it a theory of life as art.

Kuckuck subscribes to the notion that the universe is in a perpetual state of flux, with forms appearing and then disappearing only to be replaced by others. What permits this process to continue are the secret resemblances that reign between phenomena that are either past and present or at different levels of the developmental scale: "Echoes of animal physiognomy are to be found among people wherever you look. You see the fish and the fox, the dog, the seal, the hawk and the sheep. On the other hand, the whole animal kingdom . . . strikes us as humanity disguised and bewitched [*als Larve und schwermütige Verzauberung des Menschlichen*]" (*Confessions*, 271; *Bekenntnisse*, 541–42. With his theory of resemblances, Kuckuck approaches a notion of being similar to Nietzsche's in *The Birth of Tragedy*. All forms in nature correspond to each other since all are expressions of the same life force. In a passage with strong Nietzschean overtones, Kuckuck declares,

This interdependent whirling and circling, this convolution of gases into heavenly bodies, this burning, flaming, freezing, exploding, pulverizing, this plunging and speeding, bred out of Nothingness and awaking Nothingness . . . all this was Being, known also as Nature, and everywhere in everything it was one. I was not to doubt that all Being, Nature itself, constituted a unitary system from the simplest inorganic element to Life at its liveliest, to the woman with the shapely arm to the figure of Hermes. (*Confessions*, 274)

Nature can be a unity and still contain an infinite array of phenomena, since all phenomena stem from a common source. They are images of what Nietzsche called the primordial One, *das Ur-Eine*, which constitutes the unity of all apparent opposites. Everything in nature is a manifestation of the ground that not only enables it but also sustains it, and, because all phenomena share this ground, they also dissolve into each other, "crossing the line from one domain into the other" (274).

The theory of the unity of the manifold is not only reported but also enacted in the text. Indeed, the ostensible narrator of this passage is not Kuckuck but Krull, who at this point communicates Kuckuck's entire lecture from memory. Yet even this assignation of the narrator may not be entirely correct. It would perhaps be more accurate to say that Venosta narrates what he heard on the train partially in the form of reported speech and partially in the form of a recollection. What is significant is that all three personae blend into one, since none occupies a privileged position outside the diegetic space as the narrator and supposed author. Put otherwise, all are locked in the world of semblance. In such a world, it does not matter who speaks; every person is a mere reflection of another, as we learn in Krull, Kuckuck, and Venosta's shared discourse on the cosmos. According to this lecture, being emerges from nothing, which is not merely the negation of everything animate and inanimate, but also the negation of time and space in which everything first appears individuated. The price of appearing as a discrete phenomenon is being subject to time, which dictates that whatever appears must disappear to be born anew. With the emergence of being from nothing, then, change first comes about. And change, as the speaker notes in a comment with strong Nietzschean overtones, always implies a dissolution of the boundaries dividing individuals: "Perhaps the 'when' of passing was not so very far ahead. . . . Meanwhile, Being celebrated its *tumultuous festival* in the measureless spaces that were its handwork" (*Confessions*, 272, emphasis added).

It is this "tumultuous," if not Dionysian, "festival" that is at stake in the third book of the novel. What motivates it is "the knowledge of beginning and end" (*Confessions*, 276), which, according to Krull, Kuckuck, and Venosta's shared discourse, is a form of knowledge limited to humans. Only humans recognize the transitoriness of all phenomena by virtue of their intelligence. More significant than their knowledge, however, is that they feel "universal sympathy" (277) with all of nature, which Kuckuck interprets as a capacity to inhabit another's being and to experience the pleasure and burden, *"Lust und Last"* (*Bekenntnisse*, 547) of that being. Both pleasure and burden are the consequences of individuation, as Nietzsche himself understood in *The Birth of Tragedy*.

There he argued that the tragic spectacle offers metaphysical consolation to the viewer who sees the tragic hero suffer under the weight of his individuality. The demise of the hero reveals "that life is at the bottom of things, despite all the changes of appearances, indestructibly powerful and pleasurable" (*Birth*, 59). He reiterates this point in a more jubilant tone later when describing the mystical doctrine of tragedy as "the fundamental knowledge of the oneness of everything existent, the conception of individuation as the primal cause of evil, and of art as the joyous hope that the spell of individuation may be broken in augury of restored oneness [*als die Ahnung einer wiederhergestellten Einheit*]" (*Birth*, 74; *Geburt*, 62). For Nietzsche, the same forces that destroy the individual also hold open the promise of his redemption, albeit not as a solitary figure, nor even as a bearer of life, but as life itself which does not recognize any distinctions between entities. That this redemption is postponed is evident from the statement, insofar as the knowledge of it comes in a work of art that is itself an individuated phenomenon. Indeed, every tragedy is a particular example of an ontological struggle; in every tragic play the hero pays the price for overstepping his bounds. He breaks the law, for which he is punished with dismemberment, either actual or symbolic, such as Oedipus's blinding of himself. Key for Nietzsche is that the destruction of the hero is a cause for joy in that the destruction reveals that he was only the appearance of a force larger than himself: "The metaphysical joy in the tragic is a translation of the instinctive unconscious Dionysian wisdom into the language of images: the hero, the highest manifestation of the will, is negated for our pleasure, *because he is only a phenomenon*" (*Birth*, 104, emphasis added).

It is significant in this context that Krull's birth as Venosta comes at a cost. For all the riches he receives in this Faustian bargain, he loses the freedom to do what he wants. This loss is all the more striking given the ease with which he assumes the role of Venosta both in public and in private. One chapter, for instance, is devoted to a letter he writes home to his parents in Luxembourg without a single editorial comment that would indicate that Krull is still there as a narrator-cum-author to observe his performance as Loulou, the Marquis's doubled nickname. The absence of such self-reflection indicates that Krull does more than impersonate the Marquis; he becomes this persona, which is to say a pure mask without any position apart from or outside this performance. The only time this pattern is interrupted is when the issue of marriage comes up. Krull then returns in his role as narrator, to declare the impossibility of this prospect, since a wedding would require the presence of the Marquis's parents, who would recognize that he is not their son. On at least two occasions Krull addresses this impasse. Upon arriving in Lisbon, he invites himself into the Kuckuck family and immediately falls in love with both the mother and the daughter, who, like the twins on the balcony in Frankfurt, represent a double image. A further charm of the daughter is her doubled name, Zouzou, which is reminiscent of the name of Venosta's Parisian mistress, Zaza. The idea of marrying Zouzou is thus particularly enchanting for Krull, as it would be a continuation of Venosta's affair with Zaza, which this time would earn the parents' approval. When the idea of marriage first occurs to Krull, he tosses it up to the persistence of his Krullian ego even in his new form. He then concedes, "The delicate ambiguity of my existence, its ticklish double aspect [*ihr heikles Doppelgängertum*], completely ruled out any such excursion into reality" (*Confessions*, 311; *Bekenntnisse*, 584). In the penultimate chapter of the novel, these forbidden marriage dreams emerge again with unexpected vehemence. In the midst of a lengthy conversation with Zouzou on love, Krull reminds us in an aside, "It was simple enough for me to say that love has no ulterior object and does not think beyond a kiss at most, because *in my unreal state* I could not permit myself to come to grips with reality" (*Confessions*, 355, emphasis added). According to Krull's representation, reality prohibits the fulfillment of his dream. Were he truly Venosta, he could marry Zouzou, and were he able to appear in public as himself, he could elope with her. Yet his insistence that reality obstructs his desires raises the question anew of how true Krull is in any form, be it as a charming con artist, a reclusive memoirist, or a young Luxembourgian nobleman given to infatuations.

In each case one could say he suffers under the weight of his individuality. Born without money, he has to learn to earn his keep; prematurely aged, he can only charm others through his writing, not in person; and, masked as a person he is not, he cannot seduce or marry anyone. In each of these guises Krull is forced to bear predicates that result from what Nietzsche would call his individuation. The fact that he is, by profession, a trickster complicates but does not alter this scheme. As demonstrated previously, the tricks Krull plays on others are always represented in the text in a manner that divides his initial performance as a character from his current performance as a narrator before the reader. Krull may fool military boards, doctors, hotel guests, and priests, but not the readers, whom he needs to confirm his performance and to admire his self-fashioning. This is where his limitations as an individual become his strength. To the extent that his being lies in his appearance, he can also imagine himself to be a figure larger than life, and his writing enables him to achieve this objective. As long as another individual is present who views him as he views himself, he becomes this imagined figure, this beautiful vision, this magical persona.

As an appearance, then, his fantasies are realizable under two conditions. First, they must pertain to him, and, second, another figure must be present, like Houpflé, whose fantasies intersect with his. Under such conditions the individual suffering under the yoke of individuation can attain freedom. It is a freedom, however, that comes at the price of all companionship and community, not to speak of all Dionysian intoxication, as Krull notes in book 2: "An inner voice had warned me that close association, friendship, and companionship were not to be my lot, but that I should instead be inescapably compelled to follow my strange path alone" (*Confessions*, 106).

What changes in book 3 is that Krull no longer follows his own path but the path of the Marquis, and, as this outgoing and sometimes careless character, he suddenly seeks out friendship and relies on others for comfort and affection. In short, he becomes the opposite of the cunning Krull we knew in books 1 and 2. In book 2 he no longer aims to be the wondrous image, middle world, or intermediary being between the narrator and reader. In his new life as Venosta, he seeks union in a kiss that he describes as "the pledge of that marvellous release from separateness [*Aufhebung der Getrenntheit*] and from the fastidious refusal to be interested in anything that is not oneself" (*Confessions*, 364; *Bekenntnisse*, 641). Love, he continues, is the mystery that "two become one and "the actual oneness of two lives" (*Confessions*, 364)—both definitions that, in their number play, recall Krull's earlier comment on coupling: "We were not alone and even less were we as two" (113). This statement was motivated by the logic of the *inter-esse*, the Apollonian intermediary being that joins two figures that are otherwise separated. The dissolution of all figures, however, destroys this common interest, leaving behind nothing but the infinite One that constitutes the Dionysian unity of all that is contradictory.

Such a unity can scarcely be represented in a narrative work that reports what individual characters think, do, and say. If such a Dionysian merger is to be represented, it can only happen in a text in which each and every character stands out precisely as an illusion—a *Betrug* in Krull's vocabulary, and a *Schein* in Nietzsche's. The third book meets this criterion to the extent that Krull is replaced by Venosta, who functions as his dream of himself. All of the principle figures, with one exception, have doubled names (Zouzou, Loulou, Kuckuck), which frames them as characters on a stage. As dramatis personae they all voice lengthy monologues that have been placed in their mouths, since their only purpose is to parrot words written for them by an invisible hand. The invisible hand dictating their speech and actions belongs to Krull, albeit not as the conspicuous narrator of the text who in books 1 and 2 orchestrated events from afar to aggrandize himself. Rather, it belongs to the Krull who in book 3 disappears from the work to reappear as each and every character, or, more broadly, as the entire fictional space. Krull's being floods the work as an invisible unity expressed in a multitude of figures that are all masks, guises, or semblances.

The only character who stands beyond Krull's reach is Mme Kuckuck, also called Dona Maria Pia, who is consistently referred to in terms that equate her with untamed nature and a universal maternal force, as her given name Maria already implies. She stands as the visible symbol of the invisible ground of being, which in the case of book 3 is the unknown Krull, the Krull who never appears except in the guise of the entire social world of Lisbon. Not surprisingly, Dona Maria Pia has the final word in this unfinished work. Having caught Venosta with her daughter, she decides to make him her conquest instead. She jumps him with the call of the Matador, "Holé! Heho! Ahé!" (*Confessions*, 384). This is the call of the mothers to whom Faust in *Faust II* descends in pursuit of the primal unity of existence, the ontological foundation of all that is. It is a symbol that Nietzsche himself recalls in *The Birth of Tragedy* when describing the Dionysian impetus for art: "In Dionysian art . . . nature cries to us . . . 'Be as I am! Amid the ceaseless flux of phenomena I am the eternally creative primordial mother, . . . eternally finding satisfaction in this change of phenomena'" (*Birth*, 104). It is a sign of the Dionysian turn of this novel and its debt to Nietzsche that it ends with a fierce mother conquering all and destroying the differences that had contributed to the text's aesthetic play.

Postscript

To return to my initial set of questions: Would we care what happened to a figure who renounced his claim to existence and told us he was merely an invented figure? This is the situation in book 3 of *Felix Krull*, in which the characters never amount to more than the image of an image or the appearance of an appearance, since they bear no relation to a point outside the fictional space. In the first two books, Krull provided this perspective as the narrator and self-proclaimed author of the work, in a structure typical of pseudo-memoirs, which dramatize the production of any text. The fact that Krull is a confidence man only amplifies this process, as it underscores the fabrication involved in any self-representation. The fabrication occurs at two levels: Krull regales us with stories of how he deceived others in the past at the same time that he deceives us in claiming to be a ruthlessly honest narrator—that is to say, he takes us into his confidence, insisting on the truthfulness of his account, while at the same time recounting how he tricked others in exactly the same manner in the past. We indulge Krull in this fantasy, as he indulges us, each of us deriving pleasure from the aesthetic spectacle, the deception understood as a deception that functions as the common interest between us.

In the third book, however, Krull relinquishes his position as narrator and author and this leaves us without a privileged vantage point from which to view the fictional world from the outside. Instead we are confronted with a set of characters who turn away from us, as they are each the projection of an invisible hand to which we can never gain access. Because of the novel's form as a pseudo-memoir, we are able to trace Krull's retreat as narrator and return as each and every character— indeed, as the animating force that fuels them. This is fiction at the limit of fiction. What the third book makes apparent is the process of appearing that for Mann and Nietzsche defines life. For both life consists in appearing and attesting to the hidden ground of being. We ourselves are witness to this process in a pseudo-autobiographical work that "imitates" life in its doubled semblances, its image of images, and its dreams of dreams that are unending.

2   The Narrator

Robert Walser's *Jakob von Gunten*

Robert Walser's third and most popular novel is often referred to in abbreviated form. The standard title for it in the secondary literature is *Jakob von Gunten*. Yet the full title *Jakob von Gunten: A Diary* is arguably more complex, given the inclusion of the name of a person followed by a genre determination. The extended title has typically been interpreted to mean that the text that will follow is a diary written by an imaginary figure named Jakob von Gunten. Insofar as the author of the diary is fictional, so too is the work, in keeping with the principle that a cause should be consistent with its effect. The full title, however, allows for another interpretation, which is more disturbing for the assumption that Walser invented a character who kept a diary in turn. Jakob von Gunten could also be construed as the author of a fictional work—a novel entitled "A Diary" that poses as an authentic journal. In this chapter I will claim that the relation of Jakob to his diary is at least as complex as the relation of the historical author Robert Walser to his narrator and doppelgänger Jakob von Gunten.

In his now-classic study "The Autobiographical Pact," Philippe Lejeune proposes a radical scheme to resolve one of the major sticking points in the theory of autobiography.[1] He offers a definition of the genre that does not depend on the intent of the author to produce an account of his life such as he remembered it. Previous efforts to define the genre invariably foundered on this point; critics relied on the supposed sincerity of the author to distinguish autobiography proper from a fictional narrative inspired by the author's life. Lejeune, by contrast, defined the genre on the basis of the immanent features of the text. His innovation was to view autobiography from the perspective not of the writer but of the reader of the work. According to him, what distinguishes the genre, on the one hand, from all first-person fiction and, on the other, from all historical narrative is that autobiography is the one narrative form in which the author, narrator, and protagonist are identical *in name*.[2] That their identity is based in their name rather than in their person, in discourse rather than in reality, is due to the strict formalism of Lejeune's approach, which takes account only of textual features.[3]

In keeping with this formalist approach, he argues that the name of the author is included in every autobiography—if not in the body of the text, then on the title page and in the copyright notice, which, in his view, are integral parts of the work. The inclusion of the author's name on the title page functions for Lejeune as a guarantee that there is someone who takes responsibility for the statements uttered in the text as statements about himself (or, more precisely, a character bearing the same name as him).[4] The "autobiographical pact" Lejeune speaks of in the title of his study is finally the contract between the person named in the work and the reader who picks up a book designated as an autobiography. On the basis of this label, the reader has the right to expect that the author will feature in it as both the narrating and narrated subject: as the teller of his own tale. If not, the reader can claim a breach of contract, which is a legal claim, not a psychological one. It means that the autobiographer has refused to honor his pledge to give an account of his life such as he remembers or imagines it.

With the exception of Gérard Genette, few critics have noted the striking parallels between Lejeune's theory of autobiography and Käte Hamburger's analysis of the problems associated with first-person narration in her monumental study *The Logic of Literature*.[5] At the time of its publication, in 1957, the study generated controversy, not least because of its categorical claim that a story told in the first person can never be fictional, no matter how imaginary or invented it may be.[6] Yet this position, for all its counterintuitive punch, is nothing but the inverse of Lejeune's claim that the first person in autobiography refers to the name of the author, which in turn refers to a "real person." Hamburger in fact reinforces Lejeune's argument at its weakest point where it defers to the real as a guarantee of the authenticity of a memoir. For Hamburger is far more concerned than Lejeune with the reality of a statement—that is, with the ways in which it constitutes the real as discourse or linguistic representation.

True to the phenomenological tradition, Hamburger argues that the reality of a statement lies not in the object, but in the subject.[7] It inheres in the experience of an "I," whom she alternately labels the "statement-subject" and the "I-Origo," a term borrowed from the psychologist Karl Bühler.[8] Although the subject is central to the statement, it does not have to be explicit in it; it does not have to be designated with an "I." Nor does it have to be implicit as the unannounced speaker of a statement, such as "It's cold," which could always be expanded to read, "I say it's cold." Hamburger cautions that the statement-subject is neither the speaker nor the cognitive subject, which is a logical category that refers to the consciousness that forms the basis for all judgments and propositional utterances.[9] The statement-subject, by contrast, is a specifically linguistic concept. It represents the point *from which* a statement originates in space and time and gives the statement a locus *from which* it can say something about something else, a position *from which* it can have an object. This assertion can be as simple as "The book is over there," which merely indicates that the book is not "here" where the subject is at the moment. Or it could be the more complex assertion that "Napoleon died in 1821," which indicates that his death took place in a past, which is not part of the immediate past of the subject.[10] Dorrit Cohn defines the statement-subject as the "zero point (or center of orientation) in space and time determined by the here-and-now of the speaking subject."[11] The explanation is accurate except for its final provision, which Hamburger herself refutes. The subject does not have to speak to be a statement's "center of orientation" in space or time. With or without a speaker, a statement is anchored in space and time, since a statement always refers to the position or vantage point of its subject. Hamburger thus concludes that the essence of the statement, or, in her vocabulary, the "reality statement" (*Wirklichkeitsaussage*), is nothing other than "the statement-subject's field of experience."[12]

The reality statement so defined represents the basic structure for all linguistic acts except epic fiction, which, for Hamburger, means specifically fiction narrated in the third person, for reasons that will become apparent shortly.[13] In the case of epic fiction, the basic logic or grammar that governs utterances changes: the reference is no longer to the here and now of the subject, but to the position of the characters in the work.[14] The consequences of this shift are too numerous to summarize here, but a few are worth highlighting, as they represent the grounds for the distinction between epic fiction and first-person narration. The system of spatial and temporal organization in epic fiction is different than in all other linguistic acts, since the statement is narrated from the perspective of the characters, although the characters themselves remain in the third person (i.e., they are referred to as "he," "she," or "they"). Hamburger offers numerous examples to demonstrate this point, such as the following, which she admittedly makes up for didactic purposes: "*Today* he *roamed* through the European port city for the last time, for *tomorrow* his ship *sailed* for America."[15] The simple past can be combined with the adverbs "today" and "tomorrow" in this sentence, since the past does not derive its meaning from the present of a subject but, rather, the present of the character roaming the city. Precisely because this present is fictive, it can be narrated in the past tense. The rules governing the organization of space and time in reality statements do not apply to fictional language. Hamburger can consequently claim that the primary index of fictionality is the use of the epic preterite to signal a character's immediate experiences. The other index is the representation of other minds as precisely the minds of others narrated in the third person.

As indicated previously, Hamburger does not include first-person narratives in the category of fiction for reasons that are likely more apparent now. First-person narratives do not qualify as fiction because they proceed from a subject that claims to be real, even if it is only an imaginary figure. The narrative therefore adheres to the same laws or grammatical principles as the reality statement, which originates in a subject situated in a discrete space and time. First-person narratives do not create a fictional universe, only an alternative reality. They imitate the reality statement as instances of mimesis, which is why they constitute literature for Hamburger, but with a statement-subject that is "feigned," which amounts to saying that it pretends to be real, although it has no basis outside the text.[16] "Feint" (*Fingiertheit*) rather than fiction is thus Hamburger's term for the illusion created in works narrated in the first person.

I have offered this lengthy preamble on the theory of first-person narration and autobiography in order to draw attention to a problem in both that is central to Robert Walser's 1909 novel, *Jakob von Gunten: A Diary*, and the genre of the pseudo-memoir more generally. Both Lejeune and Hamburger assume that the first person is a unified phenomenon in the sense that it occupies only one here and now. As a result they can identify the first-person narrator with the author, who is either a real person or an imaginary figure, depending on whether the name designates anyone in the world beyond the text. For both critics the genre of Walser's *Jakob von Gunten: A Diary* is unambiguous. Insofar as the historical author of the book (Robert Walser) does not have the same name as the self-proclaimed author of the diary (Jakob von Gunten), the text is a clear instance of fiction for Lejeune and a feigned diary or reality statement for Hamburger. Such a classification, however, scarcely does justice to a work in which the narrator is not only a diary keeper, who tells his own tale, but also the mirror image of another diary keeper, who shares the pronoun "I" with him. As I will demonstrate, Jakob as narrator is split between two here and nows: the here and now of a subject that writes about its immediate surroundings, and the here and now of another subject that does not participate in this space and writes from somewhere else, from a hidden location. Such a double position is impossible in linguistic and logical terms. As Emile Benveniste insists, the "I" is a "unique instance of discourse" that exists only at the moment of its articulation and for the duration of this articulation.[17] Yet the same constraint does not apply to the first person in fiction, where the "I" as an invented figure already speaks from more than one place and in more than one voice. Every first-person narrator in fiction is simultaneously the "I" of another "I," to recall Novalis's definition of irony: "The supreme task of education is to lay claim to one's transcendental self, to be simultaneously the I of one's I [*Die höchste Aufgabe der Bildung ist—sich seines transzendentalen Selbst zu bemächtigen—das Ich ihres Ichs zugleich zu sein*].[18] (Novalis's and Schlegel's theory of irony will be discussed at greater length in chapter 3.) To the extent that the narrating subject in a pseudo-memoir is the "I" of another "I," whenever it speaks it does so as imagined by another ego that is not directly accessible to the reader. The novel *Jakob von Gunten* expands Hamburger's definition of fiction to include at its extreme a work in which the narrator is also a character posing as a statement-subject—or, in Benveniste's terms, a supposedly unique instance of discourse.

This chapter proposes that Jakob is both the homo- and heterodiegetic narrator of the text. On the one hand, he participates in the world that he represents: a servant school where he has enrolled to learn a vocation belonging to a bygone era. On the other hand, he produces this environment from afar, or from a vantage point not visible to the reader, since he is not only the author of a diary but also the author of a feigned diary, a fictional journal, in which he appears as or assumes the guise of a pupil. What enables Jakob to occupy these two seemingly incompatible positions is his stated aim to become a servant whom no one notices and who has no particular qualities. As a result of this ambition, he is able to escape the constraints of the first-person pronoun that would normally confine him to one place and time. An analysis of his desire to become a servant is thus a prerequisite for an understanding of the narratological dimensions of this novel, which does not fit into any established mold. *Jakob von Gunten: A Diary* represents a conundrum for narrative theory, because it does not seek to create the semblance of life, but a life beyond all semblance. In this it differs from *Felix Krull*, which culminates in a life that is nothing but a semblance, because the narrator relinquishes the role he occupied in the first two books of the novel as the supposed author of his own confessions. In *Jakob von Gunten*, by contrast, the narrator engineers his escape from the pages of his notebook by marking the notebook itself as a fanciful enterprise or fiction. The form of the pseudo-memoir, with its emphasis on the writing process, enables him to leave behind the illusion he himself created as a seemingly guileless writer.

The Freedom of a Servant

Jakob von Gunten was the third novel that Walser wrote in the brief period between 1907 and 1909 when he lived in Berlin before returning to his native Switzerland in 1913.[19] Although Walser is rumored to have written several other novels, no additional manuscripts have been found except the unfinished novel *The Robber* (*Der Räuber*), which was discovered after his death in 1956. Walser's preferred genre was the literary portrait, or sketch, in which an object is wrested from its context to be examined in its myriad aspects. This proclivity is also evident in *The Tanner Siblings* (*Die Geschwister Tanner*) and *The Assistant* (*Der Gehülfe*), which were the first two novels in Walser's so-called Berlin Trilogy. *The Tanner Siblings* chronicles Simon Tanner's adventures as he moves from job to job and place to place. The narrative framework would suggest that he moves in time as well, yet nothing that comes "before" contributes to what happens "afterward" in the text. Simon remains the same no matter what happens to him, like the hero of *The Assistant*, Joseph Marti, who is accused by a friend of never changing.[20] Both characters pass through the world rather than with it, locked in a perpetual adolescence, which makes them immune to life's disappointments as well as to all fraternal bonds and filial attachments. Regarding the peripheral figures one encounters in Walser's work, W. G. Sebald remarks, "At the moment of their appearance, they possess a wondrous presence but as soon as one tries to look at them more closely, they vanish. . . . They pass through Walser's fragmentary stories and embyonic novels likes people in dreams pass through our heads at night, failing to enter their names in any register and departing immediately after arriving, never to be seen again."[21]

A similar transitoriness marks the characters in *Jakob von Gunten*, albeit with the caveat that the hero would appear to move in time, even if he stays in the same place—the boy's school (*Knabenschule*), named the Institute Benjamenta. That the institute is referred to as a boy's school would seem to imply that the mostly adult students are overgrown children whose bodies have matured faster than their minds.[22] Nonetheless, the desire to become a servant gives them an aim and allows Jakob's diary to appear to move in a particular direction. Perhaps for this reason, Robert Walser is reported to have said that *Jakob von Gunten* was his most successful lengthy work.[23]

Already, in his first diary entry, Jakob considers what will happen to him in a comment that is as much in jest as it is in earnest: "One doesn't learn much here. We're short on teaching staff. And we boys from the Institute Benjamenta won't amount to anything. We'll be very small and subordinate later in life [*Und wir Knaben vom Institut Benjamenta werden es zu nichts bringen, das heißt, wir werden alle etwas sehr Kleines und Untergeordnetes im späteren Leben sein*]."[24] In a manner typical of Walser's heroes, Jakob does not promise much, save his eventual insignificance, should he reach a ripe old age, when his years will no doubt outnumber his accomplishments. "We won't amount to anything," he notes with peculiar certainty, given that the subject in question is the future that is not given him to see. Yet the form of the novel requires such a projection: it requires the horizon of a future to establish the present as the interval in which the protagonist becomes what he was meant to be from the outset. In this manner the text alludes to the tradition of the bildungsroman, as does its location in a school or what in German could be called a *Bildungsanstalt*.[25] In keeping with this tradition, Jakob promises his evolution over time. In contrast to it, he predicts not his eventual formation as an autonomous subject, capable of participating in bourgeois society, but his degeneration into a mere subordinate, subject to the whims of others. He longs to shed the aristocratic privilege still embedded in his name (*von* Gunten) and to become what Erica Weitzman calls a person "without consequence," a servant "to whom the *vita activa* is as strange as it is unavailable."[26] In short, he anticipates "amount[ing] to nothing," which would rank as a failure in any other work, save in this one, where becoming nothing is an extraordinary achievement, the next closest thing to godliness.

The Institute Benjamenta is a servant school that, according to Jakob, once enjoyed considerable renown, although its reputation has waned in recent years. Among the chores assigned to the students is to dust the few decorative objects hanging in the school. These include a sword and sheath and an iron helmet, items that hark back to an earlier age when there were still kings, lords, and masters. Wim Peeters contends that this hierarchy is fundamental to any social system; drawing on the work of Pierre Legendre, he argues that every political order posits a mythical past when the symbolic father established the law.[27] For Peeters the novel *Jakob von Gunten* represents nothing less than a crisis in the social system. Neither Jakob's real father nor his symbolic fathers in the form of his teachers possess any authority. Jakob, in fact, remarks early on in his diary that his teachers are asleep: "Or they're dead, or apparently dead, or turned to stone [*Oder sie sind tot, oder nur scheintot, oder sie sind versteinert*]" (*JVG*, 9). It matters little if they are actually dead or only apparently so, since "one hasn't heard a peep from them [*man hat gar nichts von ihnen*]" (9). The position of paterfamilias has long been vacated, and the task therefore falls to Jakob to find someone he can install as an authority over himself and his schoolmates.[28]

Peeters is not the first critic to note the dialectical nature of the relationship between Jakob and the institute's reclusive director, whom Jakob chooses as his ersatz paternal figure.[29] Although Jakob is the supposed subordinate, he must *compel* Herr Benjamenta to assume the role of lord and master (*Herr*). Bernhard Malkmus summarizes this dynamic succinctly when he states, "[Jakob] subjects himself to the institutionalized gaze of his school, which he, at the same time, claims to have created (or dreamed) himself."[30] As I will explain in what follows, it is precisely the desire for freedom that leads Jakob to attend, if not create, an institution in which hierarchy is of paramount importance.[31]

According to Jakob the Institute Benjamenta is trapped in a bygone era, whereas the city around it is caught in the throes of republicanism, whose central tenet is that all men are created equal. Equality, Jakob implies, is a form of enslavement, insofar as it deprives the individual of the ideals necessary for the exercise of freedom.[32] Jakob does not, admittedly, express this sentiment directly. He puts it in the mouth of his brother Johann, whom he encounters on the street in that signature trope of modernity, the crowd, or what Jakob calls the "human swarm [*Menschengewimmel*]" (*JVG*, 65). Johann warns his younger brother, "The masses, that's today's slave, and the individual is slave to the grand idea of the masses. [*Die Masse, das ist der Sklave von heute, und der Einzelne ist der Sklave des großartigen Massengedankens.*] There's no longer anything beautiful or outstanding. You'll have to dream something beautiful, good and upstanding for yourself. Tell me, do you know how to dream?" (67). The condescending tone of Johann's comment notwithstanding, the critique he makes of modernity follows a line of argumentation that is consistent with Nietzsche's own critique of republicanism. Insofar as the masses no longer have any ideals (e.g., the beautiful, the good, the upstanding), they are enslaved, as they have no occasion to demonstrate that they are free. Freedom inheres in the effort to embody ideals that are by definition hierarchical—that is, of a higher nature than nature. Faced with this paradox of republicanism, Jakob can only heed his brother's advice to dream. He dreams of becoming a servant who is master of his own destiny.

A servant is master of his fate because he is free—free to serve whoever is in need. Jakob takes particular pleasure in imagining situations where he can help someone who is, as he puts it, "of no concern to him": "To serve someone you don't know and who isn't even of concern to you [*der einen gar nichts angeht*]—that's delightful, it lets you peer into God's misty paradise" (*JVG*, 23). To give without being asked affords one a glimpse of the heavens for reasons that become apparent in the remainder of the passage. Jakob admits that no human being is ever *entirely* divorced from him, but he means this only in the most literal sense, as his next statement indicates: "People who walk past me [*die da an mir vorübergehen*], they concern me somehow [*die gehen mich irgend etwas an*], that's clear" (23). If someone walks past me (*mir vorübergeht*), they concern me (*sie gehen mich an*), because they occupy my space. The link between the intransitive verb *vorübergehen* and the transitive *angehen* reduces the latter to a mere physical relation. Strangers concern me when they are "in my face," when they are near enough to me that I feel their presence. If offering them a service is uplifting, if it enables me to transcend my station, it is because in such cases I move from being a victim of chance to a master of the situation. Jakob offers the example of a dog that gets tangled in its leash: "And then I bend, and the great, great misfortune is resolved. Now, the lady-master of the dog [*Herrin des Hundes*] marches over to me. She sees what's up and thanks me . . . 'Thank you, sir [*mein Herr*].' Oh, she made me into a gentleman [*Herr*]. Yes, if you know how to comport yourself, you're a gentleman" (23).

The mere repetition of the word "Herr" in this passage indicates that more is at stake in the term than a translation of it as "sir" or "gentleman" can convey. Jakob has afterall just resolved "a great, great misfortune," as he would have it. He has intervened to set matters aright like a deus ex machina that descends from the sky to resolve the crises created by humans. More important, he intercedes on behalf of a person he does not know and who does not know him. The latter point is crucial, as it draws attention to an asymmetry in the master-servant relation. Strangers may concern Jakob, but Jakob does not concern them, since they can do nothing for him; he is not in need of their services. He thus becomes the stranger in the scene, the one about whom the lady will later ask, as Jesus's disciples did of him, "Who was he?"[33]

The similarity between the figure Jakob imagines and Jesus is not incidental, even if it is not stated explicitly. Indeed, the novel never makes overt reference to the Christian messiah, although his example pervades almost every page. Jesus is the model servant, in that he devotes himself to the salvation of others, who need him, although he is not in need of their services, in keeping with the asymmetrical nature of this relation. Jakob draws on this model of service in the above-cited passage, albeit to pervert it for his own ends. Service does not require a sacrifice on his part; on the contrary, it elevates and enlarges him by allowing him to become a being that no one notices and that consequently is not confined to any one place. Nowhere in particular, Jakob is everywhere potentially. This reversal informs every aspect of a servant's life, including his temporality.

A servant, as Jakob sees it, has access to eternity insofar as his work is never done or his service is never complete. Accordingly, the two virtues emphasized in the institute's curriculum are patience and obedience, each of which opens up to a potentially endless horizon: "The instruction we enjoy consists primarily in two things: to impress on us patience [*Geduld*] and obedience [*Gehorsam*], two characteristics which promise little or no success. Inner successes, yes. But what does one get for that?" (*JVG*, 7). Although patience and obedience are usually characterized as passive dispositions, the definition does not do justice to them. Neither virtue consists in the surrender of will or the suspension of desire, as is commonly assumed. On the contrary, the two are arguably the most willful dispositions on the grounds that they require that the subject attend not only to the present but also to what may come in the future. For this reason patience and obedience can never be mastered or obtained. One never finishes with the initial exercise of either, unless one is of course impatient or disobedient. In this vein Blanchot writes, "True patience does not exclude impatience. It is intimacy with impatience—impatience suffered and endured endlessly."[34] Both patience and obedience stretch out over an eternity. As a result they never yield any rewards, save the reward of the exercise itself, the continuous effort to attain them. Jakob refers to this reward as an "inner success," to distinguish it from external rewards like the accumulation of wealth.

Inner and outer, however, are complicated terms in a work, where rules are said to "hail, flash, snow and rain" (*JVG*, 84), and people waft like scents in the air—in short, where individuals and institutions are represented as forces of nature. The tension in the language in the text is reflected in the instruction at the school, which is divided into a theoretical part and a practical one, although the former is not described at any length. We only know that the students memorize the maxims contained in the school's one textbook, which is appropriately entitled with a question: "What Purpose Does the Boy's School Serve [*Was bezweckt die Knabenschule*]" (83). The bulk of the instruction takes place in the practical section, which includes such exercises as gymnastics, dance, and role-playing. According to Jakob the purpose of these lessons is to give shape to the body, but it is also to give life to the law, so that the law may guide the lives of the students long after they leave the institute. Jakob indicates as much in his description of the learning process:

> We learn one thing after another, and if we've mastered it, it sort of possesses us [*so besitzt es uns quasi*]. We don't possess it, on the contrary, what we would seem to have taken possession of dominates us [*was wir scheinbar zu unserem Bestizt gemacht haben herrscht dann über uns*]. . . . The law that commands, the pressure that compels, and the many unrelenting rules [*Vorschiften*] that give us direction and taste—that's what's great, not us pupils. (63–64)

To the extent that the students incarnate the law, that they let it take possession of them, they are placed in another dimension, where time stands still even as it continues to pass for everyone around them. For, each time the students do as the law commands, they are returned to this one moment in the classroom, as if it had never passed. Conversely, this one moment lives on in them as them as their inextinguishable youth and abiding innocence. For this reason none of the characters in the work is said to live, only to "live on" (*dahinleben*). All the residents of the school "live on" without direction or orientation in a dimension where time never passes and no one grows old and withers.

Freed from the constraints of time, the students become riddles to each other and to themselves, as Jakob himself notes in his first diary entry: "Since coming to the institute, I've already managed to become a riddle [*Rätsel*] to myself" (*JVG*, 7). What Jakob finds inscrutable—*rätselhaft*— is his newfound contentment, which is not unlike the serenity of Kraus, the model student at the school, whose ordinary name belies his exemplarity.[35] Although Kraus is dim-witted, plodding, and physically unattractive, Jakob reveres him all the same, since in his commitment to service Kraus has become a riddle, which is as much an an epistemological as a theological quandary. I quote the passage in full in German and in English, given its importance for delineating the paradox of service:

> Ja, man wird Kraus nie achten, und gerade das, daß er ohne Achtung zu genießen dahinleben wird, das ist ja das Wundervolle und Planvolle, das An-den-Schöpfer-Mahnende. Gott gibt der Welt einen Kraus, um ihr gleichsam ein tiefes unauflösbares Rätsel aufzugeben.

Nun, und das Rätsel wird nie begriffen werden, denn siehe: man gibt sich ja gar nicht einmal Mühe es zu lösen, und gerade deshalb ist dieses Kraus-Rätsel ein so Herrliches und Tiefes: weil niemand begehrt, es zu lösen, weil überhaupt gar kein lebendiger Mensch hinter diesem namenlos unscheinbaren Kraus irgendeine Aufgabe, irgendein Rätsel . . . vermuten wird. Kraus ist ein echtes Gott-Werk, ein Nichts, ein Diener. (81)

No one will ever notice Kraus, and it's exactly this—that he'll live on without enjoying any attention or respect—which makes him wondrous and part of some plan and a reminder of the Creator. God gives the world a Kraus to present it with a deep unsolvable riddle as it were. Now, the riddle will never be understood, because no one will ever bother to solve it, and this is what makes this Kraus-riddle so glorious and profound. No one cares to solve it, since no living human suspects a riddle behind this nameless, inconspicuous Kraus . . . Kraus is a true work of God, a nothing, a servant.

As Jakob repeatedly underscores, what makes Kraus a mystery is precisely that no one suspects a mystery there. His distinction is that he is inconspicuous or indistinct, which resonates with scholastic definitions of God as the One who is divided from all creation by virtue of his indivisibility.[36] Kraus is a riddle because he has no particular qualities. So thoroughly has he internalized the lessons of the school that he no longer stands out as an individual, but blends in with nature as a natural phenomenon. In this respect he is a "reminder of the Creator." One does not see Kraus when he performs a service, but nature in his stead, since Kraus's work is to reestablish the order of things as God created them. If he is noticed at all, it is at best as a scent in the air, which is a recurring motif in the work. Herr Benjamenta, for instance, notes that when Jakob came to the institute he was "fresh and blooming and fragrant with unspoiled sensations [*frech und blühend, duftend von unverdorbenen Empfindungen*]" (*JVG*, 156). And Jakob himself imagines that when he dies he will be transformed into a blossom: "One day, a scent will rise from my being and beginning; I'll be a flower and leave a light fragrance [*Eines Tages wird von meinem Wesen und Beginnen Duft ausgehen, ich werde Blüte sein und ein wenig . . . duften*]" (144). All of these examples reveal the force implicit in the seemingly banal claim "Good comportment is a blooming garden" (83), which is the one maxim from the school's textbook cited in the work.

At a structural level, Kraus's function is not only to illuminate what Jakob wants to be, but also to exemplify what he becomes, if one takes the conclusion of the novel seriously—which is to say if one trusts Jakob as narrator. There is of course the possibility that his diary is a ruse, a collection of stories invented to gratify the author, who could be either Jakob von Gunten or Robert Walser. Jochen Greven argues along these lines, as does Dagmar Grenz, that Jakob is not only Kraus's likeness, but also his antithesis in his penchant for irony and verbal play.[37] Yet the full extent of Jakob's irony only comes to the foreground at the novel's end when he becomes, like Kraus, "a nothing, a servant" (JVG, 81).

The final pages of the novel are marked by a rapid series of events, which stand in stark contrast to the preceding sections.[38] After a lonely life in which her love was never requited, Fräulein Benjamenta suddenly dies. Her death precipitates the disbanding of the school, which Herr Benjamenta admits he had used as a refuge from the world. All the students are dispatched to posts around the globe, with the exception of Jakob, who stays behind as the director's chosen companion. Before leaving the institute, the students gather one last time around Lisa Benjamenta. Kraus holds a eulogy that encapsulates the lessons of the school on the rewards of service:

The thoughts that you impressed on us and the lessons and knowledge that you secured in us will always remind us of you, the Creator [Schöpferin] of everything good in us. Of their own accord [Ganz von selber]. Whenever we eat, the fork will tell us how you wanted us to use and handle it . . . Your commands, life, lessons, questions and voice will continue to rule and sound in us [In uns herrschest, gebietest, lebst, erziehst und fragst und tönst du weiter]. (JVG, 152)

Fräulein Benjamenta is able to live on in her students because they live through her. She is the author of all that is good in them, which is simultaneously all that they can call their own. For they will live their lives without any social recognition or monetary reward. The only reward they can claim, hence, is that they fulfill or embody the law. Put otherwise, the law is its own reward. This is the meaning of the phrase ganz von selber (self-evidently, of its own accord), which plays on Jakob's family name "von Gunten," as does the phrase *ganz von unten*, from the very bottom (69), that occurs earlier in the novel when Jakob muses about his preferred social station.[39] At stake in this play is that the law compensates those who serve it "of its own accord." It grants *die Guten, ganz von unten*, eternal life, albeit at the price of any recognition for their accomplishment.

Once the students leave and Lisa Benjamenta is buried, Jakob and Herr Benjamenta can depart as well. The destination of their trip is never specified as anything but a desert far from Europe, which nonetheless recalls something else: the birthplace of the patriarchs Abraham, Isaac, and Jacob, who are all mentioned in the text. Before Jakob can embark on this journey, however, he must lay down his pen. He can only venture off into the distance, if he ceases to write for reasons that become apparent in his final diary entry:

> The time's come to throw away the pen now. Away with the life of thought. I'll be going to the desert with Herr Benjamenta. I'd like to see if one can live, breathe, be, do and desire what's good, and sleep at night and dream in the wilderness. Enough. I'm not going to think any longer. Not even of God? No! God will be with me. Why do I need to think of him? God is with all the thoughtless ones. So then *adieu*, Institute Benjamenta. (*jvg*, 164)

According to the premises of this passage, Jakob must dispense with writing to start a new life, since writing, as he represents it, is a form of confinement. It imprisons one in a world of thought and, by extension, in a self that is cut off from everything around it as a self-contained and self-sufficient monad. In ceasing to write, Jakob can finally merge with the world at large. Indeed, his entire diary would seem to anticipate this moment when he retreats as a narrator from our sight to return as someone we do not notice, someone like Kraus who is "a true work of God" (81). God will be with Jakob, once he leaves us behind, because, in leaving us, he can finally fulfill his mission to serve. He can incarnate the law, which requires that he help anyone who is in need—in short, which requires that he be infinite. The Institute Benjamenta is disbanded and yet it remains intact, literally *à Dieu*, with God, who represents the world outside the confines of this text.

The Double Fiction

If there is something disconcerting in this conclusion, it is that it is all too gratifying for Jakob. He engineers or orchestrates his disappearance, so that he may gain access to eternal life, or at least to a life in which he is no longer constrained by the threat of disappearing, dying, being annihilated.[40] A servant whom no one notices cannot die. He cannot disappear when he only ever appears as a force of nature (a scent) or a deus ex machina (a miracle). For this reason Jakob's descriptions of himself as a flower or a stranger, as in the scene with the dog, are not merely whimsical remarks but part of a concerted strategy to prepare the reader for his own eventual departure from the work as a narrator and a character. Jakob would have us believe that he retreats from the very pages of the book we hold in our hands to emerge on the other side of writing— that is, in life as someone we fail to acknowledge. The two instruments he uses in this undertaking are his pen and us. We, the readers, are the necessary witnesses to his passing into eternal life.

Seen in this light, Jakob's diary is nothing but an archway or threshold—"a charming, perfectly spherical zero [*eine reizende, kugelrunde Null*]" (JVG, 8), to cite one of his favorite expressions. He passes through the circle—the institute—that he draws on the page to be born anew in another world. This passage through the school is written into the very architecture of the text. As Rüdiger Campe observes, Jakob's diary begins with his arrival at the school and ends with his departure with Herr Benjamenta, which means that Jakob speaks as a diarist only from the space of the institution.[41] Put otherwise, the space of the institute and the diary are one and the same, which raises the question if the school is not in fact a fantasy *within* the diegetic space. That is to say, in the fiction of the existence of someone named Jakob von Gunten lies another fiction: that Jakob attends a servant school, which he portrays in his diary. The text is arguably structured as a series of concentric rings, in which the diary of a pupil is enclosed within the diary of another person bearing the same name. We will see the idea of a text within a text again in chapter 3 in the discussion of Thomas Bernhard's *Extinction*, which identifies itself from the outset as a posthumous memoir prepared for publication by another hand.

Andreas Gößling develops a hypothesis regarding the mise en abyme structure of the novel, albeit for different reasons. In his interpretation Jakob draws on the classic genre of the bildungsroman to generate and fashion himself as a work of art.[42] Jakob, the pupil, is in his opinion a constructed figure modeled after the hero of *Wilhelm Meisters Lehrjahre*.[43] Because the narrator of the diary is constructed or sketched by another hand, the text has to be conceived as a double fiction with two narrators. A hidden writer named Jakob represents himself as a pupil who writes a diary in which he also represents himself. To bolster this speculative claim, Gößling points to the number of passages in which Jakob's knowledge exceeds that of a normal diary keeper. For instance, early in the text Jakob writes, "I will have to say a lot about Kraus" (*JVG*, 25), as if he already knows what direction his diary will take. A few pages later he comments, "I have to go back to the beginning once again" (29), as if it were necessary to inform others that he is retracing his steps. And, throughout the text, Jakob wonders how readers will respond to what he writes. He begins one entry with the statement "I have to report something now which may generate some doubt" (53). And later he jokes, "I'm blathering a bit again, aren't I? I don't mind admitting that I'm blathering, since the lines have to be filled with something [*Ich schwatze wieder ein wenig, nicht wahr? Geb' es gern zu, daß ich schwatze, denn mit etwas müssen doch Zeilen ausgefüllt werden*]" (105). All of these remarks lend credence to Gößling's claim that the diary is marked as fictitious within the very space of the text.

Yet for all the strength of these examples Gößling fails to address the significance of the double fiction for Jakob's self-formation. His analysis bypasses the naïve but fundamental question regarding what Jakob stands to gain in pretending to be a pupil who writes a diary, however artificial or implausible this diary may be. This question is not merely one of form; it bears on the content of the work. It concerns how the work understands its form and exploits it for its own ends. This moment of self-reflection comes as Jakob enters the "inner chambers" (*innere Gemächer*) that stand as much for the mystery of the school as they do for the mystery of Jakob's diary.

The "inner chambers" are the rooms where the Benjamentas reside. The only student allowed to see them is Kraus, who never breathes a word about them. But Jakob is suddenly, magically transported there one evening when Fräulein Benjamenta appears behind him and puts her hands on his shoulders, as if bestowing a blessing on him. Jakob then finds himself in a cavernous space underground with Fräulein Benjamenta as his guide. Although the two claim to walk from room to room, it would be more appropriate to say that each room blends into the other like shifting stills or camera frames. However cinematic this effect may seem, I do not believe it was inspired by the films of Walser's day. The rooms are too literary in one respect to be viewed as citations of film technology. Each room is the translation of an allegorical figure; each represents a particular phrase or mood as a physical environment. So, for instance, when Jakob bumps his head against a wall, Fräulein Benjamenta says, "Go and kiss the wall. It's the wall of tears [die Sorgenwand]. It will always stand before your gaze" (*JVG*, 100), and, when he is almost blinded by a light, she tells him that this represents joy, which one has to learn to take in moderation. The list of translations of allegorical figures could be extended, but these examples suffice to show that each room is the externalization of an inner state, a mode of being, or habitus, made literal.

The inner chambers are significant because they mirror the work as a whole. As the chambers are projections of inner states, so too the Institute Benjamenta is an expression of Jakob's fantasy. This becomes apparent when Jakob enters the chambers again and this time discovers only sparsely furnished rooms with a fish tank as the one flourish. Jakob had already hinted that the chambers were a fantasy during his first stay there, by playing on the two meanings of the noun *Gemach* (room and comfort) as well as its negation, *das Ungemach* (adversity).[44] He has Fräulein Benjamenta ask him:

Hörst du, wie es zornig einherdonnert und—rollt? Das ist *das Ungemach*. Du hast jetzt in einem *Gemach* Ruhe genossen. Nun wird *das Ungemach* über dich herabregnen und Zweifel und Unruhe werden dich durchnässen. (*JVG*, 102, emphasis added)

Do you hear, how it's thundering and churning darkly? That's adversity. You've enjoyed peace and quiet in a chamber. Now adversity will rain down on you and doubt and anxiety will soak you.

As soon as Fräulein Benjamenta utters the noun *das Ungemach*, Jakob is whisked from the chambers and plunged into a "river of doubt," as he puts it. That the word would have such incantatory power is not un-usual in the context of the scene. Throughout the episode the phrases that Fräulein Benjamenta utters magically appear as diverse settings. What is unusual in this case is that "das Ungemach" does not mate-rialize as a new setting; rather, it destroys the very illusion of place by exposing the chambers as nothing but an effect of language, a vision based in words and nothing else. Peter Utz thus calls the inner cham-bers "empty places" and compares them to a balloon that is popped in the course of the novel.[45]

The puncturing of Jakob's illusion is simultaneously a puncturing of ours. It calls into question whether the Institute Benjamenta ever exist-ed, or if it was just a product of Jakob's fantasy—that is, a fiction created out of words, as the inner chambers were translations of allegorical fig-ures. What is dispelled or lost with the chambers, however, is not only the fiction of the school, but also the fiction of the author as a naïve and guileless pupil. Jakob cannot be a student who writes of his experiences at school if the school does not exist anywhere outside his text. This is where the episode in the inner chambers again becomes significant. Jakob's pas-sage through the narrow and winding corridors of the chambers ends in a pool of grief—more precisely, "a river of doubt" (JVG, 102)—in which he almost drowns. Rarely in a work has birth been described in such direct and dramatic terms, and rarely has it been so completely overlooked in the secondary literature. Two entries before this one on the inner cham-bers, Jakob writes after an encounter with Herr Benjamenta, "It was as if I were home. No, it was as if I hadn't been born yet, as if I still swam in something pre-natal [etwas Vor-Gebürtigem]" (95). The passage through the inner chambers is a birth, albeit not the birth that Jakob wants, which is why it ends in grief; the birth he wants comes at the end of his diary. Indeed, it would not be unfair to say that the entire fiction of the school is meant to promote the fantasy of a birth without blood or water, a lit-eral self-formation (Selbstbildung). We indulge Jakob in this fantasy. We serve him by creating or opening a space outside of the fiction of the school into which he can slip once he stops writing. The reader in effect legitimizes Jakob's claim "The Institute Benjamenta is the antechamber to the rooms and exquisite halls of life in all its expansiveness [Die Schule Benjamenta ist das Vorzimmer zu den Wohnräumen und Prunksälen des ausgedehnten Lebens]" (64–65).

The Limits of Narrative Theory

In narratological terms Jakob is split between the two orders of the text. On the one hand, he participates in the world that he represents. On the other, he produces this world from afar, from a vantage point not visible to the reader. In Genette's vocabulary he is both the homo- and hetero-diegetic narrator of the text, although he uses the first person throughout, which would usually make a heterodiegetic position impossible. Yet in this work the pronoun "I" refers at one and the same time to Jakob's position inside and outside the diary, which is also inside and outside the institute. Jakob is both a pupil at a school that he writes about and also a writer who fantasizes about being at such a school—in other words, an author who produces what Gößling rightly calls a "feigned" diary.[46] These two positions cannot be entirely disentangled from one another. But there are moments when Jakob suggests that the pronoun "I" must be understood as at least dual in its reference: "I lead a curious double life, regulated and unregulated, controlled and uncontrolled, simple and highly complex [*Ich führe ein sonderbares Doppelleben, ein geregeltes und ein ungeregeltes, ein kontrolliertes und ein unkontrolliertes, ein einfaches und ein höchst kompliziertes*]" (*JVG*, 140). Jakob's life is a twofold adventure, a union of opposites, since he is both the narrating and the narrated subject of this diary within a diary.

As Käte Hamburger might put it, he is a fictional character at the level of the internal narrative and a feigned statement-subject at the level of the frame (i.e., the space outside the institute but in the book). The distinction between feint and fiction, however, is at best murky in a work in which the narrated subject (the pupil Jakob) writes a diary and the narrating subject (the hidden author Jakob) keeps silent. Formal criticism is limited in its ability to account for this dynamic, since it represents a perversion of the rules governing both ordinary language and fictional utterances. But as a perversion it also has a thematic component that can be expounded in any reading. *Jakob von Gunten* offers this component in its treatment of service, which informs every aspect of the novel, including finally the characters' names. Although Jakob is a pupil and by extension a son, he bears the name of the biblical patriarch, whereas his teachers and symbolic parents bear a name related to the patriarch's son Benjamin.[47] Within the school Jakob is a minor, but outside it he is the father of a nation. At the novel's conclusion, he disappears with the children he sires with his pen—that is, with the fictional progeny he produces with the aid of the reader as nurse or midwife.[48] He slips into the world beyond the institute as a word made flesh or as the embodiment of the institute's impersonal principles. Klaus-Peter Philippi has complained that Jakob's sole ambition in the novel is to be.[49] Yet it is a remarkable achievement for a character to engineer his departure from the page and entrance into life, if only as an anonymous being. With Jakob's disappearance, the semblance of life in the text gives way to a life beyond all semblance, which is also a life beyond all formal constraint. Jakob achieves his freedom by abandoning the fiction that he creates. He persists long after the conclusion of the novel by virtue of not appearing, by forsaking all self-representation. In a brief essay on Walser published in 1929, Walter Benjamin cites Walser's statement regarding his characters: "And if they have not died, then they are still living today."[50] According to Benjamin Walser's characters display a curious joy that only someone recovering from great suffering could experience. It is a joy so quiet that hardly anyone takes notice of it. This is how Jakob lives on following his self-orchestrated birth: as a forever young and *almost* innocent servant who asks for nothing but the pleasure of his own nothingness.

3 The Work
Thomas Bernhard's *Extinction*

In a 1981 essay entitled "Narrative Versions, Narrative Theories," Barbara Herrnstein Smith offers a flip but suprisingly sharp definition of narrative. What constitutes a story, in her view, is that "someone tells someone else that something happened."[1] The nature of the event is immaterial for her; what matters is that something happened in the past that a narrator then communicates to an audience in the present. For all the merits of Smith's succinct formulation, her definition suffers from a prejudice against the modern novel in which the identity of the narrator is often uncertain and the central or mobilizing event is not consigned to the past. Smith shares this bias with theoreticians of the novel as diverse as Georg Lukács, Roland Barthes, and Käte Hamburger, who all turn to the nineteenth-century realist novel to define fiction. For all the above-mentioned critics, the novel is unquestionably a mimetic genre that represents a series of events that take place in a setting that is at least plausible for the reader, even if fictive or imagined.[2] More important, for Barthes and Hamburger, the novel is narrated in the past tense. The "epic preterite," as they call it, signals that world of the novel is self-enclosed, which also means that it is distinct from the world inhabited by the reader.[3]

Many modern novels question these assumptions about narrative. Volumes could be written on the critique of omniscience in twentieth and twenty-first century fiction, or the disappearance of plot as a structuring device. It is not my intention, however, to cite examples that challenge Smith's thesis. I recall her compact formulation as it focuses on two events that collapse into one in Thomas Bernhard's fiction, if his prose work can be called that. The first is the supposedly antecedent occurrence that a story documents, the second the communication of this occurrence orally or in writing. The consistent question of Bernhard's fiction, by contrast, is whether it will happen at all—whether it will ever be written down, recorded on paper, so that it may constitute a work in the future.

Bernhard's prose work is invariably concerned with its afterlife, which is understood as the life it will achieve if it ever crystallizes on the page as something apart from its producer. For this to happen, however, its producer must die. Bernhard's fiction subscribes to the notion that a work can come to be only if its author vanishes. This is evident in the destiny of some of his more memorable characters, such as the philosopher and amateur builder Roithamer in *Correction* and the failed pianist Wertheimer in *The Loser* (*Der Untergeher*). Neither character, it should be noted, serves as the narrator of the text. In both cases, a narrator sets out to recover the literary remains of a friend who has recently committed suicide in dramatic fashion. In *Correction* this pursuit takes the narrator to Roithamer's attic apartment, where he discovers a manuscript that has been all but blotted out, corrected to the point of incoherence. As a final correction to Roithamer's attempt to edit himself out of existence, the narrator publishes the posthumous papers of his friend in all their disarray and confusion. In so doing he "corrects" what would seem to be the course of nature—namely, decay—by preserving the literary corpus of his friend precisely as the detritus of existence.[4] In this he mirrors Roithamer's landlord Höller, a taxidermist by trade, who devotes his days and nights to preserving the corpora of rare birds and other natural curiosities.

According to the logic of *Correction*, Roithamer remains a name for us because of his death. His suicide enables him to become an author posthumously by halting his efforts to destroy everything associated with his person. Yet, in the eyes of the reader, Roithamer is not primarily an author, but a narrated figure. In other words, he is a figure that is talked about (an object) but does not talk directly to us (a subject), even if the final section of the novel contains his belated opus. This distinction is significant insofar as it points to a discrepancy between the structure of the novel and its ostensible theme. *Correction* explores the idea that an author must perish for his work to survive, but does not put this idea to the test through its own example. This test comes in Bernhard's pseudo-memoirs: his fictional texts in which a first-person narrator undertakes to say something about his life. These texts differ from Bernhard's five-volume autobiography, published between 1975 and 1985, in that none of the works in this series question their belatedness.⁵ That they are posterior to the events they document is taken as a matter of course. Barbara Herrnstein Smith might say that, as an autobiographer, Bernhard "tells someone . . . that something happened" in a past now eclipsed by the present. Only in the pseudo-autobiographical works is the posteriority of writing itself addressed with attention to the issue of whether autobiography is possible at all—whether life lends itself to its narrative representation.

Bernhard wrote three principal texts in this vein, all later in life. The first was *Concrete (Beton)*, published in 1982; the second *Woodcutters (Holzfällen)*, published in 1984; and the third *Extinction (Auslöschung)*, published in 1986. All three draw attention to their belatedness as productions that materialize after the fact—after the moment of their composition, which is recounted in some detail in these texts. In *Woodcutters* this concern is more or less explicit, while in *Concrete* and *Extinction* it is a subtler matter, which ultimately calls into question how we understand narrative. If, as Aristotle would have it, a narrative is supposed to produce a semblance of life, then no material would seem more suited for narrative representation than lived experience, which is what we have come to expect from an autobiography.⁶ Yet for Bernhard life and writing never do coincide, as the closing words of *Woodcutters* pointedly demonstrate: "I will write *at once (sofort)* about this *artistic dinner* in the Gentzgasse, it doesn't matter what, only that I write about *this artistic dinner* in the Gentzgasse *now, at once (gleich und sofort)*, I thought over and over again as I ran through the Inner City, *now, at once, now, now (gleich* und *sofort* und *gleich* und *gleich)* before it's too late."⁷ The narrator's insistent repetition of "at once" *(sofort)* and "now" *(gleich)* cannot mask the fact that the declaration that he makes comes too late, after we have read what he wrote in a prior moment. In other words, the "now" of which he speaks has already passed; what remains is merely the record of a thought that is no longer current, or an impulse that has long since receded into the past.

Bernhard's prose work confronts the reader with the echo of voices that no longer speak "at once" or "now." This is the case even in his most breathless monologues, which is how his work is frequently characterized.⁸ If his prose nonetheless repeatedly takes the form of a monologue or address, it is because the narrators of his fiction struggle to say something with whatever means they have available. They aim to tell stories or to narrate events, even when the only event is the act of storytelling itself. As a result Bernhard's prose has two principal characteristics that would seem to be at odds. His fiction is, on the one hand, morose and, on the other, frantic or charged with the need to find a story that would revitalize writing and moor the text in life. I will explore this dimension of Bernhard's fiction through an analysis of his final novel *Extinction*, in which we know from the outset that the narrator has died.

The Order of the Text

Both the opening and closing sentences of *Extinction* differ from the remaining sentences in this five-hundred-page novel insofar as an anonymous editor intervenes to identify the narrator by name in almost bureaucratic fashion. The first extended sentence is interrupted by the remark "writes Murau, Franz-Josef," as if he were a historical person. Similarly, the final sentence contains the editorial comment "writes Murau (born 1934 in Wolfsegg, died 1983 in Rome)."[9] Taken in isolation, neither comment would seem significant. *Extinction* would hardly be the first text to present itself as a historical document as opposed to a novel, a memoir as opposed to a work of fiction.[10] But what stands out here is the intervention of a foreign hand in the body of Murau's text, which is written entirely in the first person. The intervention draws attention to the narrator's absence, indicating that he is not there to vouch for his words in the manner in which the authors of most memoirs do: by having their name printed on a title page. As discussed in chapter 2, Philippe Lejeune argues that the appearance of the author's name on the title page and copyright notice functions for the reader as a guarantee that the person named in the text exists outside it, however accurate or inaccurate, self-serving, or self-negating his portrayal may be.[11] The fact that Murau's name is printed in the text, but not in the paratext, thus implies that the work that will follow is fictional, since the author does not exist outside the pages in which he speaks of his supposed life. The novel *Extinction* begins by extinguishing its author as a presence apart from the page. His absence, his death, is the condition for the work.

The framing of Murau's absence coincides with the news of another loss that forms the occasion for the narrative. The first sentence of the novel bears quoting in German and English, given its length and meandering syntax, as if designed to mirror the narrator's footsteps:

Nach der Unterredung mit meinem Schüler Gambetti, mit welchem ich mich am Neunundzwanzigsten auf dem Pincio getroffen habe, schreibt Murau, Franz-Josef, um die Mai-Termine für den Unterricht zu vereinbaren und von dessen hoher Intelligenz ich auch jetzt nach meiner Rückkehr aus Wolfsegg überrascht, ja in einer derart erfrischenden Weise begeistert gewesen bin, daß ich ganz gegen meine Gewohnheit gleich durch die Via Condotti auf die Piazza Minerva zu gehen, auch in dem Gedanken tatsächlich schon lange in Rom und nicht mehr in Österreich zuhause zu sein, in eine zunehmend heitere Stimmung versetzt, über die Flaminia und die Piazza del Popolo, den ganzen Corso entlang in meine Wohnung gegangen bin, erhielt ich gegen zwei Uhr mittag das Telegramm, in welchem mir der Tod meiner Eltern und meines Bruders Johannes mitgeteilt wurde. (*Auslöschung*, 7)

Following the appointment with my student Gambetti, whom I met on the 29th on the Pincio after returning from Wolfsegg, writes Murau, Franz-Josef, to make arrangements for our May lessons and whose fine mind continues to impress me and excite me in such a refreshing manner that I decided, instead of walking home in my usual manner along the Via Condotti to the Piazza Minerva, to cross the Flaminia and the Piazza del Popolo and proceed down the whole length of the Corso, the whole time cheered up by the thought that I was back in Rome and no longer in Austria, before reaching my apartment, where I received around 2:00 pm the telegram informing me that my parents and brother Johannes had died.

Even without the editor's comment, this sentence would already be complex. Murau extends the moment leading up to the news of his parents' and brother's demise by tracing his path through Rome that day in some detail. In so doing he delays arriving at the narrative present, which is the situation that the speaker supposedly occupies and that determines his outlook or perspective. In this case, however, the narrative present is murky at best. It is at once the afternoon that Murau spends in his apartment with the telegram in hand as well as the moment in which he writes of that afternoon, as the editor informs us. Logic would dictate that Murau can only record his impressions of that day *after* it has passed, but the same does not hold true for the temporality of the text.

The editorial intrusion opens up a gap between the events recounted and the moment of recounting that cannot be undone, no matter how long Murau's monologue continues without a break. For the intrusion signals that Murau's narration is already done—that it has already been written down and prepared for publication by an editor before it has even started for us. In a meditation on W. G. Sebald's *Rings of Saturn*, Carol Jacobs remarks that the narrator at the outset of Sebald's novel stands at a juncture between the end of a particular journey in life and the beginning of a journey in writing.[12] Even the distinction between life and its depiction, however, hardly applies in a text like *Extinction* in which the narrator speaks to us from a moment that has already passed, or, more pointedly, in which he begins his narration after his death. As we will see, this reversal of beginning and end, or life and death, makes it possible for Murau to write, to find the first sentence for his memoir that had always escaped him in the past.

Murau is a failed writer, like so many of Bernhard's other protagonists, who either never begin to write or who destroy what they write before they have even finished a draft.[13] Indeed, Murau tells us that he and his friend Maria burned his manuscripts, in an apparent allusion to Kafka, who on his deathbed asked Max Brod to burn his papers. Unlike Bernhard's other heroes, however, Murau has succeeded in writing academic papers and essays for the feuilletons. What has escaped him is the memoir of his family he would like to write and that he would entitle *Extinction*. The mere fact that the book that we hold in our hands has this title would at first glance suggest his success in this endeavor. The memoir *Extinction* exists regardless of whether he agreed to its publication, and one might be tempted to say that it exists precisely because Murau did not live long enough to burn it. Yet such an interpretation assumes that the text we read is the memoir he wanted to write. Put otherwise, it assumes that the work published under the title *Extinction* is identical with Murau's intended memoir *Extinction*.

Nothing in the text would support this assumption. In fact everything Murau says in it would suggest that he is incapable of starting his autobiography, as he confesses to his student Gambetti: "The difficulty is always how to begin such a report and where to find an actually workable first sentence. In truth, Gambetti, I've failed many times with the very first written sentence" (*Auslöschung*, 155). This passage is one of several in which Murau underscores the challenge of finding an appropriate first sentence, as if the first would automatically yield the last and he faced no other obstacle. Astonishingly few critics have taken Murau at his word regarding his writer's block; most assume that the published work indicates that he eventually overcame his impasse and composed the text we now read as his autobiography.[14] The only evidence for this claim comes in the novel's final sentence, when Murau refers to Rome as the place "where I wrote this *Extinction*" (508), as if pointing to the manuscript in front of him. Yet the demonstrative article "this" is not as unequivocal as it may seem. Every "this" implies a "that," an opposing term, which in this case would be another *Extinction* besides the one presented to the reader. Murau gestures in this direction throughout the work in reflecting on what he *cannot* write. He does not so much begin his memoir as write a memoir of his problems beginning. In this manner he bypasses the irritating question of how to start his autobiography.

The detour he makes, however, comes at a cost. What he produces is an embarrassment to himself as a writer, "eine Selbstblamage" (*Auslöschung*, 479), in his words. He humiliates himself:

> Now and again we convince ourselves that we're capable of an intellectual effort [*Geistesarbeit*] like *Extinction*, which is yet to be written down, but then we shy away from it because we know that in all likelihood we will not be able to keep it up. Then, when we have perhaps made good progress, we suddenly falter and all is lost, not only the time we spent and wasted on this project . . . rather we have made fools of ourselves, if not in front of everyone, then at least in front of ourselves [*sondern uns dann auch noch wenn schon nicht vor aller Welt, so doch vor uns selbst auf die entsetzlichste Weise blamiert haben*]. (479)

While Murau would like to believe that his humiliation is private, the fact that we have an occasion to read his confession indicates that it is public already. This is true for every statement in the novel, which makes this one passage paradigmatic for the entire work. Murau is condemned to fail in the task he sets for himself: he will never begin, much less complete, the memoir of his family he would like to write on account of his death, which is announced through the editorial intrusion in the novel's final sentence. What remains, then, is merely a prolegomenon to a work that will never be. The published text *Extinction* is a preliminary study that will never triumph in a final study. This, paradoxically, is its success.

Murau chooses the title he does for his memoir to signal his aim. His text should destroy everything he associates with his birthplace, Wolfsegg, including its National Socialist past, its stifling Catholicism, and its general disdain for learning: "The one thing I know definitively, I said to Gambetti, is the title *Extinction*. The sole purpose of my report is to extinguish everything described in it, everything I understand under the name Wolfsegg, everything that Wolfsegg is, everything. Do you understand me, Gambetti? Really and truly everything. Following my report everything associated with Wolfsegg must be extinguished" (*Auslöschung*, 156). As if to underscore this point, he reiterates a few pages later, "I will call this report *Extinction*, I said to Gambetti, because in this report I will in fact extinguish everything I write down. Wolfsegg will be extinguished in my report in my own fashion, Gambetti" (158). However forceful Murau is in declaring his intent, everything in the text would seem to refute his aim. Wolfsegg enters the annals of literature as a result of his vivid descriptions of it. His writing to this extent preserves his birthplace rather than extinguishes it. Numerous critics have accordingly noted the paradoxical, if not preposterous, nature of Murau's venture. Writing as a form of fixation memorializes whatever it touches, including what it sentences to oblivion. This is true even when the text in question pitches itself as a negation of negation, which *Extinction* does insofar as its narrator engages in what Bernhard Sorg calls the "complete verbal condemnation" (*Auslöschung*, 139) of Austria as a land of unregenerate Nazis. Murau brooks no obfuscation on this point, as is evident in a statement about Austria like "The obliterators [*Die Auslöscher*] are at work, the killers [*die Umbringer*]" (89).[15]

In this spirit Murau tells the story of the miner Schermaier who was sent to a concentration camp for the crime of listening to a prohibited Swiss radio broadcast during the war. Murau is quick to note that the injustices Schermaier suffered did not end in 1945. Schermaier was given a piddling sum to compensate for his imprisonment, whereas the collaborators received generous pensions from the state and were honored for their service to the nation. In a passage striking for its sentimentality in an otherwise acerbic work, Murau remarks, "[It] is my duty in *Extinction* to speak of them [the victims of National Socialism] and through them for the sake of so many other [*stellvertretend für so viele*] who do not talk about their suffering during the National Socialist period" (*Auslöschung*, 358). While Murau would appear to depict his project as an effort to expose a past hidden by perpetrator and victim alike, the strategy he outlines is more complex than can be summed up in formulas like "breaking taboos" and "silencing silence" associated with the push to work through the past (*Durcharbeitung der Vergangenheit*) in the 1980s and 1990s.[16] Schermaier will feature in his text as a quasi-symbolic figure, "taking the place of so many others [*stellvertretend für so viele*]" (358), which is a dubious distinction, given that it robs him of any individuality as a face for the faceless or a name for the unknown.

Gerhard Scheit and Burghard Damerau both observe that Bernhard did not explicitly address Austria's National Socialist past until late in his writing, and even then the gesture is ambivalent for a variety of reasons, including the philosemitism of a text like *Extinction*, which ends with Murau's gift of his family's estate to the Jewish community of Vienna in what can only be described as an act of reparation.[17] (Earlier in the text we learn that his parents hid ss officers in the children's playhouse at Wolfsegg both during and after the war.) Irene Heidelberger-Leonard is likewise critical of the novel's conclusion, which she claims erases the past by exchanging the suffering of the victims for the property of the perpetrators, as if the latter's guilt could be discharged in this fashion.[18] Heidelberger-Leonard's concern is legitimate, and it is no accident that Damerau also claims that there is "something grotesque" about Murau's gift.[19] Yet what is at stake here is not a quid pro quo, in which Austria cancels its guilt (or *Schuld*) by repaying its debts (or *Schulden*), but the capacity of literature to do justice to the *Realitäten* it has inherited (a term I will discuss shortly).

In a bout of insomnia the night before his parents' and brother's funeral, Murau considers what to do with his family's estate, which includes not only a house but also a chapel, several additional structures, and a large tract of land, all encapsulated in the name "Wolfsegg." Murau finds himself in the unlikely position of being the sole heir to the estate as the one surviving male member of his family: "For over two hours I tossed and turned with these thoughts. I didn't think about *what will happen to Wolfsegg* but *what should I do with Wolfsegg* that with the death of my parents actually and in the truest sense of the phrase 'fell on my head' and now threatens to crush me. Wolfsegg's fallen on me with its gargantuan weight [*mit seiner ganzen ungeheuerlichen Wucht*], I thought" (*Auslöschung*, 484). What keeps Murau awake is not "Wolfsegg" the physical place, but the legacy it represents, which he subjects to unsparing verbal rebuke in typical Bernhardian fashion. In asking what he can do with Wolfsegg, as opposed to what will happen to it, he draws attention to his power as a writer, who makes things with words. Earlier in the scene he depicted himself as "a kind of literary realtor [*eine Art literarischer Realitätenvermittler*]" (481) in a comment that is tongue in cheek but that acquires particular weight when Murau is faced with the question of how to purvey and convey (*vermitteln*) the real estate holdings and realities (*Realitäten*) that constitute his inheritance.[20] The symbolic status accorded Schermaier as a surrogate for all other Austrian victims of the Holocaust comes to serve as a model for the account that Murau will write of his personal and familial past. It will be a memoir that takes the place of another that could not come to pass, but that curiously demands our attention in spite of its absence.

To produce such a memoir, Murau must distinguish between Wolfsegg "as he sees it" and Wolfsegg "as it is." Franz Eyckeler attributes this strategy to Bernhard's perspectivalism, which places the point of view of the speaker (e.g., his situation, mood, and relation to the subject matter, as well as the occasion and purpose of his speech) over any supposedly objective statement.[21] The consistent, if not exclusive, focus on the perspective of the speaker elevates him above the world that he portrays. According to Eyckeler all statements of a narrator like Murau amount to the exercise of a "will to power" that ultimately fulfills "Nietzsche's project of the decimation of truth."[22] Yet it is hard to hear the exercise of power in a pronouncement such as this: "Since my immediate family has neither the intention nor the skill to describe Wolfsegg as it is and as it has always been, the task falls to me. I will at least make an effort to describe Wolfsegg as *I* see it, since a person can only describe what *he* sees and how things appear to *him*" (*Auslöschung*, 154–55, emphasis in original). Murau draws not on his strength but on his incapacity and weakness to make a point. Wolfsegg "as it is" will never be registered in the pages of literature because Wolfsegg "as Murau sees it" makes it impossible for him to write anything but this one provisional work that costs him his life. Murau mentions throughout the text that he suffers from a chronic lung condition not unlike Bernhard's tuberculosis.[23] The fact that he dies a year after the family funeral would imply that the reencounter with Wolfsegg chokes him literally and figuratively.

In death, however, Murau is able to accomplish what he could not in life. He extinguishes Wolfsegg by extinguishing the possibility that it could ever be documented in a memoir entitled *Extinction*. Here is where Murau's failure becomes a success, albeit not a success for Murau but for those who survive him—for his readers. Murau destroys his birthplace not through what he writes, but what he marks as withheld: the definitive account of Wolfsegg that would depict the estate as it has always been, if only its author lived long enough to draft it. For this reason the novel must begin and end with the editorial comment announcing Murau's death. As the embodiment of Wolfsegg and its sole remaining male heir, Murau takes the family estate to the grave with him as something unwritten, something that has been erased from the public record. In this manner he achieves his aim. He sets Wolfsegg down on paper as "das Ausgelöschte," as that which has been stricken from memory.[24]

The destruction of Wolfsegg does, however, depend on one factor that exceeds even Murau's death. It depends on the presence of a reader who is willing to read the text from its conclusion to maintain the illusion that Murau wrote it from the beginning in chronological fashion. Murau's death, which is intimated in the first sentence and declared in the last, allows the reader to construct what is perhaps an all-too-gratifying circle, in which the text we read is assumed to be not the memoir Murau wanted to write, but the one he ended up with after putting pen to paper. In other words, it enables us to look at the text as Murau's ersatz memoir. But *Extinction* is also a novel and is marked as such if read from the beginning as a text written from its end, from the death of its principle character. In his essay "The Storyteller," Walter Benjamin argues that novels in contrast to stories are constructed from their end. To demonstrate this point, he cites Moritz Heimann's seemingly absurd pronouncement that "a man who dies at thirty-five is at every point of his life a man who dies at thirty-five."[25] No twentieth-century text would seem to bear out this dictum more than Bernhard's *Extinction*. Thanks to the initial editorial comment, Murau is marked as absent from the start; the novel indicates in its first sentence that its narrator does not exist and consequently has no place outside it. The genre of the novel is frequently criticized for constructing a self-enclosed world based on the temporal paradox that its end precedes its beginning or its conclusion determines its outset. Yet Bernhard turns precisely this dimension of the novel to his advantage in *Extinction*. Insofar as Murau does not exist outside the text, neither does his birthplace. Both are marked as fictive for the sake of another kind of extinction: of Austria from the last days of Murau's namesake Emperor Franz-Josef to the rise of Kurt Waldheim, elected president of Austria in 1986, which was also the year that *Extinction* was published.[26] Literature is limited in its means to extinguish or destroy. Whatever it names it ushers into being, except if it frames it as fictitious, as something "allegedly factual [*ein vermeintliches Tatsächliches*]" (*Auslöschung*, 374) in Murau's vocabulary. *Extinction* frames the place that haunts its narrator as a fiction to destroy it in the end, to reduce it to "ridiculous strips of paper" (22), which is how Murau describes the photograph, the "devil's instrument" (190) of the late twentieth century. The novel presents Austria in its most grotesque and exaggerated form to convert it into something that belongs only in a book or a curio cabinet. The model for literature in this text, as in *Correction*, is the handicraft of the embalmer, who records the history of nature through its oddities and monstrosities, which it preserves at the moment of their extinction.

Snapshots

Murau does not hesitate to declare that his depictions of Wolfsegg are caricatures. With a certain pride he reports that his student Gambetti has donned him "a typical Austrian doom-sayer" and "a boundless exaggerator" (*Auslöschung*, 97) because of his litany of complaints against his homeland. Exaggeration is his art. Yet Murau's clearest statement about his method comes from his reflections not on writing but on photography, in particular his reflections on the few photos of his family he has kept in his Rome apartment. The first is a picture of his parents in London in 1960; the second, of his brother on his sailboat; the third, of his two sisters in Cannes during a visit to their Uncle Georg. All three show the depicted subjects in the most perverse light. Murau notes that his mother's neck in the first photo is stretched out too far; his brother's efforts to look nonchalant in the second come off as tortured; and in the third his sisters' expressions are at once sarcastic and sullen. The snapshots lead him to conclude that photography is an affront to nature and "the most misanthropic art" (24) not because it robs its subjects of dignity, but because it preserves them in their indignity long after they are gone.

And yet for all its apparent crudeness, analog photography serves as a model for Murau's writing. Murau never claims to recount episodes or tell stories; rather, he reports, transcribes, and documents events. The only storytellers he mentions are the forest workers, who in his youth were always prepared "to *tell* [him] about themselves [*von sich zu erzählen*]" (*Auslöschung*, 108).[27] Murau is a writer who seeks to capture events with the stroke of his pen, like a photographer who can always rely on the click of her camera to capture a moment. And this strategy has consequences not only for Murau's depictions of Wolfsegg but for the novel as well: for *Extinction* as a fictional work that arouses a curious melancholy in its readers, given that its protagonist does not exist apart from the page.

In his now-canonical study *Camera Lucida*, Roland Barthes underscores that it was the poignancy of some personal photos that first drew him to the subject of photography.[28] The emotional response that a photo of his late mother elicits leads him to assert that there can be no general method for interpreting photographs, only a *mathesis singularis*, a science of the singular.[29] Part of the poignancy derives from the analog technology to which Barthes and Bernhard are wedded, as two authors who knew only the 35-mm film camera and the typewriter for text production. Barthes repeatedly notes that the photography of his era is an art of contingency. A photographer happened to be where the photo was taken, no matter how deliberate or staged the setting. Barthes underscores that whether the setting is real or artificial, authentic or contrived, the photograph still bears witness to the fact something existed in a certain spot, in a certain light, in a certain position—in short, in a certain moment that has elapsed. It is for this reason that Barthes insists that analog photography always carries its object. "The referent adheres," as he puts it, to the extent that it leaves an impression in photosensitive film that is reproduced on photosensitive paper in turn.[30] Yet it should be noted that the trace of the object is not material; it is a pattern of light. And, more important, what adheres to the photo is not the thing itself but its image, which is unique precisely because the moment in which it appears is irretrievable.

The truth of the photograph, consequently, is not spatial but temporal. Barthes stresses that the photograph brings to the foreground death at work, "immobilizing," "embalming," "arresting," and "mortifying" whatever it touches.[31] This in his view is what makes the photograph poignant. The photograph "pierces," "pricks," "wounds," "bruises," and "lacerates" the beholder with its testament to what has been.[32] Barthes invokes all these terms when describing the *punctum*, which is the essence of the photograph, as opposed to the *studium*, which is its general interest or the subject matter that it showcases. Derek Attridge explains the difference between the two in semiotic terms. The punctum, he says, is the accidental or unintentional element in the photograph that "escapes all the codes of reading."[33] The studium, by contrast, is the topos defined by these codes and conventions. Barthes himself sums up the punctum of photography in the phrase "that has been," which is his shorthand for the fact that "'the photographic referent' is not the *optionally* real thing to which an image or sign refers but the *necessarily* real thing which has been placed before the lens."[34] Every photograph stands as evidence that "*the thing has been there*" before the camera.[35]

Barthes's emphasis on the evidentiary nature of the photograph clarifies what has proven to be one of the more difficult aspects of his argument. He remarks that the punctum "cannot in any way constitute the visible object of a science. It cannot establish an objectivity, in the positive sense of the term."[36] This, however, does not mean that it is a purely subjective phenomenon. Michael Fried elaborates that the punctum is given in the photographic image but is not depicted or shown.[37] In other words, it is not something the photographer chose to highlight because she herself was not aware of its presence. The same holds true for the beholder: the punctum catches her unawares as an element in the photograph that conveys the fragility of the referent, its mutability, or transitoriness. Such an experience is for Barthes incommunicable in that it exceeds all subjective intentionality, which is why it requires something as contradictory as a science of the singular to elucidate it.[38]

It may seem odd to refer to Barthes's reflections on photography in the analysis of a literary work, due to Barthes's insistence that the punctum is incommunicable. In one of the most frequently quoted passages from the essay, he states, "What I name cannot really prick me."[39] Moreover, literature, in his view, suffers from a dearth of images in withholding its referent, whereas photography carries its referent in its depictions.[40] Yet Bernhard's *Extinction* invites this comparison for two reasons: first, Murau's comments on his family photographs echo those of Barthes; and, second, the text is organized, if not as a photograph, then as a phonograph. Murau's voice speaks in a manner that is not reducible to his own intentions or writing.

Like Barthes, Murau claims that the photograph immobilizes its subject in time. He explains that he chose to take the photos he did to Rome, "because they reproduce my parents and brother exactly as they were the moment I took the pictures" (*Auslöschung*, 22). Moreover, he recognizes that the moment captured in the photos is one in which his family will always reside, not because all the members are dead—his sisters are in fact alive—but because they persist in these pictures as images alone, or what could be called ghosts or specters. Murau gestures on numerous occasions to the kind of afterlife photography grants its subjects. Like Barthes, he would seem to confuse visual data with material remains, images with the body. For instance, he returns almost obsessively to the issue of his parents' photographed size; he notes that they are a mere "ten-centimeters tall" (22) in the photos, as if they had literally been shrunk down to miniatures. And they subsist now as "ridiculous strips of paper" (22) rather than as creatures of flesh and blood. This in his view is what makes photography such a falsification of nature and such "an absolute insult to human dignity" (22). Yet what he labels a falsification is nothing other than the fact that one's image can be preserved long after one is gone—or, to put it another way, that one's face can so readily become a death mask.

Falsification in the case of photography, then, is not untruth, but brutal honesty. It punctures the illusion that humans can ever have a natural life—a notion that Murau invokes with astonishing frequency.[41] For nature, as Murau understands it, is nothing but an ideal. He proudly reports his Uncle Georg's romantic opinion that "the *ideal* view of nature presupposes an *ideal* concept of art" (*Auslöschung*, 28, emphasis added). According to this line of reasoning, art is necessary for the appreciation of nature because it reveals the world in its infinite greatness. The photograph, by contrast, displays the world in its finite pettiness. It is this dimension of photography that makes the pictures of Murau's family so haunting for him. The punctum dispels whatever illusions he still had about his origins. Astonishingly, Murau identifies the detail that in Barthes's vocabulary "pricks" and "bruises" him: his mother's outstretched neck in the photo from 1960. Later in the text this detail comes to encompass an entire history. In a long passage on the numerous ways in which his parents collaborated with the National Socialists, he remarks in passing that his mother sprained her neck while removing the Nazi flag from the house minutes before the Americans arrived in the village at the end of the war (152). We later learn that his mother's body cannot be displayed at the wake since she was nearly beheaded in the car accident, save for a few sinews in her neck. When placed in this context, the detail of Murau's mother's neck may seem overdetermined. The pictures no doubt contain other features that encapsulate Murau's family for him in ways that cannot be so readily interpreted. But the key issue is that the detail is pregnant with meaning *for him*. It would be insignificant for any other viewer, although it is there for all to see. For Murau, as for Barthes, the punctum is given in the photograph, but its facticity never amounts to objectivity, since it will never be evident to two viewers in the same manner. As a result of this difference between the given and the universal, Murau can claim that in documenting Wolfsegg "as he sees it," he also documents Wolfsegg "as it is." His gaze immobilizes a set of features that are there for all to see, but that will never have the same significance for other viewers, as it escapes the intentionality or cognitive grasp of any individual.

The same dynamic, I would argue, applies to Murau's voice, which is the trace or residue that Bernhard's text carries with it. We know from the start of the novel that Murau has died, or, at least, that he no longer lives in the moment from which he speaks and that his present has become a past. Precisely because this moment has passed, his voice is haunting for us: it sounds and resounds as an echo of what is no longer present. This is what Bernhard's novel shares with the photograph. True to the analog technolology of his era, one would call it a phonograph. The voice of the narrator speaks from a temporal distance as the face in a photo peers out from the past, and it touches the reader in those places where it brings Murau's particular vulnerability to the fore.[42] I would not claim that the place where I locate the punctum is where anyone else would do so; the punctum is a feature that is given but not universal, as I have underscored. Murau, moreover, is not a historical figure but a fictional character. As a result the text cannot attest to his existence, as the photograph attests to the "that-has-been" of its subject. Nonetheless, in this fictional auto-biography, in this memoir-cum-novel, a voice is created that adheres to the printed word as the trace of a mortal being. To read this novel without paragraph breaks is already to respond to a voice that is fading from the start and embodies as such the essence of Murau's finitude.

The Novel as a Whole and Beyond

Much like Barthes, Murau wonders whether a work of art can touch the real, though he eventually decides that this is a delusion, cooked up no doubt by art critics. Every representation destroys "das Tatsächliche," the real or factual (*Auslöschung*, 374), in his vocabulary by transforming it into "ein vermeintliches Tatsächliches," something allegedly factual (374). This is true even of thought, itself a form of representation, as Murau indicates in a comment, whose comic force should not detract from its seriousness: "When we think and think without cease, what we call *philosophizing*, we eventually arrive at the conclusion that all our thoughts were wrong [*daß wir falsch gedacht haben*]" (122–23). While Murau would appear to thumb his nose at philosophy, he, in fact, pays tribute to the tradition by alluding to the Socratic motto that the starting point for all knowledge is knowledge of one's own ignorance. Murau merely turns this supposed starting point into philosophy's end. The pursuit concludes with the knowledge that it has attained nothing, which, paradoxically, is the truth of human existence for Murau:

They all got it wrong, no matter their names or the texts they wrote. They didn't give up on their own, I said to Gambetti. No, it wasn't their will but the will of nature. It was sickness, madness, and death that got them in the end. They didn't want to quit . . . But they advocated for false conclusions, I said to Gambetti, in the end for nothing, regardless of what this nothing is, I said to Gambetti, about which we know that it is nothing but at the same time cannot exist. Everything runs aground, everything comes to a halt. Everything in the end comes to naught [*am Ende doch für nichts, gleich, was dieses Nichts ist, hatte ich zu Gambetti gesagt, von welchem wir wissen, daß es zwar nichts ist, aber doch gleichzeitig auch nicht existent sein kann, an welchem alles scheitert, an welchem alles aufhört, zu Ende ist am Ende*]. (123)

Murau can quip that "everything in the end comes to naught" because of the dual function of naught in this passage. On the one hand, it is the culmination of all philosophical pursuits, which miss their mark and, in lieu of discovering the truth, veer off in multiple, fruitless directions in keeping with the logic of *ein Zerfall* (decay, disintegration, unraveling), which is also the subtitle of the novel. On the other hand, it is the nothingness of existence itself that stymies thought and brings every effort to understand it to a sudden but decisive conclusion, in keeping with the logic of *eine Auslöschung* (extinction), to recall the novel's German title. The play on the letters "z" and "a" in the statement that "[alles] *zu* Ende ist *am* Ende" (emphasis added) could be interpreted as an allusion to the letters of the novel's title words *Auslöschung: Ein Zerfall* (emphasis added) that span the alphabet. (I will return to this at the end of the chapter.) Whether or not the line is an allusion, the passage as a whole makes plain that the senselessness of existence redefines philosophy as a mere fiction or a form of madness.[43] The same holds true for *Extinction*, whose narrator searches in vain for a transcendental principle or overarching purpose in a world bereft of sense.

In *The Theory of the Novel* (1914/15), Lukács argues that the novel arises at a juncture when the sense of life is no longer given in the world of experience. This world belonged to the Greeks in the epic age, when everything physical (*sinnlich*) was simultaneously saturated with meaning (*Sinn*), or, what amounts to the same, when everything that existed had a proper place. Whatever the merits of Lukács's characterization of the Greeks, his argument still obtains, since the ancients serve primarily as a foil for the moderns in his analysis. The novel cannot be understood as a genre without a past from which it breaks, due to Lukács's understanding of genre as a form that expresses the "transcendental topography of spirit."[44] With this Hegelian formulation, Lukács refers to the conception of the universe that defines any one period and determines the horizon of possible experiences. The Greek epic, as he sees it, attests to an age in which the subject and object have yet to be divided, as they are made of the same substance.

The homogeneity of the Greek world ensures that nothing ever goes astray: everything has a preassigned place that determines its meaning and function within the social context. This meaning, as Lukács underscores, is not concealed. If anything, it is written on the surface, as the

Greeks do not recognize any distinction between inside and outside or essence and appearance: "There is not yet any interiority, since there is not yet an exterior, anything 'other' than the soul" (Lukács, 22). To the extent that the soul has no other, nothing stands opposed to it. Whatever it wills, it eventually accomplishes, as is evident in the fate of Odysseus. Fate may place Odysseus far from Ithaca's shores; it may prolong his journey home by putting several obstacles in his way. But that he will return home is never a question throughout Homer's epic, because he belongs there in more than one sense. Odysseus is anchored in Ithaca not merely as a son of the soil, but as a father, husband, and king, and it is the latter two social and political relations that constitute his place in the world, which, for the Greeks, is something transcendent. More precisely, it is something that, although transcendent, is manifest in life, because life is in every aspect permeated by a transcendental force that governs it. In short: the world *is* as it *ought* to be.

This is the "topography of spirit" that gives rise to the epic. It is one in which what is given (*das Sein*) is consistent with the ideals or norms held by the community. As a result every particular instance is simultaneously a general rule. Every isolated phenomenon is simultaneously universal in its significance. Every part constitutes a whole, because the whole is manifest in every part as the meaning or substance that underlies existence: "Totality as the formative basis of every individual phenomenon means that something closed in on itself can be complete [*vollendet sein kann*]—complete because everything occurs in it, nothing is excluded from it, and nothing refers to a higher order outside it. It can be complete because everything in it ripens to its own perfection and, in attaining itself, it submits to the larger relationship" (Lukács, 26). According to the logic of this statement, every individual epic is complete because it is a metonymy for life, which the Greeks experienced as a totality, owing to the presence of transcendental purpose in every aspect. Consequently, they could assume that everything that existed had been ordained to be exactly what it was: this entity fashioned in this or that form and situated in this or that place in the cosmos. Even "something closed in on itself [*etwas Geschlossenes*]" could participate in the fabric of life, since the outside was present within it as its calling, as that which it was meant to be from the outset. Lukács thus emphasizes that individual phenomena need not refer to a higher reality: the transcendent order is present within them, which makes them not only complete and fully formed (one meaning of *vollendet*), but also fully evolved from within (another meaning of *vollendet*).

The completeness and fullness of the given world allows Lukács to claim that the epic period was a "blessed" age. "Blessed" is the first word of his text, which opens not with a statement but an incantation: "Blessed [*Selig*] are the times in which the starry heavens are a map of all traversible paths" (21). These are times when the poet only needed to copy what he perceived to produce a work of art, for the world was already perfectly formed as something good, true, and beautiful. That these times, if they ever existed, have long since passed is a fundamental presupposition of Lukács's text. Of interest, however, is not this idealized vision of antiquity, which is hardly unique to *The Theory of the Novel*, but the reasons Lukács gives for the decline of the epic and the rise of modern culture. Central to his argument is the view that meaning is no longer given in the world that the modern subject confronts. The ideal no longer floods the real as it once did, making transcendence immanent. Instead the subject becomes the bearer of all ideals now that all sense is based in the interior of his soul, which has no correlate in nature or the social sphere. For this reason Lukács later declares that the novel is the adventure of interiority (78). It externalizes what is at root an inner conflict: the attempt on the part of the soul to find a world that accords with higher principles. Yet what enables such a venture is a more profound ontological turn that Lukács outlines in three consecutive propositions striking for their nearly identical wording and syntax: "We have invented [*erfunden*] the productivity of spirit. We have invented [*erfunden*] formgiving [*das Gestalten*]. . . . We have found [*gefunden*] the one true substance within us" (25–26).

While Lukács would seem to arrange these propositions in logical order, the opposite is in fact the case. In carrying the "one true substance" within it, the subject is also the basis of the one true world, which differs markedly from the external environment. The subject thus faces the task of giving the world it finds within itself a form and making it appear— all acts that attest to the power of subjectivity, or, in Lukács's phrase, "the productivity of spirit." Hence, whereas the epic poet could merely copy the world, the modern artist cannot. She has to create a sphere in which all the seemingly disparate elements of life are related to one another as mutually dependent entities; she has to fashion the "totality of life" that for the ancient Greeks was self-evident, but that disappears with the advent of tragedy, then philosophy, and, finally, the verse narratives that precede the novel and novella. Each of these genres, according to Lukács, divides what in ancient times had been a unity: the unity of life and essence, immanence and transcendence, *Sein* and *Sollen*. Separated from one another, these two realms become not only different but opposing spheres. The modern artist can bridge them only by creating a work of art that is, among other things, of ethical import.

Lukács places particular emphasis on the latter point, which comes as a surprise, since he never mentions ethics in connection with the epic in the first two chapters. Yet ethics are implicated in his discussion to the extent that the Greeks supposedly inhabited a world of shared value. The immanence in life of a transcendental purpose made the issue of right and wrong superfluous for them. This is not the case with the novel, whose hero must decide what to do on his own in the absence of any transcendental purpose. Lukács notes repeatedly that the hero of the novel is alone in a world governed not by ethical norms but by assorted and rigid conventions, which are the remnants of previous efforts to locate sense in life or an order underlying existence. In one of the most dramatic passages in the work, he calls this inheritance from the past a "second nature," which replaces the natural world not as an alternative life form but as "[a] charnel house of decaying interiorities" (55). Social conventions are the remains of past interiorities to the extent that in the absence of a manifest order all ethical norms are by definition subjective constructs. Yet the novelist cannot accept this condition if she is to create a work in which the actions of the main characters are to make sense—that is to say, to accord with a higher purpose or order. The novelist has to invent a world governed by laws that are themselves manifest, so the reader can evaluate what the characters do (i.e., whether their conduct is villainous or virtuous, selfish or responsible, effective or inept) in the context of the work.

Lukács treats this demand for transparency as evidence that our mode of thinking still tends toward totality even though the totality of life is no longer given, and "the immanence of meaning in life has become a problem" (47). In such an environment, art becomes the one sphere where totality prevails, albeit not as the totality of life but as the totality of form, the wholeness of the completed work. The artwork remains whole because it is cut from life, which, according to Aristotle, is the sphere in which decisions are made and actions are taken.[45] Lukács notes this development with surprising sobriety; of greater concern to him is how the novel responds to the loss of meaning in life given that the novel is divorced from this arena. This becomes a question for him of the ways in which "the fragility of the world's construction" is carried into "world of forms" (30).

As Lukács repeatedly argues, form cannot usher into being what does not already exist. It cannot generate a totality of life, when this totality is not itself forthcoming as was the case in antiquity. Indeed, for this reason, the epic could begin and end in medias res without sacrificing its wholeness or claim to completeness. The totality of the Greek epic did not depend on aesthetic forms but on life itself, which formed its basis. The novel is likewise concerned with the here and now, not, like drama, with a higher realm, nor, like lyric poetry, interiority.[46] For this same reason, the novel cannot defer to abstract concepts to create a meaningful web of relations. If the novel is to create a totality and to produce the semblance of a meaningful life, it can do so only through irony, which in the novel is not a random element, but a constitutive practice of the genre. Irony transforms the subjective ideals of the novelist into objective norms—or, more precisely, norms that would appear to be objective (i.e., natural, organic, spontaneously arising), even if they are invented for the sake of the fiction of a meaningful life.[47]

Lukács's account of irony draws heavily on the writings of Friedrich Schlegel, and, in keeping with this tradition, he defines irony as a twofold process. In the first instance, a character attempts to impress meaning on a world hostile to sense—in other words, a world that is diffuse and heterogeneous, since no transcendental purpose is evident in it. This act necessarily fails, but not for the reasons one would suspect. Lukács implies that the subject's ends are legitimate to the extent that they were realized in the epic age, but the means that the subject has at its disposal are insufficient because the subject is not a god that can create the world ex nihilo. Instead the subject can only *reflect* on the ideals it harbors within itself that, as indicated previously, refer to the world not as it is but as it ought to be, from the subject's perspective. Reflection, consequently, draws attention to the gulf between interiority and exteriority that is characteristic of the modern age and is the problem of modern culture more generally. The novel does not so much resolve this problem as give it form through a second act of reflection that turns the initial subject into an object: the "I of another I," to loosely quote Novalis.[48]

The narrator reflects on the opposition between the subject and the object in the fictional space, which he has created by articulating his thoughts as well as reproducing elements from his external environment.[49] In so doing he absorbs the subject and the object into a third term, which contains them both despite their inherent opposition. This term is the narrator's consciousness, which suffuses every aspect of the work and is as such the transcendental subjectivity that enables the novel and endows all elements with sense. In this matter Lukács is consistent with his contemporary Edmund Husserl, who in the first volume of *Ideas* (1913) develops the method of transcendental phenomenology, which brackets the existence of the world apart from consciousness to explore instead how consciousness constitutes its objects and generates their sense.

More important, with the model of a double reflection, Lukács recalls Friedrich Schlegel's dictum in fragment 116 of the *Atheneum* that modern literature should consist of an "endless series of mirrors," in which differing or opposing elements are integrated into a new whole at a higher level.[50] The key difference is that for Schlegel the process is never complete; every reflection can be "raised to a higher power," thereby forging a progressive poetry "whose actual essence is that it is always becoming."[51] Lukács, by contrast, cannot renege on the idea of wholeness, even if he concedes that it is an impossible aim. For him the narrator makes the world of the novel whole by reflecting on it as if it were the "extensive totality of life," but that it can never be, owing to the conditions of its production. Just as the narrator surmounts the opposition between subject and object by reflecting on them both, so too another person can reflect on the unity that the narrator creates in a process that could continue ad infinitum. This is the dilemma of transcendental subjectivity: any order that the subject posits becomes an empirical instance once posited, and, as an empirical instance, it can never be a totality, only a sign of what was not attained through reflection. Lukács thus concludes, "The composition of the novel is a paradoxical fusing [*Verschmelzen*] of discrete and heterogeneous components into a continually announced organic whole"

(73). While the organic wholeness of the novel is announced again and again, it never comes to pass. The novel at best gestures toward a totality it cannot achieve, but whose promise it keeps alive.

The inability of the novel to establish objective norms and craft a meaningful web of relations contributes to the resignation of the novel, which, according to Lukács, is its dominant mood. The novel concludes not in victory but defeat: "The manner in which the novel concludes points eloquently to the sacrifice that had to be made, to the paradise forever lost that was sought and not found. The vain pursuit and resigned abandonment of this paradise complete the circle of form" (74). As Murau might put it, the novelist, like the philosopher, "advocated for false conclusions . . . in the end for nothing" (*Auslöschung*, 123). What is significant nonetheless is that in the novel "[everything] in the end comes to an end [(*alles*)] *am Ende zu Ende ist*" (123): even if that end amounts to naught, to borrow from Murau's phrasing yet again. The novel achieves closure not by penetrating reality but by recognizing its distance from a world that is no longer imbued with a transcendental purpose. It is in this spirit that Lukács declares that irony is both a form of negative mysticism and a *docta ignorantia* (learned ignorance) near the end of the first section of his treatise: "The irony of the poet is the negative mysticism of a godless age. It is a *docta ignorantia* vis-à-vis sense . . . and a deep certainty that can only be vaguely expressed as the certainty that in not wanting to know and not being able to know the poet has glimpsed and grasped the ultimate reality, the true substance, the present non-existent God" (79). In not wanting to know and not being able to know, the novelist arrives at a curious certainty. He recognizes the truth is that there is no truth or meaning only nothingness, "into which everything collapses" (123), as Murau puts it. This recognition may undermine the fiction he creates, but it undermines reality as well, which henceforth can only be referred to in negative terms as "sickness, madness, and death" (123), which puncture the illusion of a sense-filled and purpose-driven existence. The nothingness of the world, its paradoxical character as the presence of the absence of God, justifies the novel in hindsight as a form of recognition, not of what is, but of what is not: the totality of life in which sense is immanent.

Eva Marquardt argues that a similar strategy is at play in Bernhard's *Extinction*. The novel calls into question whether a narrative can ever be truthful through its contradictory statements, or what she characterizes as its antithetical diction.[52] Murau routinely announces a position only to negate it a few sentences later. Take, for instance, the following two statements on photography delivered in rapid succession:

> Photography shows only the most grotesque and ridiculous moment. . . . Photography is a pernicious, perverse falsification [*Fälschung*]. Every photograph . . . is . . . a monstrous falsification of nature [*Naturverfälschung*]. (*Auslöschung*, 22)

> These aren't idealized parents, I said to myself, these are my parents as they are, as they were, I corrected myself. . . . Only the factual and truthful pictures. Only what is absolutely authentic. (23)

The certitude with which Murau expresses each of these opinions has often been attributed to his fondness for hyperbole, a fondness he himself amplifies by referring to himself as an "exaggeration artist." Yet Marquardt locates Murau's artistry not in the absoluteness of his claims, but in the competing positions he presents throughout the text, sometimes in the space of a single sentence. Each of these antitheses unsettles the distinction between truth and lies; each turns the two into relative terms by juxtaposing them without further comment. Marquardt remarks, "If the opposite of the truth is true, then there is no distinction between truth and lies, which always appear inextricably linked with each other in Bernhard's work."[53] What interests Marquardt is not the indistinguishability of truth and falsehood per se, but the mediated nature of both as positions articulated in representation. According to her, Bernhard's antithetical narrative style exposes the artifice involved in any representation since representation can never reveal the truth, only a view as plausible as its opposite.

To surmount this impasse, the narrator of *Extinction* engages in a process of self-reflection. He reflects in his own belletristic work (i.e., his memoir) on art and literature in general and in so doing transcends the medium of his writing, which will never capture the truth, since the truth (*das Wahre*) for Murau is merely what is probable (*das Wahrscheinliche*).[54] In this manner he arrives at the one certainty that an artwork can convey: the certainty of art's "inability to reproduce reality," as Marquardt puts it in a comment that situates *Extinction* squarely within the modernist tradition.[55] This inability, however, serves Murau's aim to destroy his birthplace by writing about it in an antithetical fashion. In so doing he recasts Wolfsegg as an aesthetic construct with no basis in reality that exists only in his narrative and as a narrated phenomenon. For Marquardt, Wolfsegg is blotted out through its inscription on the page: "The reflection on art in *Extinction* leads to the lifting of the illusion, which nonetheless remains bound up in the fable."[56]

With this remark Marquardt would seem to be on Lukácsian terrain. The reflection within the text circumscribes the text as a fictional totality. Yet what establishes the work as fictional in her view is finally the unrepresentability of reality. The object, not the subject, is the focus of her account of Bernhardian irony, which differs considerably from Lukács's theory. In a brief but provocative article, Sylvia Kaufmann proposes that the novel's primary concern is not the past and present of Austria but the problem of transcendental subjectivity in postromantic literature.[57] Competing claims in the text say less about their object than the subject who utters them. Indeed, Murau's continual revision of his positions amounts to a revision and rearticulation of himself as a narrating subject: "The novel always reflects at a higher level on what it has previously said and is to this extent writing about writing or writing that has not come to fruition."[58] Kaufmann is perhaps the only critic to question whether Murau's envisioned memoir, *Extinction*, ever comes to pass; that she links this question to the process of self-reflection in the novel is a testament to the strength of her reading. Murau does not so much articulate his positions, as cite positions he held at different times. He bears out the stance articulated by another Bernhard protagonist: "In essence, everything said is a citation [*Im Grunde ist alles, was gesagt wird, zitiert*]."[59]

Insofar as each and every statement is the citation of a view held at a previous time, the narrating subject no longer functions as a unity but as a divided entity, if not multiple personae. Murau is both the empirical subject who said this or that at one time and the transcendental subject who meditates on these positions, as if they were divorced from him, and he no longer recognized himself in such guises. In this manner Murau attempts to free himself of all historical constraints, such as his family background, his profession, and his chosen place of residence. He writes a work in which the conditions of his narration are included in the narrative, or the "producer" is represented "along with the product," to bor-

row from Schlegel's definition of irony.[60] This practice enables him to surmount his position as an individual embedded in a particular place and
time, but the solution is only provisional, since the process must be repeated ad nauseum. For Kaufmann this is the fate of transcendental subjectivity in the modern novel: the reflecting subject becomes a historically determined or finite being once he announces a view since this view
can be reflected upon continually. Yet what makes *Extinction* a singular
achievement, in her reading, is that it recognizes this dilemma. It points
to the impossibility of transcendental subjectivity by having its narrator die—or, put otherwise, by turning its narrator into a narrated figure.

Kaufmann notes that the editorial comments at the beginning and
end of the work frame the text that follows as the work of someone who
can no longer speak for himself and consequently requires a third party to represent him. This third party transforms Murau into a historical
subject "identifiable through his name and dates of birth and death."[61]
Murau's role as a historical being can never be made to coincide with his
role as the narrating consciousness of the work except through his death,
which Kaufmann argues is a formal necessity of the novel. Murau must
die to overcome his dissolution, or *Zerfall*, into a narrated and narrating
subject as well as a collection of utterances that define him in different
ways at different moments. Hence the full title of the work, as Kaufmann
emphasizes, is *Auslöschung: Ein Zerfall*. Murau can achieve identity with
himself as an empirical subject only if he ceases to write, for only then
will he be consistent with *all* his utterances. He will be their historical
reference point, the object defined by these statements. Kaufmann summarizes this process as follows: "The speaking subject who tries to establish himself in *Extinction* reflexively through the act of self-representation
no longer exists once he succeeds in completing the aesthetic project, i.e.,
the novel. Murau's death symbolically expresses the fact that the subject
loses himself in the act of imagining himself."[62] Murau's death makes
the work whole and his project complete inasmuch as it halts the process of self-reflection that had fueled the text and made it potentially infinite, as well as forever incomplete.

This is a heavy price to pay for totality. Benjamin would seem to argue
as much when he declares in "The Storyteller" that the novel is written
from its conclusion, from the death of its principle character, and is as
a result a closed genre. The story, by contrast, remains open through its

constant retelling from generation to generation. Stories do not belong to individuals but to forms of life, to communities in which handworkers still report of journeys to distant places, and farmers recount events from the distant past.[63] In both cases what enables the story to be retold is the distance that it represents. Stories draw from the limit of the horizon that can never be known, only intuited or felt. While this would appear to be the dividing line between the story and the novel, it is in fact the place where the two meet. Both genres begin and end with the death of the narrator or prinicipal character. "The storyteller draws his authority from death," writes Benjamin in an oft-cited remark from the essay.[64] And he returns to this point again when he describes how the storyteller retreats into the distance at the end of his narration: "Just as a sequence of images plays out in the head of dying man consisting of his own views, in which he, without being conscious of it, encounters himself, so too something unforgettable [*das Unvergeßliche*] suddenly appears in the expressions and glances of the storyteller and imparts to everything related to him authority."[65] What the storyteller contributes to his story is "something unforgettable," which is a slippery concept, since the only matter that can never be forgotten is one that has also never been remembered. What is "unforgettable," consequently, is what is permanently present, what persists long after a story has been told and as such provides the impetus for its continual retelling.

For the story the unforgettable aspect of existence is death, but for the novel it is life. The life excluded from the novel by virtue of its closed form returns as an excess the novel cannot contain or circumscribe. In *Extinction* this excess is precisely Murau's voice. While Murau's death seals the work and brings his writing to a premature, if definitive, close, it also provides an occasion for him to speak from the grave—or, rather, to speak in manner he can never internalize in his own narrative and grasp in his own reflections. Like Benjamin's dying man, who sees a series of images that "without being conscious of it" represent him, so too Murau speaks throughout the text in a manner he cannot recognize as his own. What his constant process of self-reflection will never be able to capture or portray is his voice, which persists long after his death as something "unforgettable." Murau's voice has this status because it exceeds everything spelled out on the page. The text may proceed from A to Z (or from the Greek A to Ω), as its full title *Auslöschung: Ein Zerfall* implies, but there will always be something outside this whole because the text is not only a narrative but also a narration or monologue.[66] The initial and final editorial comments draw attention to the mystery that a voice can speak even after a text has been printed. It speaks as the immanence of meaning in life that can never be contained in any totality, no matter how perfectly crafted the totality may be, because it is not a formal element. This is Bernhard's variation on the structure of the novel as theorized by Lukács. It is true not only of *Extinction*, but of every pseudo-memoir in which the moment of inscription provides an occasion for a telling that succeeds and supercedes it. Yet, in contrast to Lukács's contention that the dominant mood of the modern novel is resignation, Bernhard's *Extinction* gives cause for hope that the immanent sense and quality of existence will sound and resound beyond the narrative whole. Murau's voice is the unforgettable aspect of being that the novel imparts without ever representing it or giving it a name. It is both the condition for *Extinction* and its achievement as a work of art that does justice to life in letting it be lived beyond its pages.

4 The Author
W. G. Sebald's *Vertigo*

At the outset of the second chapter of W. G. Sebald's 1990 essay-novel
Vertigo, the narrator recalls losing his bearings at the beginning of a journey that eventually brings him home but not to himself, as did the adventures of Odysseus. Displaced in Vienna for no apparent reason other than a desire to escape a difficult period in his life, the narrator soon
discovers that the change in location cannot change his relation to the
past.[1] With few, if any, demands on his time, the narrator takes to wandering the streets of Vienna from early morning to late at night. When
he later retraces his steps on a map, he realizes that the walks he took
were confined to a single crescent-shaped area: "Early every morning I
would set out and walk without aim or purpose through the streets of
the inner city, through the Leopoldstadt and the Josefstadt. Later, when
I looked at the map, I saw to my astonishment that none of the journeys
had taken me beyond a precisely defined sickle-or crescent-shaped area,
the outermost points of which were the Venediger Au by the Praterstern
and the great hospital precincts of the Alsergrund."[2] The path that the
narrator traces lends itself to an allegorical interpretation, as it represents
a map of the sky transposed onto the surface of the earth. The narrator walks back and forth in a lunar landscape—a half-moon ("a sickle-
or crescent-shaped area"), to be more precise—which stretches from the
district of Vienna known as the Alsergrund to the traffic circle known
as the Praterstern. In abbreviated form one could say that his walks take
him from the "ground" embedded in the name Alser*grund* to the "star"
embedded in the name Prater*stern*—that is, from the underworld to the
upper world where the many angels pictured in the text dwell.

This is the cosmos that the narrator inhabits during his 1980 trip to
Vienna and Northern Italy. He finds himself in this orbit again when,

in 1987, he returns to Northern Italy to discover why he suspended his previous trip so abruptly. One could even say that he inhabits this world as he looks back on his earlier adventures, since the locus of his travels is not a physical site but an allegorical space in which the dead reside, as its very emblem suggests. This emblem is the sickle wielded by the Grim Reaper, the personified figure of death, who makes an appearance in the final chapter of the novel in the form of a menacing female reaper.[3]

The narrator wanders in a netherworld populated by ghosts and shades, as he himself indicates when he reports that he dreamed of crossing a body of water not unlike the River Styx: "I felt as if I had crossed a wide stretch of water during the hours of my nocturnal absence" (V, 37–38). The novel's second chapter, "All'estero," literally begins "abroad," to translate its Italian title, but not in a foreign nation-state. It starts in a strange land, where the distinction between past and present no longer obtains, since the only residents of this land are the departed, whose sole lasting testament is their name. Perhaps for this reason, the first ghostly figure the narrator encounters in Vienna is Mathild Seelos, whose name can easily be misread as Mathild *Seellos* (Mathild without a Soul) in a slip of the tongue that the text would seem to elicit.

Although Sebald's literary work is often noted for its visual dimensions with its many reproduced images and photographs, what is perhaps most striking about his prose is that it asks the reader to see what is not there. As Julia Hell notes, Sebald's narrators routinely walk among the dead, sometimes in the face of the wreckage of history and sometimes in the face of the absence of any wreckage, which itself proves suspect.[4] For Hell what is significant is that Sebald's narrators resist the temptation to aestheticize history, which in his work is nothing other than a cycle of destruction in which human catastrophes repeat themselves without respite.[5] One wonders, however, how his work could expose such a cycle without resorting to aesthetic means, such as the construction of emblematic figures and ciphers that, as Bianca Theisen has shown, are central to his literary practice.[6] Sebald's narrators relish in creating ciphers that draw together what is otherwise separated in time; they place distant events on the same synchronous plane and, in so doing, call into question the distinction between past and present or then and now.

The above-cited paragraph is instructive in this regard. The narrator wanders through an area of Vienna that includes, among other things,

Fig. 1. Wall mural of a female reaper in Sebald's birthplace, Wertach, from
Vertigo, 256. Image from *Vertigo* by W. G. Sebald. Copyright © 1990 by W. G.
Sebald, used by permission of the Wylie Agency LLC.

the home of Sigmund Freud, which would be an insignificant detail if the text did not allude to a passage in Freud's 1919 essay "The Uncanny."[7] In it Freud recounts how he once got lost in an Italian city and repeatedly returned to a bordello-lined street, as he notes in a comment that stands out for being overly, if not defensively, discreet:

> I found myself in a quarter whose character could not elude me for long. Only heavily made-up women were to be seen in the windows of the small houses. I hurried to leave the street at the next corner, but after wandering without guidance for some time, I found myself suddenly in the same street again, in which my presence began to attract attention. In my haste to leave, I ended up returning via a different route to the same spot for a third time. Then a feeling gripped me that I can only describe as uncanny, and I was happy when I found my way back to the Piazza I had left shortly before.[8]

What in Freud's text constitutes an isolated incident becomes in "All'estero" a sustained condition precisely because the narrator never masters his disorientation, as Freud does by turning his discomfort into an object of scientific inquiry. The narrator's repeated walks in the same area remain a mystery for him even after the fact, as he acknowledges in a passage where he once again takes a bird's-eye view of his strolls, rather than a view from the ground up: "My traversing of the city, often continuing for hours, thus had very clear bounds, and yet at no point did my incomprehensible behavior become apparent to me: that is to say, my continual walking and my reluctance to cross certain lines which were both invisible and, I presume, wholly arbitrary" (V, 34). While the parameters of the author's walks may be arbitrary, they have a certain textual logic in anticipating both the places that the narrator will go and the ghosts or characters that he will meet. Of note is that his wandering extends as far as the "Venediger Au" (literally the Venice Meadow). Venice will be the next station of his journey, as it was the destination of so many Austro-Hungarian authors, including Franz Kafka and Franz Grillparzer, who are both mentioned explicitly in the text. Kafka is, in fact, there from the start in the jackdaws (*Dohlen*) with which the narrator converses in Vienna.[9] The Prague author was well aware that his name was all but indistinguishable in sound from the Czech *kavka*, meaning "jackdaw," which is a kind of blackbird.

It is worth noting that all the Italian cities that the narrator visits were part of the Austro-Hungarian Empire following the Napoleonic Wars, which feature in the first chapter of *Vertigo*, which is devoted to the life of Stendhal. This, too, is registered, if only obliquely, in the initial map of space that the narrator draws in the second chapter. At the center of the Praterstern stands the Tegetthoff Monument, named after the admiral who led the Austrian navy to victory in 1866 in the Battle of Lissa in the Third Italian War of Independence. The battle was a Pyrrhic victory: the Austrians ended up losing the war and had to return Venice to Italy. Erecting a monument to commemorate a victory in an otherwise lost war would be a typical Austro-Hungarian gesture, according to Musil. In *The Man Without Qualities* he writes, regarding the empire, "Huge sums were spent on the military, but only so much that the Empire was assured to remain the second weakest of the great powers."[10] Musil, too, plays a role in Sebald's chapter, if not to the same degree as his fellow Austro-Hungarians Kafka, Grillparzer, and Hofmannsthal. His story "The Blackbird" forms the basis for the episode in which the narrator talks to the birds of Vienna like the protagonist of Musil's story, who converses with a single blackbird.[11]

These may seem mere coincidences. It would be difficult to prove in any one case that the novel is alluding to a specific work or historical event. Yet in a text that consists primarily of references to other works, the boundary separating this one piece of writing from any other is porous to say the least; whether the boundary even exists is a question raised throughout the text. Although *Vertigo* would appear to move forward in time, it in fact circles back to the same region between Italy and Austria where many pitched battles were fought in the nineteenth and twentieth centuries. Circling back the text calls into question the chronological framework that it at the same time sets up through the almost obsessive notation of dates, as if they could lend order to experience. This technique will rise to a new level of intensity in *The Rings of Saturn*, published in 1995, but already in *Vertigo* it is clear that the novel is interested not in a linear order of time but in a circular one that joins, say, the destiny of Stendhal, who visited Riva in 1813, and the destiny of Kafka, who visited the same resort exactly one century later and, like Stendhal, sat on a boat discussing love with an unknown female companion one evening.[12]

One could add to the list of circumstances connecting these two events.

Both Stendhal and Kafka faced a personal crisis at precisely the moment that the world as they knew it was about to be overturned. Napoleon's reign ended a year after Stendhal visited Riva in 1814; likewise, World War I broke out in 1914, a year after Kafka's visit. Stendhal's companion wears a hat modeled after the one worn by the Tyrolean hunters who fought against Napoleon at the Battle of Marengo, in which Stendhal himself participated as a member of the French infantry; Kafka tells his companion that he puts "an imaginary black Napoleonic tricorne" (V, 159) over his thoughts whenever they start to circle obsessively. As this brief list indicates, the parallels between the two events are potentially infinite in number—or, if not infinite, at least significant enough that one would have to recite the entire text of *Vertigo* to enumerate them. Even this gesture, however, would prove inadequate, because the two events are not merely similar incidents separated by one hundred years; rather, they qualify as similar incidents because they overlap in this one text and in the text of history more generally. *Vertigo* subscribes to the view that the world as a whole is a text with neither a "before" nor an "after," only a series of intersecting lines that constitute particular literary works.[13] Every work borrows from the archive of literature to spin its web, which is not so much a new phenomenon as a returning (and recurring) one, even if it does not occur elsewhere verbatim. For whether or not this textual web occurs elsewhere, its incidence "here" attests to the existence of the world as discourse and, conversely, to discourse as a world, in which otherwise historically distant individuals, such as Stendhal and Kafka or Grillparzer and Sebald, can meet, as if nothing in truth separated them—indeed, as if their separation were merely an illusion.[14]

This view explains the emphasis on coincidences throughout the text. When the narrator arrives at the train station in Milan in 1987, he sees an advertisement for Hertz Rental Cars with the words "La prossima coincidenza" (V, 108–9). The fact that two young men try to mug him at this moment only contributes to his impression that this is a warning meant for him alone in an hour of danger. The narrator has convinced himself that two men have followed him throughout his 1980 and 1987 journeys, and, furthermore, that the two are members of the "Organizzazione Ludwig" (130), an unknown group that has claimed responsibility for several murders in Veneto and Lombardy.[15] While this suspicion ultimately proves false—the two murderers are, in fact, in custody at the time—it does not diminish the weight of the evidence presented in the text that coincidences constitute signs of an invisible order at work. Luisa Banki contends that the narrator displays a paranoid disposition, which she defines as "the certainty, that everything is meaningful and therefore open to interpretation," even if no fixed sense can be assigned it.[16] The melancholic, by contrast, is convinced that the search for meaning is futile in a fallen world, in which everything proves to be an empty vessel.

Both dispositions are on display in the narrator's excursus on Casanova, who himself relied on hermetic techniques of reading to determine when he should break out of his prison cell in the Doge Palace in Venice in 1755. Casanova, he tells us, wrote down a question and translated it into a series of numbers, which he then reduced to a set of three integers to indicate the exact canto, stanza, and verse in *Orlando Furioso* that he should consult for information. The numerological translation leads him to the line, *"Tra il fin d'ottobre e il capo di novembre"* (*V*, 59, emphasis in original), which he interprets as a providential sign: "This instruction, pinpointing the very hour, was the all-decisive sign Casanova had wanted, for he believed that a law was at work in so extraordinary a coincidence, inaccessible to even the most incisive thought, to which he must therefore defer" (59). While the narrator is at first hesitant to subscribe to Casanova's belief that there is a secret law governing all events, he is inspired enough to consult his calendar to determine the exact dates of his visit to Venice in 1980.[17] There he discovers—as much to his dismay as to his delight—that his trip coincided with the anniversary of Casanova's escape from the Doge Palace.[18]

This example may seem trivial. If we regard it as trivial it is because we assume it is a self-reflexive gesture in which the narrator points to his own poetic practice, or enacts his own principle of composition, in keeping with a performative logic that has dominated modern literary criticism. Casanova's experience, however, offers another possibility for interpretation. If, as he argues, the law governing human affairs is inaccessible to thought, then no human being could ever construct a coincidence that would attest to the secret order of Creation. Anyone who attempted to do so would presume to be a god—that is, a being that is at once all-knowing with respect to the law and all powerful with respect to its implementation. It may have been possible for a romantic writer like Friedrich Schlegel to declare, "The revolutionary wish to realize God's

kingdom is the elastic point of all progressive formation and the beginning of modern history," but, for a late twentieth-century writer living
in the aftermath of two world wars and at the onset of the climate crisis
evoked in *The Rings of Saturn*, such confidence is misplaced.[19] And yet
Sebald does not entirely renege on the idea of an invisible hand at work
in the course of history. Instead he gives the idea a Saturnine turn, seeing in every man-made edifice a monument to *vanitas*, and in every catastrophe a testament to the natural history of destruction.

Like Benjamin's baroque allegorists, Sebald's narrators treat the phenomena that they encounter as magical signs that hold the promise of
unlocking the mysteries of the universe. When they fail to do so, the narrator discards them and turns instead to other phenomena in a process
that could continue without end. This process is hermeneutic, and it explains why Sebald's narrators routinely find themselves drawn back to a
past, even when they would appear to move forward, as evidenced by their
obsession with dates in their chronicles of their journeys. In short, his
narrators write in an effort to untangle the web in which they find themselves. However, in attempting to unravel this web, they only spin it further, since they never gain a position outside it to decipher its mesh. Every
attempt they make to render the world transparent leads only to the production of new ciphers and figures, which undermines the self-evidence
of what is given by turning it into a placeholder for something missing.

An interesting example of this dilemma occurs in 1987 when the narrator sits down to write at a hotel in Limone not far from the spa in Riva
that Kafka visited in 1913. According to the third chapter, the stay inspired
Kafka's story "The Hunter Gracchus," which is cited throughout *Vertigo*.[20]
In what again would seem like a performative gesture, the narrator announces the steps he is taking in drafting a composition that is presumably an early version of the text we read: "I sat at a table . . . my papers
and notes spread out around me, drawing connections between events
that lay far apart [*und zog Verbindungslinien zwischen weit auseinander-
liegenden Ereignissen*] but which seemed to me to be of the same order. I
wrote with an ease that astonished me" (*V*, 94; *SG*, 107). As in *Felix Krull*,
Jakob von Gunten, and *Extinction*, we are given a window into the creative process of the author through his narrative double, the writing protagonist. Every pseudo-memoir is in this sense a double fiction: the story of its own telling. Where *Vertigo* differs from Mann's and Bernhard's

novels is in its emphasis on the absence of any space apart from the story. What the narrator represents in the above-cited passage with the utmost clarity also ranks as the height of deception: it constitutes the lie or swindle alluded to in the German title of the novel, *Schwindel. Gefühle*, which makes every artwork potentially dizzying, vertiginous, *schwindlig*. One would like to believe that the narrator sits at a table crafting the text we have at hand, which draws connections between distant events from the past. This scenario would ensure that the narrator also serves as the author of this work, which is a conceit not only of *Vertigo* but of all Sebald's writings, whose first-person narrators invariably resemble the historical author W. G. Sebald.[21] Yet no sooner does the narrator assert his role as author than another voice intervenes—indeed, at precisely the moment the narrator says "I" and in so doing calls into question the transparency of his voice and the authority of his position.

This voice belongs to the protagonist of Hofmannsthal's unfinished novel *Andreas*, which the Viennese author worked on the same year that Kafka visited Riva. Like the narrator, Andreas is consumed with the idea of "a mysterious connection" between people and events, so much so that he assumes "that a gaze from high enough would unite everything divided," and everything past would be restored to the present.[22] It would be a present in which the living would once again commune with the dead, as the narrator of *Andreas* indicates in a passage that resonates with the one cited from "All'estero" in its play on the idea of the world as a text: "Between Andreas and the dead dog there was a connection, he just didn't know what it was, so too between him and Gotthelff, who was responsible for the death of the animal. . . . Threads ran back and forth and out of them a world was spun, which lay behind the real world and was not as empty and desolate as this one."[23] Andreas believes he is part of a world woven or spun out of interlacing threads as the narrator of "All'estero" believes he is spinning or weaving a world by writing lines that connect distant events. Yet to the extent that the narrator invokes the words and images of another at precisely the moment he claims to speak for himself, his presence becomes the most elusive aspect of this scene.[24] The lines that the narrator scribbles in his notebook draw him into a web in which the "here and now" in which he writes is no longer distinguishable from the "there and then" of other figures. The past and present converge in a world that is not governed by any law except the law of coincidences, which could also be interpreted as the law of the return of the past. In such a world what previously existed can return as if it were still present, as, conversely, what is here and now can recede into the background as nothing but the double or shadow of something else. The narrator who sits down to write in "All'estero" is a double, if not for Hofmannsthal's protagonist Andreas, than for innumerable other figures, since whatever he writes will turn out to have been written before, which amounts to saying since his work will always intersect with other works in ways he cannot coordinate or determine. This coordinating function, this authorial privilege, belongs to what Casanova called the law and what this text refers to *ex negativo* as a missing person, "eine verschollene Person" (sG, 108).[25] This may not be the most original designation, with its echoes of Kafka's *The Man Who Went Missing* (*Der Verschollene*), but in its very unoriginality it underscores the disappearance of the author as an autonomous figure who records his own experiences. In "All'estero," this function falls instead to an impersonal force: a network of intersecting texts that is personified as an author. In his oft-cited essay "The Death of the Author," Barthes refers to the authorial figure constructed by the reader as the "scriptor."[26] True to its status as a novel written *after* theory—to borrow Judith Ryan's phrase—*Vertigo* dramatizes this process, whereby the author disappears as a force outside the work to linger in it as a mere ghost or semblance. As Ryan writes, "The text should not be understood as produced by an author, but rather by an anonymous 'scriptor,' a writing mechanism devoid of individuality, interiority, or intention."[27] How *Vertigo* is able to preserve intentionality without the person of an author will be addressed in the remainder of the chapter.

The Missing Author

In Limone the narrator tells the hotel proprietress that he is writing a work concerning "the reappearance of a person who had long been missing [*das Wiederauftauchen einer verschollenen Person*]" (V, 95; sG, 108). While we may be inclined to read this statement as tongue-in-cheek, we should not ignore the metaphors at play in this otherwise seemingly straightforward remark. *Wiederauftauchen* literally means to resurface or to rise from a pool of water, which would be an insignificant detail, were "All'estero" not awash in water imagery.[28] Scarcely a passage can be found that does not invoke this element. When the narrator awakens in his hotel in Vienna, he hears "the surging roar [*Brandungsgeräusche*] of traffic [*Verkehrsströme*]" (*V*, 37; SG, 44). While sitting on a train with the poet Ernst Herbeck, he looks out at the "flood plain" (*V*, 40) along the Danube. When the two finally reach Schloß Greifenstein, he pays less attention to the river than the "sea of foliage" surrounding it and the "currents of air" (41) that flow through the trees. These trees return a few pages later when the narrator recalls an earlier visit to Klosterneuburg, which is, among other things, the place where Kafka died in 1924, as mentioned on the chapter's final page. There, the narrator looks out at the crowns of the trees, whose lushness prompts him to remark, "It was like looking upon a heaving sea" (45).[29]

With this turn of phrase, the narrator refers at one and the same time to the two poles that characterize the destiny of the Hunter Gracchus in Kafka's tale by the same name. The first is the Black Forest from which the hunter hails, the second the earthly waters to which he is condemned after his helmsman fails to deliver him to the afterlife. These two poles are captured in the image of the foliage as "a heaving sea," which, as a poetic interpretation of Kafka's story, implies that the hunter was adrift long before he was sentenced to travel the waters of the earth.[30] Such an interpretation would be consistent with the overall theme of the work: vertigo as the sensation of sinking or losing one's ground even when one stands firmly planted in one place. It is thus no accident that the narrator frequently feels unmoored during moments of introspection, as in the following passage, in which he revises an earlier comment that he "sank" (*versank*, itself an aquatic term), into his memories: "Or rather, the memories (at least so it seemed to me) rose higher and higher in some space outside of myself, until, having reached a certain level, they overflowed from that space into me, like water over the top of a weir [*und flossen dann, als sie einem bestimmten Pegelstand erreicht hatten, aus diesem Raum, in dem sie sich stauten, in mich herein wie Wasser über ein Wehr*]" (*V*, 82; SG, 93–94). It would be hard to think of a passage in which the narrator could be more overt about identifying his memories with water, which, as he would have it, well up in him almost to drown him in the next instance. If nothing else, they set him adrift, to continue the water metaphor, and in so doing call into question his position not only in space but also in time.

According to the narrator, the vertigo caused by his memories functions as a prelude to an experience of time in which everything would appear to pass more quickly—or *geschwinder*, as he puts it in an apparent pun on the title of the work *Schwindel. Gefühle*: "The time passed more swiftly than I should have ever thought possible [*Geschwinder als ich es je für möglich gehalten hätte, verging mir über meinen Aufzeichnungen die Zeit*]" (*V*, 82; sɢ, 94). Time can pass quickly for the narrator as he writes, precisely because writing takes him from the steady progression of time or the perpetual ticking of the clock. Freed of this yoke, he can slip into a dimension in which there is neither a "before" nor an "after" and the passing of time is itself suspended. Thus, although the narrator asserts that time passes more quickly as he writes, the opposite would seem to be the case. He passes more quickly than he could have imagined from a time in which the present dominates as a measure for all that was and will be. He becomes, in short, the "missing person" (*der Verschollene*) about whom he claims to write, and his first words in the chapter—"I was back then" (*Ich war damals*)—become a voice from the grave, the testament of a dead man.

In *The Space of Literature*, Maurice Blanchot argues that writing always begins at a point when it is no longer possible to write, since writing deprives the would-be author of a goal, which is the most basic requirement for this undertaking.[31] Without an objective the writer cannot start a project, since he has no goal, however provisional, to motivate and direct his efforts. So opens one of the many circles in Blanchot's account of the writing process. To begin to write, one must have an aim; to have an aim, however, is to forestall the writing process, which consists in straying from everything that is known, familiar, and certain. That Sebald's text begins with the narrator walking in an allegorical space would seem to resonate with Blanchot's notion of writing as a form of wandering from which there may be no return. Yet the link between the two texts runs deeper. Both are concerned with a time lost to salvation.

Blanchot emphasizes that the time of writing is of a different nature than that required for any other task. It is not a time we have at our disposal, as he suggests in a comment on Kafka's chronic complaint that he lacks the time to work on his literary projects: "Even if one gives 'all one's time' . . . 'all' is still not enough, for it is not a matter of devoting time to the task, of passing one's time writing, but of passing into another time where there is no longer any task."[32] Blanchot speculates that while other writers may romanticize the retreat from the demands of daily life, this is not an option for Kafka because of the status of the everyday in Judaism. Kafka's faith is the faith of his fathers, understood specifically in the biblical sense, as the faith of the patriarchs Abraham, Isaac, and Jacob, as well as all who follow in their footsteps.[33] As this brief sketch indicates, it is a faith realized rather than thwarted in historical time, which is the medium in which the Law is preserved through its observance. To devote oneself to writing instead of to marriage and to family is, accordingly, to sacrifice the time in which the Law survives as a divine gift that is still bound to earthly life. It is in this respect to sacrifice God inasmuch as he inheres in the covenant and the community founded around it. Why write, then, is a question of particular urgency for Kafka, and although it does not have quite the same urgency for Sebald, it nevertheless colors his work, which is devoted to the suffering of individuals in the face of man-made catastrophes.

Blanchot is hesitant to accept the justification for writing that Kafka offers in a famous diary entry from 1914 in which he states, "If I don't save myself in a project, I am lost."[34] Kafka does not seek to redeem himself or Creation through writing, even if he sometimes suggests as much, as in the following diary entry from 1917: "I can draw occasional satisfaction from works like 'The Country Doctor.' . . . Happiness, however, only if I raise the world to the status of the pure, true, immutable."[35] Blanchot is skeptical of this justification, not because of the scale of its ambition, but because it is premised on an idea that Kafka himself rejected in his later work—the idea that writing could restore him to a hospitable world or deliver him to the promised land from which he had been expelled. Kafka was, in his own understanding, an outcast, a citizen of another world, a wanderer in the desert who, as Blanchot puts it, would never reach Canaan.[36] He was destined to remain *all'estero*, abroad, like the narrator of Sebald's text and the Hunter Gracchus. All that writing could give Kafka, since it could not give him a home, was "the consciousness of unhappiness, not its compensation."[37]

Unhappiness has a time all its own. Blanchot calls it the "time of distress" in an allusion to the question that Friedrich Hölderlin poses in the elegy "Brod und Wein": "Wozu Dichter in dürftiger Zeit?," which became the title phrase of a famous essay by Martin Heidegger on Rainer Maria Rilke. The "time of distress" is simultaneously the time of writing in which all projects are suspended, since nothing can move forward or be accomplished when time itself stagnates. In such a dimension there is no longer any distinction between moving forward and falling behind, as the protagonist of Kafka's *The Castle* discovers after arriving in the village at the foothills of the castle. Every entreaty the land surveyor K. makes to approach the castle only sets him further back, as every person he turns to deceives him either deliberately by giving him false information, or inadvertently by giving him hope when his situation is hopeless. Why, then, write? Blanchot offers a striking answer to this question: "It is as if, cast out of the world, into the error of infinite migration, [Kafka] had to struggle ceaselessly to make of this outside another world and of this error, the principle, the origin of a new freedom."[38] Error as a principle, migration as rootedness—these reversals are typical not only of Blanchot's thought but also of Kafka's and Sebald's texts insofar as all three grapple with a world that has no organizing principle and no law that ensures the felicitous outcome of events.

Kafka writes for the sake of a world abandoned by providence. To do so, however, he must renounce all hope of saving the world, which may seem like a paradoxical position but has its own internal consistency. According to Blanchot, Kafka must forsake the idea of writing as a means to achieve an end, since any aim would direct him back toward Canaan and, by extension, away from the desert in which he dwells. In other words, it would return him to the domain of the Law, from which he had been expelled through no fault of his own other than writing, which has no place in the promised land. As Blanchot observes, "Truth needs neither to be known nor to be described . . . just as earthly salvation asks not to be discussed or represented."[39] Truth and salvation do not require writing. If anything writing introduces error, by turning whatever is self-evident into something ambiguous that requires interpretation. Seen in this light, writing can be characterized as a form of error, or straying, and the person who writes wanders without hope of deliverance, like the Hunter Gracchus who is, among other things, a writer. Oliver Sill refers to him as "an emblem of the homeless writer."[40] In his audience with the Mayor of Riva, Gracchus complains, "No one will read what I write *here* [*Niemand wird lesen, was ich hier schreibe*]" ("Jäger," 288), in a surprising statement, given that he is supposed to be having a conversation with the mayor at this moment, not lying in his barge alone with a sheet of paper.[41] In an early draft of the story, Gracchus continues in this vein by asserting, "I know that and don't write to call help to my side [*Das weiß ich und schreibe also nicht um Hilfe herbeizurufen*]," which Max Brod, for inexplicable reasons, changed to "[I] don't shout to call help to my side [*ich schreie nicht um Hilfe herbeizurufen*]."⁴²

The change is disturbing to the extent that it obscures the hunter's vocation following his fall down a cliff, which is simultaneously a fall from grace. Gracchus is a writer condemned to travel the waters of the earth not in spite of but because of his vocation, which keeps him from reaching what he longs for in the netherworld. This paradox explains why he takes offense at the mayor's seemingly innocent question regarding who is at fault for his fate. I quote the original and an English translation, given its importance for Sebald's *Vertigo*:

> "Ich war Jäger, ist das etwa eine Schuld? Aufgestellt war ich als Jäger im Schwarzwald, wo es damals noch Wölfe gab. Ich lauerte auf, schoß, traf, zog das Fell ab, ist das eine Schuld? Meine Arbeit wurde gesegnet. 'Der große Jäger vom Schwarzwald' hieß ich. Ist das eine Schuld?" ("Jäger," 288)

> "I was a hunter, is that a crime? I was employed as a hunter in the Black Forest, where there were still wolves at the time. I waited, shot, hit, and skinned my prey, is that a crime? My work was blessed. I was called 'The Great Hunter of the Black Forest.' Is that a crime?"

While Gracchus may indeed be correct that he committed no crime, the question still remains why he was condemned to navigate the waters of the earth eternally instead of enjoying a final resting place. Gracchus offers a partial answer to this question in the two above-cited statements regarding his writing from a stretcher on an errant ship. Both contain a deictic gesture that is not as unequivocal as it may seem. In the first case, the gesture is overt: the phrase "was ich hier schreibe" points explicitly to the hunter's "here and now." The second is more oblique but equally significant: the pronouncement "[ich] schreibe nicht um Hilfe herbeizurufen" rotates around the speaker's present, to which help would be called, were that his intention. As is perhaps evident, both statements presuppose the hunter's here and now, his presence in space and time. Yet it is precisely this present that writing takes from him. What he writes "here" issues from nowhere and possibly no one, since, by the time we read this message, he has already traveled elsewhere, far from the place where we read his testament.

This is the predicament of the writer, according to Blanchot: "In [the] land of error one is never 'here,' but always 'far from here.'"[43] The writer leaves behind everything familiar—not for the sake of another world, but for the sake of the unfamiliar in this world. In "All'estero" the unfamiliar is identified specifically with souls of forgotten figures, who are sometimes named (e.g., Matthild Seelos) and sometimes referred to in generic categories such as "those who had faded away [*die Verblichenen*], the persecutors and the persecuted, the murderers and the victims" (*V*, 54; *SG*, 63), who haunt Grillparzer throughout his 1819 stay in Venice. (It is not accidental that the narrator's first trip to Italy coincides with All Saints' and All Souls' Day.) Yet the writer cannot approach the unfamiliar without suffering a loss—first and foremost, a loss of the ability to venture forth, since the unknown cannot be singled out as an objective. Such a gesture would indicate that it is in fact known and holds no mystery. The impossibility of approaching the unknown, however, has another consequence that bears on the figure of the author, the subject of this chapter.

Insofar as the writer is unable to seek out the unfamiliar as an object, he also cannot write. He cannot begin to draft a text when he has no overwhelming reason for doing so and nothing to compel him to exert himself in this fashion. Taken to its logical conclusion, this argument would mean that there could be no written works, for no one would ever be in a position to produce them. Every aspiring author would, like Thomas Bernhard's Franz-Josef Murau, be blocked from the start, incapable of finding a first sentence that could serve as the impetus for the remainder of the narrative. Sebald's narrators are similarly impeded in their writing efforts. In *The Rings of Saturn*, the narrator reports that he decided to tour the Northeast English coast "in the hope of escaping the emptiness that grows in [him] after having completed a larger project."[44] Yet the adventure, which presumably was intended to generate material for a later project, leaves him physically and mentally paralyzed—or, in his words, "in a condition of almost complete immobility."[45] In "All'estero" the narrator likewise travels in 1980 to Vienna and Northern Italy "in the hope that a change of place would help [him] get over a particularly difficult period in [his] life" (*V*, 33, translation modified), and here again the adventure does not spur his creativity but impedes it for seven years. Sebald's narrators, however, devise a different strategy than Bernhard's for dealing with their writer's block. Or, rather, the text does it for them, inasmuch as they are impersonations of the historical author Sebald, and sometimes even bear the same name as him, but also characters who in their fictitiousness attest to the impersonal force that drives literary writing. For Blanchot literature does not have a personal author who creates it from nothing; it happens instead when the writer loses himself and in losing himself writes as no one (we know) from nowhere (we can locate).

This dynamic answers the question "Why write?" One writes not out of free will or choice but because, in forgetting oneself, one is drawn into the realm of the unknown and unfamiliar where no rules apply, not even the rule dividing the past from the present. In this lawless realm, one is absolutely free, which can be intoxicating but also vertiginous, for without rules one loses the ground beneath one's feet. One loses even the security of the first-person pronoun "I," which no longer functions as what Émile Benveniste called a "unique instance of discourse."[46] One dwells in the dark, attempting to divine a principle behind the coincidences that confront one at every turn, since the same repeats itself endlessly, although in the absence of a rule one can no longer tell if it is the same incident or something different. Blanchot thus cautions that the land of error is simultaneously a land of false idols. For the land surveyor K., these idols promise him immediate access to the castle and to the authority that will decide his fate. For the narrator of "All'estero," the idol is literature itself, which promises to reveal the truth behind the weight of existence. Idols are famously deceptive, and yet they hold open the promise of a future in which they will no longer be necessary. Kafka's famous aphorism "The messiah will come when he is no longer necessary" would seem to encapsulate this point.[47] Yet I would turn instead to the ex libris plate reproduced at the very end of "All'estero" for an explanation of the promise that literature holds out.

It is a pyramid located curiously inside a house with a large, round sun shining through a window. The narrator refers to the pyramid in almost technical terms as a "Todessinnbild" (SG, 153), an emblem of death. If the illustration is a "Sinnbild" (emblem, or sense-image) it is because it lends itself easily to verbal translation. In the light "of books" (ex libris), as opposed to the light of truth, the dead have a home. For the sake of

Fig. 2. Ex libris plate in *Vertigo*, 172. Image from *Vertigo* by W. G. Sebald.
Copyright © 1990 by W. G. Sebald, used by permission of the Wylie Agency LLC.

these unredeemed and forgotten souls, literature is written. The "death of the author" makes this writing possible.

Ghostly Returns

The alleged author of "All'estero" dies in becoming a character in his own work. As mentioned previously, this is not an unusual strategy in Sebald's oeuvre. His fiction is filled with documentation, designed to authenticate the adventures of the first-person narrator, who sometimes bears the name W. G. Sebald. Even when he is not named Sebald, he closely resembles the historical author in terms of his biography as a German writer who has been living in England since his mid-twenties. Every reproduced receipt, ticket, newspaper clipping, postcard, and snapshot is designed to create the impression that the narrative is based in historical fact. That many of the trips recounted coincide with Sebald's known travels only reinforces the idea that his fiction is at best autobiographical and possibly not fictional at all but a stylized memoir. Whatever the case may be, the inclusion of documentary evidence in a self-reflexive narrative changes its status irrevocably. As Carol Jacobs observes, "The play of montage alters the incorporated material and puts it into new relations that cause us to see and read otherwise."[48] Documentary evidence loses its indexical function when absorbed within a work and quickly becomes a double of itself—that is, proof of what proof would look like, were the text able to reach outside itself to the nondiscursive world. It stands in for what is still outstanding, what is yet to come, which is the unvarnished truth that by definition is evident in itself and needs no explanation. The documentation presented in Sebald's work is documentation staged, which is to say the fiction of documentation, or the semblance of proof. One might call it—conscious of the oxymoron—the illusion of verification.

Nowhere is the transformation of evidence from something immediate and unequivocal to something mediated and ambiguous more apparent than in the narrator's efforts in "All'estero" to authenticate his identity. He reproduces a page from his passport containing his photograph and signature, and, as the signature indicates, it is the passport of W. G. Sebald issued by the German consulate in Milan in August 1987.

While "All'estero" is not the only text that includes a picture of Sebald—*The Rings of Saturn* does as well—it is the sole work that con-

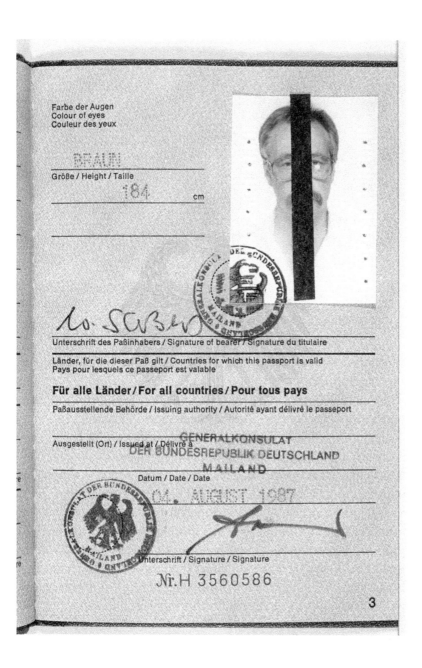

Fig. 3. Page in Sebald's passport in *Vertigo*, 144. Image from *Vertigo* by W. G. Sebald. Copyright © 1990 by W. G. Sebald, used by permission of the Wylie Agency LLC.

Fig. 4. Picture of Sebald before a cedar tree in *Die Ringe des Saturn*, 313. Image
from *The Rings of Saturn* by W. G. Sebald. Copyright © 1995 by W. G. Sebald,
used by permission of the Wylie Agency LLC.

tains his name alongside his photo in an official document: the passport
attesting to his identity.

This difference is significant. The inclusion of the author's signature
undermines the tripartite scheme that Philippe Lejeune articulated to
distinguish autobiography proper from fictional narratives. As discussed
in chapter 2, in "On Autobiography" Lejeune advances the claim that autobiography is the one genre in which the author, narrator, and protagonist all share the same name. The identity of all three in name functions for him as a guarantee that there is a person outside the text who
vouches for every statement in it as a statement about himself, or, more
precisely, a statement about his life, thoughts, and experiences. Lejeune
saves the genre by reducing the author to a legal signatory or copyright
holder whose primary function is to ensure that the text refers to a reality outside it, however murky this reality may be.

The official document reproduced in "All'estero" perverts this logic.
Already, as a reproduction, it takes the signature that is supposed to be
an author's singular trace and duplicates if not multiplies it, so that the
signature no longer has any legal authority. It is not a unique mark made
by the historical author on the page we read. However much the idea
of a singular trace may seem wedded to analog technology, it is worth

pointing out that every speaker who refers to herself as an "I" assumes the pronoun is unique in that moment. Neither analog nor digital technology changes that presumption. More striking than the reproduction of the author's signature in this case, however, is the line drawn through the passport photo that not only invalidates it as a form of identification, but also gives it several connotations that exceed the identity of the photographed subject as a unique individual with a singular face. (We use photographs as a means of identification because we assume that faces are not interchangeable.) This line could be interpreted as the Lacanian bar that bars the subject from the fulfillment of its desires; alternatively, it could be interpreted as bars in a metal gate (*Gitterstab*) that imprison the author within the world of his text; finally, it could be interpreted as a bar (*Stab*) that pictorially represents the letters (*Buchstaben*) that make up the text. While all these explanations are plausible, there is a more immediate possibility suggested in the text. The author "who drew lines connecting events that lay far apart" is now drawn into a web that he does not make but that makes him by withdrawing him from his own historical position. In other words, the line through the photo crosses the historical author out literally and figuratively, so that he can cross into a realm in which "nothing is what it seems," to cite from the film *Don't Look Now*, which Marcel Atze shows is alluded to throughout "All'estero."[49]

The narrator crosses into a realm where he exists exclusively as an *apparent* author: as a character who would *appear* to write the text, although he is powerless to do so as a fictional figure. The circumstances surrounding the loss of his passport underscore this fact. On the day he is to depart from Limone he discovers that his passport is gone. According to the hotel staff, the document was mistakenly handed to a German tourist who had left the day before. The narrator therefore travels to the German consulate in Milan to replace his lost passport. Nothing would seem extraordinary about this incident, if the narrator did not underscore that it was an inadvertent error that led to his current predicament. The proprietor of the hotel tells him that his passport was given to a Herr Doll by accident, "versehentlich" (*SG*, 114). As if to draw attention to this comment, the narrator then expands on it, this time citing the key word in Italian: "I still hear him calling out *inavvertitamente*, striking his forehead with the flat of his hand in despair at such negligence [*Unachtsamkeit*]" (*V*, 100; SG, 114, emphasis in original). The narrator's insistence on the inadvertent nature of this error should remind us of the circumstances that led to the Hunter Gracchus's fate, given the centrality of this story in "All'estero."

Gracchus describes the circumstances as follows:

> Mein Todeskahn verfehlte die Fahrt, eine falsche Drehung des Steuers, ein Augenblick der Unaufmerksamkeit des Führers, eine Ablenkung durch meine wunderschöne Heimat, ich weiß nicht, was es war, nur das weiß ich, daß ich auf der Erde blieb und daß mein Kahn seither die irdischen Gewässer befährt.

> My death ferry veered off course. I don't know why, a wrong turn of the helm, a moment of inattention on the part of the boatman, distraction caused by my beautiful homeland. I don't know what it was, only that I remained on earth and that my ferry ever since has wandered the earthly waters.

While the hunter is convinced that an error has been committed, he cannot state exactly what it was. He offers three possible reasons for why his barge veered off course, one of which resembles the reasons given for the disappearance of the narrator's passport in "All'estero." "Unachtsamkeit" (negligence) replaces the helmsman's "Unaufmerksamkeit" (inattention). Ultimately the hunter concedes that he does not know why his ship went astray, only the consequences of this mistake, committed, we might say, so inadvertently that it never registered in anyone's consciousness. The decisiveness of this error, however, cannot be overstated. Thanks to it the hunter becomes a nomad, a homeless figure who is "never here, but always 'far from here,'" to cite Blanchot again.

The same holds true for the narrator of "All'estero," the supposed author of the text. As long as he is without a passport, he is technically a stateless person. Yet, even when he obtains a new passport, he remains homeless. In this context it is worth recalling that the ostensible purpose of the narrator's 1987 trip was to revisit and to conquer the past—specifically, the disastrous trip he took to Italy in 1980 that filled him with such mortal dread that he fled back to England. It was a trip conceived as a repetition of the past, so that the narrator could overcome the vertigo that overwhelmed him the previous time. Repeating something to master it is not unique to travel; Freud would claim it is endemic to psychic life, but even on a more modest scale it is fair to assume that repetition is tied to the writing process. Literary writing does not restate what is known, but turns instead to what is still unknown to let it happen anew as well as yet again. The narrator's 1987 trip is no exception to this rule, which, properly speaking, is the rule that no rules apply when one starts writing. Although he intends to follow his previous itinerary, events take an unexpected turn. He spends a morning in Venice before deciding to travel to Verona that afternoon with a brief detour in Padua to see Giotto's frescoes, to which Freud also makes passing reference in *The Interpretation of Dreams*.[50] The change in itinerary brings about a change in his person; he no longer dictates his trip but finds himself compelled to repeat someone else's journey. Specifically, he finds himself following the itinerary of Kafka and his fictional double Gracchus.

In September 1913 Kafka visited Vienna, Triest, Venice, Verona, Desenzano, and Riva, in that order. The third chapter of *Vertigo* is devoted to this journey. That most of these places already appeared in the second chapter attests to the circular structure of Sebald's text, in which everything that will occur in a later chapter has happened already, as, conversely, everything that occurred previously in the work is still to come. In "All'estero" the repetition of Kafka's trip is not something the narrator chooses. It happens to him in a manner that makes chance the author of both his travels and his writing. Sitting on the train to Verona, the narrator is suddenly overcome by a wave of inertia:

After barely an hour of breezy travel, in which the landscape shone through the open windows [*die Landschaft leuchtete bei den offenen Fenstern herein*], the Porta Nuova came into view and as I beheld the city lying in the semicircle of the distant mountains [*Halbrund der Berge*], I found myself incapable of alighting. Strangely transfixed, I remained seated, and when the train had left Verona and the guard came down the corridor once more I asked him for a supplementary ticket to Desenzano, where I knew that on Sunday the 21st of September 1913, Dr. K . . . had lain alone in the grass on the lakeside and gazed out at the waves in the reeds. (*V*, 85; *SG*, 97–98, translation modified)

The mere fact that the narrator mentions that Kafka went to Desenzano would seem to undercut the chance nature of this event. It would suggest that, although the narrator had not planned to repeat Kafka's journey, he ended up doing so, since the Prague author was very much on his mind as he toured Northern Italy. Yet this line of reasoning assumes that we know what Kafka did—where he went and what he saw—as if his travels were limited to his physical trips, which were, in fact, few in number. Kafka's travels occurred predominantly in his writing. Rarely has there been an author who devoted his entire work to a single theme: the exile of the writer, or the homelessness of the one who lives by the pen. It is this Kafka that is evoked in the passage, a Kafka that comes by many names, including the Hunter Gracchus, whose name derives from the Italian *gracchio*, which means the same thing as the Czech *kavka*, "jackdaw," or "blackbird."[51]

As in the case of the Hunter Gracchus, the sight of something beguiling immobilizes the narrator. He does not make this claim explicitly, but implies it by recounting in some detail what he sees through the train window. Indeed, the description has a surprisingly sensual quality, especially the comment that the landscape "shines" (*leuchtet*) through the window. It is as if the distance necessary for vision is overcome through the metaphor of the landscape as a radiant body or sun that touches the narrator in his confinement on a train going nowhere. We may be reminded of the ex libris logo (fig. 2) printed at the end of the chapter, which, as mentioned previously, pictures a pyramid in a room illuminated by an iconic sun. There, too, the sun shines through a window in which we see a flat expanse and then "the semicircle [*Halbrund*] of the distant mountains." This coincidence is not incidental: it is what links the narrator with the Hunter Gracchus, who says, "The warm air of the southern night comes through a small hole in the wall" ("Jäger," 287). Otherwise he is confined to the stretcher in his "wooden cage" in the bowels of his ship.

Immobile and yet nomadic: these are the two predicates that best capture the Hunter Gracchus's situation. How he can hold these two opposing predicates is something the previously cited passage from *Vertigo* explores through the example of the narrator. Like the hunter, the narrator is distracted by a beautiful sight. His reference to the "semicircle [*Halbrund*] of the distant mountains" calls to mind the hunter's former home in the Black Forest, if only because it is the sight of his "magnificent homeland" that drives the helmsman to distraction. Yet it is worth pondering whether the helmsman was the party distracted on that fatal day when the hunter's ship got lost. A careful examination of the passage raises doubts about this interpretation: "My death ferry veered off course. I don't know why, a wrong turn of the helm [eine falsche Drehung des Steuers], a moment of inattention [ein Augenblick der Unaufmersamkeit] on the part of the boatman, distraction [Ablenkung] caused by my beautiful homeland. I don't know what it was, only that I remained on earth and that my ferry ever since has wandered the earthly waters" ("Jäger," 287). Although everything in this passage would point to a failing on the part of the helmsman, he is mentioned only once. The hunter never says who is guilty for the "wrong turn of the helm" and the "distraction caused by my beautiful homeland." In the end he cannot; as he confesses, he does not know himself why his boat lost its way. Here is where "All'estero" expands on Kafka's tale. It does so specifically as a poetic interpretation—that is, a text written as a reading of another work and as an attempt to decipher figures that only generates new ciphers. The inertia that besets the narrator and prevents him from disembarking from the train functions as a parallel to, or a repetition of, the immobility that prevented the hunter from leaving his boat when he arrived in the nether world. For, according to "All'estero," the hunter's boat did arrive at its destination, just as the narrator's train reaches Verona, which was supposed to be the next station of his journey. One would be tempted to say that it is beauty that in both cases renders the figures powerless to move (i.e., the hunter's "magnificent homeland" and the luminescent landscape streaming through the narrator's window). Yet this explanation is insufficient in that it ignores the vocation that links the narrator and the hunter: their work as writers.

Writing incapacitates both and renders them unable to participate in the world that offers itself to them, which is, in fact, the only world at their disposal. They turn their back on this world because they fall under the spell of another, which they never find, since it does not exist except as a lure or seduction—that is, as a fiction. Hence the Hunter Gracchus emphasizes in one draft of the story that it was a trap that led to his fatal fall: "If the antelope hadn't lured me . . . I would have had a long hunter's life, but the antelope did lure me and I fell and was struck dead by the rocks [*Hätte mich nicht die Gemse verlockt . . . hätte ich ein langes schönes Jägerleben gehabt, aber die Gemse lockte mich, ich stürzte ab und schlug mich auf Steinen tot*]."[52] What he neglects to mention is that the trap he falls into was of his own making, something that the narrator of the next chapter of *Vertigo* underscores when he asks the following question regarding the antelope: "Is this not one of the strangest items of misinformation [*eine der eigenartigsten Falschmeldungen*] in all tales that have ever been told?" (*V*, 165; *SG*, 180). The narrator of "All'estero" is likewise seduced by a vision that he himself dreams up: not merely the sight of Verona from the train, but of something uncanny that the text can represent only by returning to an earlier allegorical figure. The "semicircle" (*Halbrund*) of the distant mountains is a reiteration of the "sickle-or crescent-shaped area" (*V*, 33) in which the narrator wandered in Vienna nearly a decade earlier.

Confronted with this semicircle, the narrator is transported back to his past and to the space he occupied in 1980, which was one in which the dead kept returning as ghosts. Ironically it was the narrator's desire to revisit his past that prompted his journey in the first place. He believed the trip would give him an occasion to examine his memories and record his impressions. That this desire gets the better of him should come as no surprise. The repetition of the past rarely leads to its mastering, as the text itself points out in alluding to the many battles fought in the borderland between Italy and Austria in the past two centuries. Of greater significance, however, is that this repetition is also a literary one: it results from the narrator's figurative encoding of his own experience. As a result of his representation of his path in Vienna as a half-moon and a sickle at once, the sight of a semicircular mountain range can return him to this place in time. What the episode on the train reveals is that in writing the narrator is transformed into a written figure, which is not a fate unique to him—we speak about writers based on their written work—but which has particular poignancy in this text given its emphasis on the problems of authorship. In writing the narrator loses his power to write. He gets lost in the mesh of his own figures in which he reappears not as a living author but as the semblance of one—a ghost or what we call a protagonist. For this reason the narrator is unable to move from the train, as the Hunter Gracchus is unable to disembark from his boat. The means they choose to conquer space (i.e., literature as metaphor) conquers them in time, returning them to a moment that they thought they had left and that in this manner becomes eternal.

For the narrator, this moment is both 1980 and 1913. It would perhaps be more appropriate to say it is 1913 alone, since already in his 1980 trip the narrator was haunted by visions of the year before the outbreak of World War I. Yet even this qualification is unsatisfying, as it relies on a measure of time that the text declares null and void. Dates have no meaning when time is nothing but the eternal return of the same, which is why the whole framework of a 1980 and then a 1987 trip is a fiction, even if it accurately reflects W. G. Sebald's travels.[53] We are always a year before the catastrophe, according to "All'estero" in particular and *Vertigo* in general. The novel, accordingly, begins in 1813, a year before Napoleon's fall, and ends with the number 2013, which is not so much a date as a cipher in the full sense of the term. Literature is situated at this juncture; it inhabits this moment of eclipse, when "everything was moving toward a single point" (*V*, 129), as the narrator's friend Salvatore Altamura tells him. The comment carries particular weight in light of the name of the person who pronounces it. Salvatore can mean "rescuer" or "savior" in Italian, as Kafka was no doubt aware when he named the mayor of Riva who visits the Hunter Gracchus "Salvatore." The mayor asks Gracchus if he intends to stay in Riva, possibly in an effort to give this abject figure hope that he can return to the realm of the living. In his response the hunter rejects this hope for himself as he preserves it for others in an image that is an allegory for literature itself: "I'm here, that is all I know and can do. My ferry is without a helm, and it travels with the wind that blows in the deepest regions of death [*Ich bin hier, mehr weiß ich nicht, mehr kann ich nicht tun. Mein Kahn ist ohne Steuer, er fährt mit dem Wind, der in den untersten Regionen des Todes bläst*]" ("Jäger," 288). Literature is, on the one hand, the boat that tends toward but one point, death, and, on the other, the boat that indefinitely extends the moment leading up to this point because of the wind that propels it. This wind comes from the "deepest regions of death" and fills literature's mast, thus driving it from the end it seeks and the disaster it courts. In relinquishing his position as author and becoming a character in his own work, the narrator prolongs the single moment before the catastrophe that is just around the corner, as he would have it. He lets himself be cast out into the waters of the text for the sake of the earthbound—that is, the happy individuals who have a home and hence do not need to wander *all'estero*. Kafka is reported to have said, "There would be hope in infinite supply but not for us," in an aphorism that could function as the epitaph for every writer who has gone missing and never again resurfaced from the depth of his text, the pool of his writing.[54]

Conclusion
On the Value of Dissembling

The chapters in this study have been organized around what I identified in the introduction as the four fundamental requirements for fiction: the character, the narrator, the author, and the work. In the novels that I have considered, these factors have proven to be nothing more than an aesthetic illusion or semblance. It thus seems fitting to conclude this book with a brief reflection on the idea of semblance from a phenomenological perspective that has guided the meditations in each chapter.

Phenomenology concerns itself with what appears to us, and this concern means that it makes no judgment on reality, only what we take to be real. As such it is a particularly suitable method for analyzing fiction, which we also take to be real—or, rather, which we accept as true, even when we know that it is false, because it gives us pleasure to do so. Seen in this light, fiction provides us with an occasion to consider how something announces itself or makes itself seen; it presents us with the process in which something presents itself to us, which is not merely an empty tautological formulation. The doubling evinced in this statement is, rather, a reflection of the extent to which fiction stages the process of becoming a phenomenon. As we saw in the discussion of Thomas Mann's *Confessions of Felix Krull, Confidence Man* in chapter 1, fiction is unique among the discourses in that it makes the act of appearing apparent. It shows us how phenomena emerge and form, and this process is particularly pronounced in the case of Krull, who, in the first two books of the novel, regales the reader with stories of his youthful exploits only to disappear in the third book and to reemerge as the entire represented world: every character, every fixture. He does so as what we called the appearance of appearance, or the semblance of semblance, which we analyzed as a fiction that exposes the fictionality of the world as a phenomenon in the strictest sense of the term: as that which shows itself.[1] This is the truth of fiction.

Such a truth, however, depends not only on an object, but also on a subject to whom the world appears. Phenomenology posits a correlation between the phenomena given in consciousness and the mental operations performed to underscore the subjective constitution of the world.[2] As a method, it does not address what is qua ontology—only what makes a claim to being by appearing to us in any number of forms that correspond to any number of acts of consciousness. In Edmund Husserl's shorthand it analyzes the relation of various "modes of givenness [Gegebenheitsweisen]" (Ideas, 90) to different "kinds of mental processes [Erlebnisarten]" (106), as can be seen in the relation of, for example, something remembered to the act of remembering, or of something imagined to the act of imagining. The list of examples is potentially endless, but these two suffice to demonstrate the correlation between objects intuited and intuition or consciousness more generally.

In Jakob von Gunten we witness the continuous stream of Jakob's mental life, thanks to the novel's form as a diary in which Jakob chronicles his experiences at the Institute Benjamenta. Yet the reader is never able to shirk off the suspicion that the diary is a ruse, a pretense crafted by Jakob to pass himself off as an innocent or naïf in order to achieve other ends. We see this in the fact that Jakob consistently undermines the correlation between the phenomena he experiences and the mental acts in which he is engaged (i.e., remembering, imagining, daydreaming). This severing of subject and object or mind and world calls into question the validity of his diary from within the diegetic space. Within the story the diary itself is marked not as a spontaneous outpouring, but as a cunningly crafted document. In one telling instance, Jakob reports that the teachers of his youth "actually lie there quasi-deathlike in a slumber" (JVG, 9) in the Institute Benjamenta, as if they were objects of perception, only to indicate a few sentences later that they are merely fantasized figures, trifles of the imagination.

The same discrepancy is evident in his account of the institute's "inner chambers," the inner sanctum of the school where the director and his sister reside in what is possibly an incestuous relation. Jakob emphasizes that he experiences the chambers in all their sensuality and magic on one occasion, but when he returns to it a second time, he finds the most prosaic rooms with no personal touches.³ These two instances are paradigmatic for the work as a whole: Jakob repeatedly represents the world he inhabits as real only to challenge this impression a few sentences later and to imply that his surroundings are a product of his whim or fancy as a writer. In this manner he is able to engineer his escape into a sphere beyond the written word. By depicting things not as perceived entities (one form of givenness) but as fantasized objects (another form of givenness), he is able to retreat from the pages of his notebook and to emerge in life in a process that would have to be called a literary transubstantiation, as it takes a word and makes it flesh.

Such a passage from the realm of semblance into the sphere of life, nonetheless, requires a work. Jakob would not be able to journey beyond the fiction that he creates in his diary if the pages of his diary did not coincide with the pages of the book we hold in our hands. The requirement of a work, however, is called into question in Thomas Bernhard's *Extinction*, which is portrayed from the start as a posthumous text. An anonymous editor intervenes in the first sentence to announce that the supposed author, Franz-Josef Murau, has died and as a result is no longer able to vouch for the truth of his autobiographical narrative. In the course of this narrative, Murau discloses that he has for many years longed to write a memoir entitled *Extinction* that would extinguish all trace of his family and his native land, which he loathes for its hypocrisy, bigotry, conformity, provincialism, and violence. He admits that he has never been able to compose this work, because he could not find the first sentence from which the rest would follow as if by magic. As discussed in chapter 3, it would be tempting to assume that the work we read is the memoir that Murau desired to write, as if he somehow overcame his writer's block and finished this long-awaited project, his protests notwithstanding. Yet to make this assumption is to ignore Murau's stated aim, which is not to preserve but to eradicate his personal and family history through the power of the pen. To realize this ambition, Murau must fail. He can only extinguish his birthplace if he never drafts his intended memoir. This is a failure that—however curious it sounds—Murau achieves through the drafting not of a work but the semblance of one.

In the course of his extended monologue, Murau laments that virtually every modern medium turns "what is factual [*das Tatsächliche*]" into "something allegedly factual [*ein vermeintliches Tatsächliches*]"

(*Auslöschung*, 374). The culprits he names are newspapers and photography, both of which claim to reproduce the real without artifice, as if they were merely reflective surfaces. But the criticism applies to literature as well, as a mimetic medium. Murau condemns the idea of imitation as an objective act, which is hardly a surprise. What is surprising is that he relies on imitation to produce a manuscript with the power to destroy. The text Murau writes takes the place of his intended memoir *Extinction*. It extinguishes the possibility of this work by choking the only person who could ever write it—Murau, who ends up taking his secrets with him to the grave. The long-awaited memoir never comes to pass; what takes its place is an ersatz memoir, something "allegedly factual," the imitation of a never-to-be-realized manuscript.

In its mimetic function, literature mirrors not only the external world, but also the self. It gives the reader access to another person's interiority, and, as Käte Hamburger explained in *The Logic of Literature*, this access requires a fundamentally different grammar than the one operating in ordinary language, or what she calls the system of the reality statement. As elaborated in chapter 2, Hamburger refuses to categorize first-person narratives as fiction on the grounds that the underlying logic for utterances in such narratives is no different than in ordinary language; nothing distinguishes them from, say, historical narratives, which follow the rules of the reality statement. Yet, as the reading of *Jakob von Gunten* revealed, first-person narratives have a peculiar formal dimension; they introduce a split in the "I" between the recounting and the recounted subject, which is only partially illuminated by Benveniste's distinction between the *sujet de l'énonciation* and the *sujet de l'énoncé*. The *sujet de l'énoncé* is the grammatical subject in any sentence; the *sujet de l'énonciation*, by contrast, is the subject who voices the statement and, as such, is the subjectivity or consciousness that imbues it. The novel *Jakob von Gunten* makes explicit a split that is central to every pseudo-memoir. Jakob occupies two positions in his text: as a writer who imagines the Institute Benjamenta from outside, and as a figure thoroughly enmeshed in the day-to-day affairs of this environment. In W. G. Sebald's *Vertigo*, this split is pushed to the breaking point, and what causes the collapse is that the author, who ostensibly exists outside the text, is drawn into the work and becomes a fiction, the shadow of an author, a narrated character in lieu of a narrating subject.

What draws the author into the work in *Vertigo* is first and foremost the fact that he and the narrator share the same name, and, lest this seem like an incidental fact, the text reinforces it by reproducing a page from W. G. Sebald's passport. Yet the documentary evidence alone does not suffice to explain how W. G. Sebald becomes a narrated figure at the mercy of an invisible hand. The loss of autonomy that accompanies becoming a character is inextricably bound up with the theory of history propounded in this work, in which the past repeatedly returns in the present, since, for Sebald, the past and the present are nothing but discursive phenomena; both are expressions of an order that can never be revealed as such, but that still dictates the meridian lines connecting far-flung people, places, and events. As soon as Sebald starts to write, he finds himself pulled into a web that is not of his own making, as can be seen in the recurring words and phrases of other authors, from Stendhal to Kafka and Casanova to Hofmannsthal, that sound and resound in his prose fiction. These writers come to the fore as if they were still present, while, conversely, Sebald retreats into the background, as if he were nothing but the ghost of previous writers.

Sebald's admiration for Robert Walser is well documented, and yet his texts move in the opposite direction, as the writings of his self-appointed literary forebear.[4] Walser plays on the first-person narrator's position inside and outside the text to enable his heroes to move from the pages of a book to a life beyond all semblance. Sebald's narrators, by contrast, surrender their position outside the text and in so doing become fictionalized authors or semblances. As semblances, however, they reveal something otherwise hidden in any work. They function as an embodiment of the force that drives narrative; one might even say they personify it. In "The Song of the Sirens," Maurice Blanchot suggests that what both inspires and sustains song is something that cannot be named except as a mythological figure. For him this figure is the sirens, but even these legendary creatures are nothing but a guise or face for a source that literature can never account for, even though it is propelled by it. The inaccessibility of this source leads to a curious situation whereby literature, with each step, constructs a lost origin. It places ahead of itself a past it can never retrieve, as this past precedes all literary production. What every image, every representation attests to, then, is the "movement toward song."[5] Literature does not so much proceed from a beginning as wander in search of one—in search of what initiates and powers it.

Blanchot muses that the tale "'narrates' itself" ("Song," 447), by which he means that it tells the story of its own genesis and generates a myth of its own unfolding. Such a tautological process, in which what is at stake in a work is the possibility (or impossibility) of its own telling, is for Blanchot specific to the tale (*récit*). The novel, by contrast, is preoccupied not with its origins but with what is known (i.e., with the affairs of this world). Yet the distinction between the novel and the tale is not as self-evident as it would seem, as the examples chosen by Blanchot palpably demonstrate. His chief example is the siren episode from *The Odyssey*, which has long been considered the archetype for all epic narration in the West. However, even if one wants to claim that *The Odyssey* is not a single, cohesive epic narrative but a collection of tales, it is still hard to ignore that most of the works Blanchot cites to illustrate the nature of the tale are, in fact, novels. As discussed in chapter 3, theories of the novel have invariably assumed that the realist novel of the nineteenth century stands as the measure of the genre, but it would be equally plausible to assert that the realist novel constitutes an aberration in the history of the genre, which is uniquely concerned with its conditions of possibility. In underscoring the moment and the process of their composition, pseudo-memoirs bring to the fore the question that lies at the heart of any work of fiction, whether a tale or a novel: what it means to tell a story.

Blanchot's statement "The tale is not the narration of an event, but that event itself" ("Song," 417) is significant in this regard. Pseudo-memoirs do not narrate what precedes them; the past is merely an occasion for them to probe the mystery of their own narration or the enigma of their power to tell a story. This is why they focus on the figure of the writer. The narrator-cum-author is a personification of the consciousness that organizes the work, which does not necessarily belong to a person. Indeed, properly speaking, it does not. Throughout his career Husserl underscored that transcendental subjectivity is not to be confused with the mind of an individual; the latter is the subject matter of psychology. Phenomenology, on the other hand, is concerned with the consciousness that constitutes a world in which there are objects, including other minds that can be studied in the empirical sciences or imagined in fictional narratives.

It may be odd to compare two thinkers like Blanchot and Husserl, who could not be more different in method or style—the one lyrical and essayistic, the other technical and single-minded—and yet the two converge in their understanding of a foundation that can never be given as a phenomenon or rendered transparent. Such a foundation can never be relegated to the past. It stretches to the end of a horizon that cannot be obtained and in fact seems to withdraw as soon as one approaches it. Blanchot thus writes, "The tale is a movement toward a point . . . which is not only unknown, obscure, foreign, but such that apart from this movement it does not seem to have any sort of real prior existence, and yet it is so imperious that the tale derives its power of attraction only from this point" ("Song," 447). The tale pursues a point that both retreats and commands. It has this dual aspect because of the peculiar dynamics involved in approaching a source or foundation. Every step a tale makes in the direction of its origin pushes that origin away by representing it as something it is not: an image, figure, or character (e.g., the sirens). At the same time the tale's missteps necessitate a new start, a new or extended myth to convey this one elusive point. Pseudo-memoirs pay tribute to the consciousness that underlies them in creating a semblance or manifest fiction: the fiction of an author who would be the work's origin. Yet the figure does not suffice to convey the work's origin, which in the end is not a person and may not even be human, but consciousness itself. This is the power pseudo-memoirs expose and make heard. In giving a face and a voice to it, they cast a spell on us and encourage us to lose ourselves in shadows of the imagination.

Notes

Introduction

1. Robert, *Origins of the Novel*, 15.
2. The first quotation comes from Barthes, *Writing Degree Zero*, 40, the second from Todorov, *Fantastic*, 33.
3. Koskimies calls him "the father of modern novel theory," in a remark typical of German literary histories from the nineteenth and early twentieth centuries, in *Theorie des Romans*, 143.
4. Blanckenburg, *Versuch über den Roman*, 257 and 390. Blanckenburg insists throughout this five-hundred-page work that the subject matter of the novel is the hero's "inner history." He frequently makes this point when comparing the novel to the theater, which represents the polar opposite of the novel in its emphasis on the hero's actions. Consider, for instance, the following passage: "In keeping with the nature of its genre, theater can only show us already completed, formed characters whom the poet connects to produce a scene or event. Herein lies the principal difference between drama and the novel. Just as the former requires personae for an event to be maintained because, with the exception of Shakespeare's historical dramas, a unique event is the proper content of drama, so the novel has to connect several particular events that transpire over a greater span of time, and this connection can only be maintained through the formation and development, the inner history of a character" (*Versuch*, 390, my translation). Blanckenburg distinguishes the classical epic from the modern novel on similar grounds. Whereas the epic is devoted to the "public deeds" of a "citizen," the novel takes up "the actions and feelings of a human being" (17).
5. See Bareis, "Role of Fictionality," who comments in this vein: "In narrative fiction, it is mandatory that we have a narrator, since it is the narrator's act of narrating that is the essential act of imitation and representation" (157).
6. Saunders, *Self-Impression*, 7–13.
7. Campe, "Form und Leben," 193–206. Campe draws on Blanckenburg's metaphor of an "interrogation" (*Verhör*) in his *Essay on the Novel* to advance the claim that the novel arises as it interrogates itself, a process that enables

it to "set itself before its own eyes," which is the original meaning of the rhetorical category of *evidentia*. Via such self-interrogation, the novel gives form not only to itself but also to life, which it posits as the basis for its own narration, even if the latter proceeds from it. Every novel is simultaneously a theory of the genre and a theory of life. Its self-reflection and integration of other forms (e.g., ballads, idylls, letters, discourses) enables it to compensate for its own intrinsic formlessness. According to Campe, the latter point is of particular significance for Friedrich Schlegel, who was convinced the novel does not have a fixed or given form, as do other genres, and must consequently sketch one for itself.

8. In *Thomas Mann* Hamburger argues that the modern novel is rooted in Romantic irony, which is grounded in the "split between the I and the act of saying I [*Spaltung des Ich und Ichsagens*]" (27). This split is reflected in the related but opposing spheres of life and spirit or life and consciousness, which alternate with each other but can never be identical with each other in any work (27–29). It is this difference that fuels what Schlegel called "progressive universal poetry," in which each and every work is nothing but a stage in the unfolding of life and its simultaneous reflection in spirit. For Hamburger the Romantics never succeeded in overcoming this duality, whereas Thomas Mann was able to conceive the mutual dependency of life and spirit even in their opposition (*Thomas Mann*, 16–30). Whatever the merits of Hamburger's evaluation of Thomas Mann, she isolates a moment critical to the reception of the novel. To the degree that the novel alternates between the positing and the negation of a world, and the positing and the negation of the self, it is constantly theorizing its own production as it proceeds. See also Campe, "Form und Leben," 193–97. Campe points out that it is only through the process of internal reflection that the novel acquires form—as a prose genre it has no external criteria—but the process applies to life as well, which emerges as something formed only in and through its own narration.

9. Husserl, *Ideas Pertaining to a Pure Phenomenology*, 160. Hereafter cited parenthetically in the text and the notes as *Ideas*, followed by the page number.

10. Mann, *Confessions*, 3, translation modified. Hereafter cited parenthetically in the text and the notes as *Confessions*, followed by the page number. Quotations from the German original will also be referred to parenthetically in the text as *Bekenntnisse*.

11. Coleridge, *Biographia*, 2.

12. Defoe, *Jonathan Wild*, n.p., emphasis added.

13. Defoe, *Jonathan Wild*, n.p., emphasis added.

14. Wieland, *Geschichte des Agathon*, 4, my translation, emphasis added.

15. Beckett, *Malone Dies*, 179. Hereafter cited parenthetically in the text as Beckett.
16. OED *Third Edition*, s.v. "tell," accessed July 19, 2016, http://www.oed.com .proxy1.library.jhu.edu/view/Entry/198787?result=3&rskey=bxm8qj&.
17. I am indebted to Lisa Montanarelli for drawing my attention to this pun.
18. It is possible that in showing the first person's status as a supplement that is always in excess of the count it takes, *Malone Dies* alludes to Russell's paradox concerning whether the set of all sets contains itself as a member. For a consideration of the import of Russell's paradox for narrative theory, see Rimmon-Kenan, *Glance beyond Doubt*, 75–92.
19. Watt, *Rise of the Novel*, 9–34. Watt also sees a coincidence between Cartesian dualism and the story of a story typical of the fictional diary and the autobiographical novel as practiced by Defoe and Sterne. He notes that the split between life and its writing, which is central to this genre, parallels the split in the self, which takes itself as its own object in Descartes's writing. See, especially, *Rise of the Novel*, 294–95.
20. Lejeune, "On Autobiography," 3–30.
21. Descartes, *Meditations*, 13. Hereafter cited parenthetically in the text as *Meditations*.
22. Rousseau, *Reveries*, 1. Regarding Bernhard, the narrators in his fiction are often the sole surviving member of a family or a circle of friends. The narrator of *The Loser* (*Der Untergeher*) survives to tell of his friend Wertheimer's descent into madness; in *Concrete* the narrator, Rudolph, recalls a woman he met in Mallorca only to discover her name engraved in the concrete wall of a mausoleum after she evidently committed suicide; and in *Correction* the narrator returns as the literary executor of his friend Roithamer's estate to review his manuscript regarding the building he designed for his sister, which led to her death and eventually his. To the degree that the narrator functions in part as an editor, his role is consistent with the narrators of numerous eighteenth-century novels, who likewise insist that they do nothing more than edit existing documents.
23. Hamburger, *Logic of Literature*, 81–84.
24. The first quotation stems from James, *Wings of the Dove*, 5, the second from Kafka, *Das Schloß*, 114.
25. Cohn, *Transparent Minds*, 5–6.
26. A historical argument can also be made for the convergence of the novel and Descartes's philosophy of the subject. Gallagher notes that the term "fiction" came to mean a narration of imaginary events and not simply a deceit at the end of the seventeenth century. See Gallagher, "Rise of Fictionality," 337–39.
27. Hamburger, *Logic of Literature*, 134–42.

28. See Banfield, *Unspeakable Sentences*, 183–223.

29. Banfield, *Unspeakable Sentences*, 212.

30. Foucault, "Dream, Imagination, and Existence," 59, emphasis added.

31. The meaning of "apodictic evidence" is discussed in §6, Husserl, *Cartesian Meditations*, 14–16; and *Cartesianische Meditationen*, 16–18.

32. Husserl, *Crisis of European Sciences*, 73. Hereafter cited parenthetically in the text and the notes as *Crisis*, followed by the page number. As will become evident in this introduction, Husserl's stance vis-à-vis Descartes is ambivalent. While he acknowledges the indispensability of the French philosopher for the development of his own method of transcendental phenomenology, he also believes that Descartes completely abandons everything that is radical in his project with his embrace of rationalism.

33. This expression returns throughout Husserl's later work; see *Crisis*, 79. The original expressions can be found in Husserl, *Krisis*, 81.

34. Each of these pairs is equivalent. Husserl did not introduce the terms *noeisis* and *noema* until 1913, in the first volume of *Ideas Pertaining to a Pure Phenomenology*.

35. See Grimm, *Sprache der Existenz*, 65. Grimm is one of the few critics to connect the form of the novel with Descartes's philosophy. As far as I know, she is the only critic to consider the modernist experiment with perspective in light of Husserl's notion of the *epoché* and the analysis of the supposedly objective world as a subjectively constituted phenomenon.

36. See, especially, *Crisis*, 78–80.

37. Husserl discusses Galileo's role in establishing intelligible nature as a mathematical sphere in *Crisis*, §9, 23–59.

38. The figure of "natural light" appears throughout the *Meditations* as an emblem for reason, which illuminates truth or truths otherwise obscured by appearances.

39. As Derrida writes, "Total derangement is the possibility of a madness that is no longer a disorder of the body, of the object, the body-object outside the boundaries of the *res cogitans*, outside the boundaries of the policed city, secure in its existence as thinking subjectivity, but is a madness that will bring subversion to pure thought and to its purely intelligible objects, to the field of its clear and distinct ideas, to the realms of the mathematical truths which escape natural doubt" ("Cogito," 53). This form of madness ends up being far more dangerous than the madness of doubting one's immediate sense impressions, which Foucault emphasizes based on his reading of the First Meditation. For Derrida this kind of doubt does not challenge the cogito itself and is as such far less destabilizing to the subject or the world constructed on its basis.

40. Beckett, *Company*, 46.

41. Wieland, *Geschichte des Agathon*, 5, my translation.

42. The narrator in *Geschichte des Agathon* emphasizes the absence of any measure for truth and its resulting arbitrariness in the paragraph immediately following this one. He points to the biographical data we have to assume as true, since there is no evidence to justify it. Of note is that the recurring phrase in the paragraph is "gesetzt, daß," which is normally translated as "assuming that" but that could be rendered equally well as "let it be posited that," which underscores the arbitrariness of the frame for the narrative. See Wieland, *Geschichte des Agathon*, 3: "*Gesetzt*, daß wirklich einmal ein Agathon gewesen, . . . *gesetzt* aber auch, daß sich von diesem Agathon nichts wichtigers sagen ließe, als wenn er geboren worden, wenn er sich verheiratet, wie viel Kinder er gezeugt, und wenn, und an was für einer Krankheit er gestorben sei: was würde uns bewegen können, seine Geschichte zu lesen, und wenn es gleich gerichtlich erwiesen wäre, daß sie in den Archiven des alten Athens gefunden worden sei" (emphasis added).

43. Lukács, *Theorie des Romans*, 70. Hereafter cited parenthetically in the text and the notes as Lukács, followed by the page number; all translations of Lukács are my own.

44. Lukács's brief and dense, but also highly provocative, interpretation of romantic irony can be found in chapter 4 of the *Theorie des Romans*, 64–67.

45. Larmore, "Ethics of Reading," 50.

46. See Iser's discussion of the relation of overdetermination in a Freudian sense to indeterminacy in *Act of Reading*, 48–50 and 163–179. Iser himself describes his method in an article that appeared at the same time as *Act of Reading* as a "phenomenological approach" to literary works. Drawing on the work of Roman Ingarden, he argues that what is "concretized" in the reading process is the structure of the text's realization, which is to say the reader's consciousness. See Iser, "Reading Process," 279–99.

47. Rimmon-Kennan, *Glance beyond Doubt*, 22.

48. Frederick, "Self-Destruction of the Enlightenment Novel," 168.

49. Sterne, *Tristram Shandy*, 10–11.

50. See Rimmon-Kenan, *Glance beyond Doubt*, 7–8, where she succinctly demonstrates the link between notions of reference and the split between story and discourse in twentieth-century narrative theory.

51. Barthes, *Writing Degree Zero*, 39.

52. Mann, *Betrachtungen*, 70. The full statement reads: "The talent suited to the novel is comprised of synthetic-plastic and analytic-critical tendencies and is not properly speaking German, nor is the novel itself a genuinely German genre. For the time being it is unimaginable that in this 'unliterary

nation,' an author, prose writer, and novelist would rise to a representative position in the national consciousness in the same way a poet, a lyricist, or a dramatist would be able to."

53. Auerbach, *Mimesis*, 455.

54. See Schegel, *Athenäums-Fragmente*, 127. Schlegel makes this recommendation for modern literature in Athenaeum Fragment 238, where he also states, "There is a kind of poetry whose essence is the relation of the ideal to the real and which should be called by analogy to philosophical language transcendental poetry. . . . Much as we would dismiss a transcendental philosophy that was not critical, did not present the producer along with the product, and did not simultaneously contain within the system of transcendental thought a characterization of transcendental thinking, so too should [transcendental] poetry . . . represent itself in each of its representations and be everywhere at one and the same time poetry and the poetry of poetry" (my translation).

1. The Character

1. See Coleridge, *Biographia Literaria*, 2. As I indicated in the introduction, Coleridge coined the phrase "shadows of the imagination" in reference to literary characters in his *Biographia Literaria*, which is also the source for the frequently cited phrase "the willing suspension of disbelief" concerning the stance of a reader vis-à-vis a fictional text.

2. For the authoritative analysis of human society and culture as play, see Huizinga, *Homo Ludens*, 46–75. Callois builds on Huizinga's insights in *Man, Play, and Games*. For his commentary on Huizinga, see Callois, *Man, Play, and Games*, 3–10; and, for his four-fold classification of games as *agon* (competition), *alea* (chance), *mimesis* (imitation), and *ilinx* (vertigo), see 11–36. In contrast to Huizinga, Callois extended mimcry to the animal kingdom, specifically insects. See Callois, "Praying Mantis," 69–81.

3. Aristotle, *Poetics*, 52.

4. Arendt, *Human Condition*, 187.

5. In a meditation on Arendt and Sebald, Cavarero makes the case that while we reveal ourselves to each other in speech and action, we do not necessarily know who we are. For this we require a storyteller, either to tell us our identity or to preserve our life story from extinction, as can be seen in Sebald's work. Cavarero argues that his fiction is devoted to reconstituting the memories of those traumatized by the Shoah; see Cavarero, "Narrative Against Destruction," 1–16, and, especially, 2–3, where she states, "In order to know who I am, I always need others: whether spectators, to whom I actively, though occasionally, reveal my distinct uniqueness through ac-

tion, or the narrator who, by telling my life story gives shape to my personal identity through words and makes it survive my own death." What is notable in the third book of *Felix Krull* is that Krull turns his back on the audience and becomes oblivious to all others, as he becomes a pure fiction divorced from all reality.

6. See, for example, the following comment in Arendt, *Human Condition*, 95: "The whole factual world of human affairs depends for its reality and its continued existence, first, upon the presence of others who have seen and heard and will remember and, second, the transformation of the intangible into the tangibility of thing." Arendt identifies writing as that which records and bears witness to past events and constitutes the medium that turns something as intangible as the past into something as concrete as print. Regarding the importance of speech for defining the human *as* human, Arendt writes the following in *The Human Condition*: "A life without speech and without action . . . is literally dead to the world; it has ceased to be a human life because it is no longer lived among men" (176).

7. Arendt, *Human Condition*, 181.

8. Arendt, *Human Condition*, 184. Arendt states categorically, "Nobody is the author or producer of his own life story." We act in, enjoy, and endure our lives but do not make it as a work. The only figures she claims who do so are the Greek national heroes, as epitomized in Achilles, who is able to rise to the level of the author of his life by dictating the terms of his death. See Arendt, *Human Condition*, 193–94. Cavarero amplifies this point by making a distinction between the "story" that arises from our words and actions and the "narration" that preserves that "story," though she also admits that not every story is immortalized in a written narrative. See Cavarero, *Relating Narrative*, 28–29.

9. Hobbes, *Leviathan*, 217.

10. I rely principally on Wysling's account of the genesis of the novel in "Archivalisches Gewühle," 234–57.

11. See, for instance, Mann, *Betrachtungen eines Unpolitischen*: "Schopenhauer, Nietzsche, and Wagner: a triumvirate [*Dreigestirn*] of eternally united spirits. Germany, the world stood under its sign until yesterday, until today, even if it will no longer do so tomorrow" (79; my translation). Lukács is suprisingly mild in his criticism of Mann for the nationalism epitomized in *Reflections of a Nonpolitical Man*. In the preface he wrote to accompany *Theory of the Novel* in 1962, he muses on the conditions that lead up to the World War I in 1914, when he was writing the work. Mann's *Reflections* exemplify a "romantic anti-capitalism" that could not find, or even disdained, a concrete political outlet and thus became "a form of apology for

the political-social backwardness of the Hohenzollern empire." See Lukács, *Theorie des Romans*, 13.

12. Adorno and Mann, *Briefwechsel*, 96.

13. In Denver Lindley's translation, the subtitle is "The Early Years" (*Confessions*, unnumbered front matter).

14. Wysling, "Archivalisches Gewühl," 236.

15. Downing, *Artificial I's*, 226. Downing's rich and probing reading of the novel first drew my attention to this important detail.

16. See Heidegger, "Die Frage nach der Technik," 11, where he states, "Only where such unveilling [*Enthüllen*] occurs does truth happen [*ereignet sich das Wahre*]." In *Der Ursprung des Kunstwerkes*, he analyzes how art in particular sets truth to work or puts it at play. Consider the statement "We, however, hold the setting into work of truth [*das Ins-Werk-Setzen-der-Wahrheit*] as the essence of art" (44).

17. Nietzsche, *Birth of Tragedy*, 50. The original can be found in *Geburt der Tragödie*, 38. Both texts will be referred to hereafter parenthetically in the text under the heading *Birth* for the English translation and *Geburt* for the German original.

18. Mann, *Doktor Faustus*, 527.

19. Krull's distinct memory of his birth could be a reference to *Tristram Shandy*, the urtext of all pseudo-memoirs, whose narrative portion likewise begins with Tristram's recollection of his birth.

20. Malkmus, *German Picaro*, 104. See also Freud, "Zur Einführung des Narzissmus," 37–68. Freud traces a passage from prenatal and infantile autoeroticism to primary narcissism and then secondary narcissism in adult life, in which a person takes herself as her own erotic object.

21. Puns based on the two meanings of the verb *scheinen* (to shine and to appear) abound in the German tradition. The most famous play on the verb's dual meaning occurs in the closing verse of Eduard Mörike's ekphrastic poem "Auf eine Lampe": "Was aber schön ist, selig scheint es in ihm selbst."

22. In *Thinking with Tolstoy and Wittgenstein*, Pickford argues that Nietzsche's account of music echoes Schopenhauer's position in *The World as Will and Representation* that music "is a copy of the will itself," which is not an object but the inner nature or striving that fuels all phenomena. Music moves us to lose ourselves in its unfolding and in this respect functions as an equivalent in the aesthetic realm to compassion in the ethical sphere. As Pickford writes, "Because music is non-representational, appealing to neither actual objects (referents) or abstract entities (Platonic Ideas), it is non-inferentially, immediately, and universally understood, and provides unique intuitive insight into the noumenal essence underlying the illusion of phenomena tran-

scendentally conditioned by our cognitive faculties of sensibility and understanding. Music therefore is the *aesthetic* counterpart of *ethical* compassion
(*Mitleid*)" (*Thinking with Tolstoy and Wittgenstein*, 79).

23. Even typographically this statement would seem to perform the shattering
of individual forms or elements. The possessive pronoun "Sein" contains
the same letters as "Eins," which then return as the nominalized verb "Sein"
at the end of thie quoted excerpt.

24. Nietzsche, "Über Wahrheit und Lüge," 314. The original passage reads:
"Was ist also Wahrheit? Ein bewegliches Heer von Metaphern, Metony-
mien, Anthropomorphismen, kurz eine Summe von menschlichen Rela-
tionen, die, poetisch und rhetorisch gesteigert, übertragen, geschmückt
wurden und die nach langem Gebrauch einem Volke fest, kanonisch und
verbindlich dünken."

25. Nietzsche "Über Wahrheit und Lüge," 314. There are other notable similarities between Nietzsche's rhetoric in "On Truth and Lies" and Kuckuck's
discourse or the words imputed to him in book 3. Krull, for instance, states,
"Er hatte von Neugier, einer *Neubegier* gesprochen" (*Bekenntnisse*; 537, emphasis added), which echoes Nietzsche's own use of the same neologism:
"[Die Natur] war den Schlüssel weg: und wehe der verhängnisvollen *Neubegier*, die durch eine Spalte einmal aus dem Bewusstseinszimmer heraus
und hinab zu sehen vermöchte." In addition Krull speaks of the stimulation (*Reiz*) that Kuckuck's discourse exercises on his "most secret fibers or
chords [*heimlichste Fibern*]" (*Bekenntnisse*, 537), which recalls Nietzsche's
emphasis throughout this essay on the stimulation of the nerve fibers that
generates words as the first form of metaphor production.

26. Downing, *Artificial I's*, 116.

27. Heftrich, "Der unvollendbare *Krull*," 99.

28. Heftrich, "Der unvollendbare *Krull*," 103. Heftrich's provocative insight regarding Mann's possible play on his name in this novel raises the question
of how much this play is part of Mann's practice throughout his oeuvre. For
the purposes of this study, it is noteworthy that a fictional confession or
pseudo-memoir can also function as an autobiography.

29. Downing likewise notes the "de-emphasized role of the narrator" in the
third book in *Artificial I's*, 212.

2. The Narrator

1. My discussion of Lejeune is based primarily on his essay "The Autobiographical Pact," although he did revise his views on the first-person pronoun and the name of the author considerably in a later essay. See Lejeune,
"Autobiographical Pact," 8–21.

2. Lejeune, "Autobiographical Pact," 12.
3. DeMan's criticism of Lejeune amounts to the claim that Lejeune is not formal enough in his analysis. DeMan argues that Lejeune bases his definition of the genre on the reader's power to judge the author's signature. This power of discernment is assumed, but has no textual basis. See DeMan, "Autobiography as De-Facement," 71–72.
4. Lejeune, "Autobiographical Pact," 11.
5. Genette, "Fictional Narrative, Factual Narrative," 757n5. Regarding the similarity between Lejeune and Hamburger, Genette writes, "Lejeune, like Käte Hamburger, observes no difference between autobiography and the autobiographical novel 'if one remains at the level of the internal analysis of the text.'"
6. Hamburger, *Logic of Literature*, 311–37. Hamburger's dismissal of Hans Vaihinger's theory that fiction presents a world *as if* it were real proved to be equally controversial. Hamburger insists that Vaihinger's "as if" thesis reduced fiction to a deceptive imitation; this, she argues, mistakes its nature, which is not to present an imitation *as if* it were real, or to introduce a falsehood *as if* it were the case, but to represent something *as* real, even if it is only a semblance. See Hamburger, *Logic of Literature*, 55–59. Michael Scheffel offers a remarkably succinct summary of Hamburger's argument and a review of its reception history in "Käte Hamburger's *Logik der Dichtung*," 140–55.
7. For her discussion of the reality statement, see Hamburger, *Logic of Literature*, 45–51.
8. Hamburger discusses the difference between the I-Origo and the I-Origenes in *Logic of Literature*, 67. The I-Origo represents the implicit or explicit subject position from which any and every statement issues, even seemingly impersonal statements of fact or propositions such as "Socrates is a man." The I-Origenes, on the other hand, is a subject whose internal mental processes are represented in the third person. Such representation, according to Hamburger, is impossible in any discourse save epic fiction.
9. What Hamburger calls the "cognitive subject" could also be understood phenomenologically as the consciousness that underlies any statement. See Hamburger, *Logic of Literature*, 29–31.
10. Hamburger, *Logic of Literature*, 36–37. What makes statements of fact more complex is their impersonality. The past is not placed in relation to the subject's present, as it would be if the statement were to read "Napoleon died last year," "last month," or "some time ago." Hamburger thus calls the subject of such impersonal or factual claims a "theoretical statement-subject." The theoretical statement-subject is understood not as an individual, but in generic terms, as the kind of person who would make such a claim. In this case the theoretical subject is a historian who, based on the evidence

gathered, is able to make a claim in the present about a past he did not experience. The category of the theoretical statement-subject is important, because it extends the notion of a statement-subject beyond the stating subject—or, in Benveniste's terms, the *sujet de l'énonciation*.

11. Cohn, *Distinction of Fiction*, 24. Cohn also quips that some of Hamburger's expressions like "'the I-originarity of a third person' are not catchy phrases but the technical nature of her vocabulary ensures that her concepts are precise and powerful."

12. Hamburger, *Logic of Literature*, 51.

13. The idea that the modern novel represents a continuation of the classical epic has a long history in German literary theory. See Behler, *German Romantic Literary Theory*, 189, where he observes the connection between the epic and the novel in German romantic thought, especially as articulated by Schlegel: "One can observe a tendency in German criticism at that time to derive the classical epic and the modern novel from the same source, namely epic narration, and to consider the epic and the novel as different manifestations of one and the same type of narration. Schelling, Hegel, and even Goethe shared this opinion, which still dominates Georg Lukács's theory of the novel." I discuss Lukács's conception of the novel and how it draws on as well as departs from the Greek epic in chapter 3.

14. Hamburger, *Logic of Literature*, 74. To distinguish the fictive statement from the reality statement, Hamburger claims that the former refers to an "I-Origenes" and the latter to an "I-Origo." The characters in epic fiction constitute the I-Origenes of a statement. This "I," she specifies, has "nothing to do with a real I who experiences fiction in any way—in other words, with the author or reader."

15. Hamburger, *Logic of Literature*, 71, emphasis added.

16. Hamburger, *Logic of Literature*, 311–37.

17. Benveniste, "Nature of Pronouns," 217–22. In claiming that the "I" is an "instance of discourse," Benveniste essentially concurs with Hamburger's and Lejeune's assessment that the first-person pronoun refers to the speaker who invokes it at any one moment; it is to this extent singular in its reference. While this approach frees discussions of the first person from questions of identity, it also limits how the first person can be understood in works of fiction in which the first-person narrator is a constructed figure.

18. Novalis, *Werke*, 329, my translation.

19. For a brief but informative account of Walser's life and the history of his publications, see Harman, "Introduction," 1–14.

20. Walser, *Der Gehülfe*, 139.

21. Sebald, "Promeneur solitaire," 145–46, my translation.

22. Kreienbrock argues that the pupils are "neither children nor adults" because they never master anything. He points out that their instruction consists in the repetition of a few exercises that could in principle continue ad infinitum, since the process of learning to become nothing is not one that can ever be completed. See Kreienbrock, *Kleiner. Feiner. Leichter*, 169.

23. When asked about the novel, Walser said, "For the most part it's a poetic fantasy. A little daring, no? Among my lengthier works, it's also my favorite." Quoted in Seelig, *Wanderungen mit Robert Walser*, 13, my translation.

24. Walser, *Jakob von Gunten*, 7, my translation. Hereafter cited parenthetically in the text as *JVG*, followed by the page number. All translations of Walser's work in this chapter are my own.

25. Several critics have noted that the novel alludes to the genre of the bildungsroman. Philippi argues that the novel invokes this tradition not to revive but to parody it, in "Robert Walser," 121–22. Gößling claims that the work is at almost every turn a play on *Wilhelm Meisters Lehrjahre*, the classic text of the bildungsroman tradition; the second half of his study *Abendstern und Zauberstab* is devoted to the question of the ways in which Walser's novel forces us to reinterpret Goethe's text. See Gößling, *Abendstern und Zauberstab*, 169–234. Borchmeyer claims the novel turns the bildungsroman on its head and perverts the entire tradition in an effort to show that it is no longer valid in a capitalist age in *Dienst und Herrschaft*, 27–28. Grenz concurs with Borchmeyer's assessment of the social critique that runs through the work, noting that Jakob does not venture out into the world, as the typical hero of the bildungsroman does, but instead withdraws into a school hermetically sealed off from the world around it. See Grenz, *Die Romane Robert Walsers*, 90–116. As I indicate in the final section of this chapter, Jakob does indeed eventually enter the public realm as a new if not fully formed person.

26. Weitzman, *Irony's Antics*, 81.

27. Peeters, "Wenn kein Gebot," 179–81.

28. Peeters discusses the absence in the position previously reserved for the paterfamilias in "Wenn kein Gebot," 186–87.

29. The relationship between Jakob and Herr Benjamenta has inspired a wealth of criticism. Regarding the reversal of the positions of master and servant in this relation, see Magris, "In den unteren Regionen," 347; and Philippi, "Robert Walser," 127–28.

30. Malkmus, *German Picaro*, 67.

31. It seems to me that Hiebel overstates the case for Jakob's willful, if not gleeful, submission to Herr Benjamenta at the price of a consideration of what Jakob gains through this submissive posture. See Hiebel, "Robert Walser," 308–45.

32. Borchmeyer identifies this critique as central to the text in *Dienst und Herrschaft*, 29–30. As to the rejection of republicanism in particular, see the passage in the novel about the Weibel brothers who supposedly torment Jakob in his youth because of the way his family treated a servant: "They slandered Mama and me in the most distasteful manner. Like true boys, yes, but also like true small republicans, for whom the idea of letting personal and rank-based favor or disfavor rule is a disgrace and an object of scorn. . . . Just as the Weibel brothers judged me, so today a whole world judges" (*JVG*, 70).

33. See, for instance, Mark 4:41: "And they feared exceedingly, and said one to another, What manner of man is this, that even the wind and the sea obey him?"

34. Blanchot, *Space of Literature*, 173.

35. In a reading attentive to the ontological and epistemological dimensions of the novel, Plug emphasizes the paradox implicit in the utterance "Since coming to the institute, I've already managed to become a riddle to myself." He argues that either the "I" that makes this statement is, in fact, no longer a enigma to itself, which undoes the statement, or, alternatively, any "I" that is truly enigmatic would no longer have the status of an "I." It would drown in its own "enigmaticity": "The 'I' that speaks of having completed a task assumes a position that is immediately undone by the very proposition in which it asserts its knowledge and history." See Plug, *They Have All Been Healed*, 141. I agree with his contention that the "I" that is a riddle to itself can persist only as a remainder, which the text frequently describes as something like a scent in the air that is at once too immaterial to attract our attention and yet too material to be dismissed as nothing.

36. Beierwaltes has examined with stunning clarity the paradox that what singles God out in Meister Eckhart's theology is that God is indivisible or inseparable from everything. Only a being that is its own cause has the ability to permeate not just itself but everything that would appear to exist outside it. A being that owes its existence to another force will always be distinct from its source and from every other phenomenon to which its source gives rise. See Beiewaltes, *Identität und Differenz*, 97–104.

37. Greven, "Figuren des Widerspruchs," 173; Grenz, *Romane Robert Walsers*, 141–42.

38. Grenz also observes this change in rhythm or pace in *Romane Robert Walsers*, 90.

39. I am indebted to a number of critics for drawing my attention to this pun. See Siegel, *Aufträge aus dem Bleistiftgebiet*, 16; Utz, "Robert Walser," 203; and Middleton, "Der Herr Niemand," 24.

40. A similar structure is at play in Walser's *Der Spaziergang*, where the narrator draws attention to the act of writing at the start of his account only to depart from his text at the end with a rhetorical adieu or bow: "Es war schon spät, und alles war dunkel." See Walser, *Der Spaziergang*, 77. For a discussion of the narrator's disappearance from the text, see Tobias, "Walking Is Not Writing," 39–49.

41. Campe, "Walsers Institutionenroman," 24. Campe reflects on the novel in terms of what it tells us about the genre of the novel more generally, and *Jakob von Gunten* proves to be a particularly salient example because it presents the novel at its eclipse. With its focus on a school that has been reduced to nothing but a few meaningless exercises repeated ad nauseum, Walser's novel demonstrates the role that institutions play in giving form to life and providing the parameters in which it can be narrated. What *Jakob von Gunten* narrates is nothing other than the institutional nature of a novel in which a coming-of-age story would be possible, were such a form (or institution) still to have credibility. For Campe it is crucial that the institution of the novel creates an occasion for a fictional diary or confession. See Campe, "Walsers Institutionenroman," 235–50. I appreciate the depth of this insight, but adopt a different perspective. In my reading it is the strictures of writing that enable Jakob to pass into life, which is itself formless and tangential to, but also outside, the scope of art.

42. Gößling, *Abendstern und Zauberstab*, 170–79.

43. Gößling refers to Jakob as both a "medial reader" and a "medium of *Wilhelm Meisters Lehrjahre*" (171). For the purposes of the present analysis, it is significant that he sees the pupil and diary keeper Jakob as a compendium of allusions to Goethe's classic novel. It is on this basis, I assume, that he calls Jakob a medium: Jakob is the vehicle through which a hidden narrator makes evident how he reads and understands another literary work.

44. To my knowledge Peter Utz is the only critic to remark on the significance of the reference to "das Ungemach" during the episode in the inner chambers (*innere Gemächer*) in Utz, "Robert Walsers *Jakob von Gunten*," 496.

45. Utz, "Robert Walsers *Jakob von Gunten*," 496.

46. Gößling, *Abendstern und Zauberstab*, 170–75.

47. For a discussion of the reversal of the biblical names, see Peeters, "Wenn kein Gebot," 219; Campe, "Walsers Institutiontenroman," 244–45; and Malkmus, *German Picaro*, 83–85.

48. Pleister provides a comprehensive revew of the literature pertaining to the conclusion of the novel from the 1950s to 1992, when he published his article. See Pleister, *Jakob von Gunten*, 87–103. According to him most critics have emphasized either the utopian or politically resigned nature of Jakob's

departure from the page: either the hero achieves freedom by abandoning all expectation of becoming somebody or he resigns himself to the exploitative conditions of modern society. Pleister sides with the latter interpretation. As I have tried to show, readings that emphasize only the political dimensions of the novel ignore its narratological aspects; they treat the novel as a manifesto or political treatise rather than a literary work. As a result they fail to explore the participation that *Jakob von Gunten* demands from its readers, which would be the place to start for any political analysis of the the text.

49. Philippi, "Robert Walser," 131.
50. Quoted in Benjamin, "Robert Walser," 328.

3. The Work

1. Smith, "Narrative Versions," 228.
2. See Lukács, *Theorie des Romans*, 25–29, where he addresses the subjectivity at the root of the novel, which also makes its representations comprehensible for other readers. Regarding the plausibility of the novel, see Barthes, *Writing Degree Zero*, 39; and Hamburger, *Logic of Literature*, 55–59.
3. See Barthes, *Writing Degree Zero*, 34–38; and Hamburger, *Logic of Literature*, 64–80.
4. In *Correction* the narrator often spies on Höller as he embalms birds at night. In more than one way the narrator performs in language what Höller performs with things. He ensures a body can be seen in its exact condition the moment before its death. See Bernhard, *Korrektur*, 153–57.
5. The titles of the five volumes are as follows: *Die Ursache: Eine Andeutung*; *Der Keller: Eine Entziehung*; *Der Atem: Eine Entscheidung*; *Die Kälte: Eine Isolation*; and *Ein Kind*. All five are printed in volume 10 of Bernhard's collected works.
6. See Aristotle, *Poetics*, 52. I have admittedly compressed two aspects of Aristotle's argument in the *Poetics* into one. Aristotle defines all poetic forms, including tragedy, comedy, epic narratives, and music of the lyre, as modes of imitation (49–51). Tragedy, comedy, and the epic imitate "men in action" (52) or "persons acting and doing" (53). What is, however, unique to both the tragic and epic form is that they represent not "what has happened, but what may happen—what is possible according to the law of probability or necessity" (68). Aristotle famously devises a series of seemingly contradictory formulas to indicate the appropriate material for the tragic and epic plot. "Probable impossibilities" are preferable to "improbable possibilities" (109–10). Here is where critics normally locate Aristotle's demand for verisimilitude in the dramatic and narrative arts. Yet it is important to note that

the epic has considerably more leeway in absorbing implausible or unlikely events than tragedy. An element of wonder is essential to both genres. At first Aristotle argues that the epic can account for irrational events better than tragedy because it does not have to represent it before the viewer's eyes. But he later states that the epic can include irrational elements, since it is probable that in life improbable events happen. With this second claim, Aristotle would seem to suggest that epic narrative is closer to life than tragedy, as it is not limited by its form to seeming truths or plausible fictions.

7. Bernhard, *Holzfällen*, 199, emphasis in original. All translations of Bernhard's work in this chapter are my own.

8. See Anderson, "Fragments of a Deluge," 130. He describes Bernhard's narratives as "spoken performances" and "funeral orations" in a concise but remarkably comprehensive article on the Austrian writer's work.

9. Bernhard, *Auslöschung*, 7 and 508. Hereafter cited parenthetically in the text and the notes as *Auslöschung*, followed by the page number. All translations of Bernhard are my own.

10. This tradition of fictional historical documents can be traced back to Henry Fielding at least. Bernhard himself employs this structure in *Concrete*, which begins and ends with the editorial insertion "writes Rudolf." See Bernhard, *Beton*, 7, 131. Wirth argues that the idea of the author not as a fiction writer but as the editor of a treasure trove of documents is central to the novel around 1800 and enables the transitition from the anonymous legends of antiquity to the literary productions of autonomous authors in modernity. See Wirth, *Die Geburt des Autors*, 19–48.

11. See Lejeune, "Autobiographical Pact," 8–21. Lejeune's theory of autobiography is treated in greater detail in chapter 2.

12. Jacobs, *Sebald's Vision*, 39.

13. One need only think of the narrator Rudolf in *Concrete*, Roithamer in *Correction*, Wertheimer in *The Loser*, and Konrad in *The Lime Works*, to cite but a few examples.

14. Schlichtmann's comment that "Murau, who long held the wish of writing [his memoir], had previously 'failed in the very sentence he wrote down.' Now, however, the writing succeeds," is typical in this regard. Schlichtmann, *Das Erzählprinzip "Auslöschung*," 31.

15. Sorg sees Murau's invective as an effort to gain an upper hand over an empirical world, with which he never truly grapples but only uses as a foil to establish himself. He interprets the narrator's tirades against Austria, painted in the most lurid—if not ludicrous—light as part of a rhetorical strategy in which a subject is able to rise to prominence as long as it sits in judgment of a fallen world (Sorg, "Strategien der Unterwerfung," 135–42).

16. Schlichtmann advances the theory that *Extinction* contributes to memory by ending the deliberate silence and forgetfulness that has characterized both official and unofficial accounts of Austria's role in National Socialism in Schlichtmann, *Das Erzählprinzip "Auslöschung,"* 111.

17. Damerau argues that, although World War II and traumatic memories play a large role in Bernhard's prose from "Amras" to "Der Italiener" and *Frost*, the references to Austrian complicity with the National Socialists and genocidal acts remain indirect. The theme is not developed until his later novels, albeit with emphasis on the failure of Austria to reckon with its murderous past, either through outright denials or through the public ritual of "working through," which often ends up functioning as a scarcely veiled form of self-exoneration. See Damerau, *Selbstbehauptungen und Grenzen*, 130–36. Scheit points out that novels like *Frost* and *Verstörung* refer to the trauma of war but fail to identify the perpetrators, in "Komik der Ohnmacht," 147–51. *Extinction* stands out in Bernhard's oeuvre in its explicit statements about Austrian participation in the Holocaust, albeit for purposes besides remembering and reckoning, as I will discuss shortly.

18. Heidelberger-Leonard, "Auschwitz als Pflichtfach für Schriftsteller," 184.

19. Damerau, *Selbstbehauptungen und Grenzen*, 133.

20. I am indebted to Naqvi's analysis of this term and the link she draws between real estate and the process of mediation central to education as well as that between buildings and *Bildung* throughout his oeuvre. See Naqvi, *How We Learn*, 3–29.

21. Eyckeler, *Reflexionspoesie*, 157. Eyckeler points out that Murau himself draws attention to the perspectival nature of all utterances in the text. He notes the dishonesty, unctuousness, and self-congratulatory aspect of Cardinal Spadolini's comments regarding his mother, who was the cardinal's lover. He observes that Murau's statement "[Spadolinis] Wie hat immer das Was zugedeckt, dachte ich" (*Auslöschung*, 574) could just as well be applied to Murau's own rhetoric. See Eyckeler, *Reflexionspoesie*, 157–60.

22. Eyckeler, *Reflexionspoesie*, 159 and 167.

23. The narrator Rudolf in *Concrete* also suffers from a lung disease which he refers to in the novel's opening page as "morbus boeck"— in English, sarcoidosis, which is an inflammation, usually affecting the lungs, that causes wheezing, shortness of breath, and pain in the chest. See Bernhard, *Beton*, 7. The similarities between Rudolf and Murau are not incidental: in both texts a narrator intervenes in the first and last sentences to indicate that the narration that follows is itself famed and narrated by an editor. Both texts have the aura of posthumous works. The link between Bernhard's illness and the act of writing is already embedded in his name, whose initials T B

spell out the common English abbreviation for tuberculosis. Bernhard, who studied in England, would in all likelihood have been aware of this. Moreover, the issue of his name was by no means something he would take for granted, given that he was forced to take on his mother's maiden name, even though she was married, as a child born out of wedlock.

24. Murau's full statement is "Das, was ich zu Papier bringe, ist das Ausgelöschte" (*Auslöschung*, 424).

25. Quoted in Benjamin, "Der Erzähler," 456.

26. In this context it is important to note that there is a village and castle named Wolfsegg in Austria owned by aristocratic friends of Bernhard. I would argue that this fact does not change my interpretation. If anything it reinforces it, by drawing attention to the difference between the historical or actual Wolfsegg and the Wolfsegg that Murau sketches in his text to destroy it in turn. In this novel, as in most of Bernhard's other works, elements from the author's social milieu are incorporated into a constellation that is neither fictional nor nonfictional. As Theisen has shown, Bernhard consistently blurs the line between autobiography and fiction. See Theisen, "Im Guckkasten," 246–65. I am also indebted to her insight into the historical resonances of Murau's first name, Franz-Josef, in the Austrian context in which the play on Kaiser Franz Josef would be unmistakable. What is important in *Extinction* is that Wolfsegg, as Murau sees it, consumes him so entirely that this burns any reference to a reality apart from his writing or a place apart from his representation. What is not and cannot be represented in the text is Wolfsegg in its actuality. A similar strategy is at play in the representation of the topography of Rome in the novel's first sentence. The landmarks Murau passes during his walk home all exist, but not in the locations he suggests. It would seem that Bernhard has picked well-known place names from a map of Rome and thrown them into a new configuration. Hence Murau's setting would appear to be Rome and has the aura of reality, even if it is a fictitious place. I thank Sabine Wilke for pointing out that the places cited in the first sentence are not contiguous. For a discussion of the historical Wolfsegg and its role in Bernhard's work, see Honegger, *Thomas Bernhard*, 176.

27. Murau uses the verb *erzählen* all of three times in the work, once in reference to the gardeners; another in reference to the hunting lodge in Wolfsegg, about which he says, "Ich könnte noch ganz anderes über dieses Jägerhaus erzählen" (*Auslöschung*, 154); and once indirectly in connection with the Archbishop Spadolini whose highly exaggerated, if not utterly untrue, depiction of Murau's father is described as an "Erzählung" (431). The scarcity of this verb is all the more striking given that Murau's narration

consists in large part of his memory of statements he made to Gambetti. In this text, as in most of Bernhard's other works, the repeated and punctuating utterance is "sagte ich." With respect to his intended family portrait, Murau never says that he will tell the story of his family—only that he will document and report it. Consider, for instance, the following statement: "[Ich] will doch darangehen, alles über das *aufzuschreiben*, das mir, Wolfsegg betreffend, keine Ruhe läßt . . . ich dürfte mich nicht davon abhalten lassen, es zu *dokumentieren*. . . . Jahrelang denke ich, ich muß diesen *Bericht* über Wolfsegg *schreiben*" (155, emphasis added).

28. Within the context of this study, it is interesting to note that, according to several critics, *Camera Lucida*'s genre is perched between an essay and a novel. Shawcross identifies it with what Barthes called in *The Rustle of Language* a "third genre" between the essay and fiction; cited in Shawcross, "Roland Barthes," 68. She adds, "*Camera Lucida* develops or unfolds like a mystery novel told from an autobiographical point of view" (71). In the context of this study, it fits the definition of pseudo-memoir. Attridge also ponders whether Barthes's first-person statements should be taken at face value or considered fictional utterances. Regarding the famous Winter Garden photograph that is never actually shown in the text, Attridge asks, "What if there is, was, no Winter Garden photograph?" ("Roland Barthe's Obtuse, Sharp Meaning," 86). In Barthes's terminology the reality effect of first-person utterances is so strong and the investment in the subjectivity of the narrator so complete that, in a text in which the author and narrator bear the same name, it is all but impossible to differentiate a memoir or reflection from a work of autofiction.

29. Barthes, *Camera Lucida*, 8.

30. Barthes, *Camera Lucida*, 6.

31. The respective page references for these terms are: Barthes, *Camera Lucida*, 33, 14, 79, and 11.

32. The respective page references for these terms are: Barthes, *Camera Lucida*, 26, 27, 27, 27, and 94.

33. Attridge, "Roland Barthes's Obtuse, Sharp Meaning," 77.

34. Barthes, *Camera Lucida*, 76.

35. Barthes, *Camera Lucida*, 76.

36. Barthes, *Camera Lucida*, 73.

37. Fried, "Barthes's *Punctum*," 146.

38. Attridge underscores that Barthes's text is premised on a contradiction. On the one hand, it argues that the punctum exceeds all cognitive categories and is as such incommunicable in words and, on the other, tries to communicate to the reader where the punctum in specific photographic images is located.

Attridge generalizes this contradiction to make a broader statement about art, which issues "a demand for translation" that can never be adequately met but that even in this failure makes its underying essence felt: "Indeed it might be said that [the details that bruise or pierce Barthes] are only fully constituted in their incomprehensibility in the necessary attempt to render them comprehensible, that their specificity actually depends on the words (or other codings) by which the viewer acknowledges and attempts to artic-ulate them—in the first place to himself or herself. They thus appear only in the moment of disappearance" (83–84). With this insight Attridge is able to acknowledge the singularity of the punctum, while allowing for its interpre-tation, and thus indirectly aligns Barthes's theory of photography with Kant's notion of the universal communicability of judgments of taste.

39. Barthes, *Camera Lucida*, 3.

40. See Barthes, *Camera Lucida*, 89 and 76–77.

41. See, for instance, Murau's comment: "Jahrhundertelang ist ein tatsächliches natürliches Leben in Deutschland und Österreich nicht mehr möglich, weil es von der Zeugnis-und Titelsucht aufgefressen und ausgelöscht worden ist" (*Auslöschung*, 65).

42. Fried notes the temporal distance between the photographer, who captures a present that neither he nor his subject perceive as being past, and the be-holder, who views this frozen or immobilized moment as something irre-trievably lost: "Time, in Barthes's sense of the term, functions as a *punctum* for him precisely because the sense of something being past, being histori-cal, cannot be perceived by the photrapher or indeed by anyone else in the present" ("Barthes's *Punctum*," 150).

43. Murau's nominalization of "nothing" and treatment of it as something that both does and does not exist echoes and parodies Heidegger's peculiar philosophical idiom. In *Alte Meister* the protagonist Reger calls Heideg-ger, among other things, "the ridiculous Nazi bourgeois in his knickers [*der lächerliche nationalsozialistischen Pumphosenspießer*]" and a "measly thinker of the Alpine foothills [*Voralpenschwachdenker*]," in Bernhard, *Alte Meister*, 55–56.

44. Lukács, *Theorie des Romans*, 24. Bernstein argues that the epic does not constitute the real ancestor to the novel. Lukács presents it in this way since the epic is the past written into the present of the novel; it is the paradise lost the novel implies to explain the challenges it faces. For Bernstein, con-sequently, the section on the epic is not significant for what it says about the epic but what it indicates about the novel that follows it. See Bernstein, *Philosophy of the Novel*, 44–49. I am indebted to his remarkably lucid dis-cussion of Lukács's compact and often dense text in this section.

45. Aristotle, *Poetics*, 52. For Aristotle art imitates "men in action" because it imitates life. Lukács is making the case that with the rise of the novel life and art no longer coincide.

46. In a fragment from the period 1797–1798, Novalis writes, "The novel is about life; it represents life [*Der Roman handelt von Leben—stellt Leben dar*]," in Hardenberg, *Werke*, 391. The comment could have inspired Lukács: he cites Novalis's aphorisms at least twice in the work.

47. Bernstein posits that the norms established by the novel are not objective, only apparently so. He views this as a weakness in Lukács's theory of irony, which was inspired in large part by Schlegel: irony produces not objectivity, only an objectivity effect. While I agree with this interpretation, I do not think it differs significantly from Lukács. As I indicate in what follows, irony enables the novel to create the appearance of an organic whole where none exists. In my reading what Lukács means when he refers to irony as the "objectivity of the novel" (79) is the knowledge of the negative that it breeds: the knowledge that the world in its current condition is bereft of sense.

48. I have slightly altered Novalis's statement to fit Lukács's account of a double reflection, which for Novalis is always a process of a subject reflecting on itself. His full statement in the *Blütenstaub* fragments is: "The highest goal of one's education and formation is to lay claim to one's transcendental self and to be simultaneously the 'I' of one's own 'I' [*Die höchste Aufgabe der Bildung ist—sich seines transzendentalen Selbst zu bemächtigen—das Ich ihres Ichs zugleich zu sein*]." See Hardenberg, *Werke*, 329.

49. In the first chapter of *Aesthetic Theory*, Adorno likewise underscores the heterogeneous composition of art. He advances the the theory that art is neither pure spirituality, as the Idealists would have it, nor pure sensuality or materiality, as hedonism would claim. Rather, diverse elements from the external world—be it the empirical or social world—are always included in art and integrated into its form, although such absorption does not mean that fractures are covered over. He further claims that art cannot be reduced to or defined exclusively by reference to its form, for such a move would strip art of anything other than itself. In other words, it would spiritualize art by removing from it any trace of empirical or social content. See Adorno, *Aesthetic Theory*, 1–22.

50. Schlegel, *Athenäums-Fragmente*, 114.

51. Schlegel, *Athenäums-Fragmente*, 114 and 115, respectively.

52. Marquardt, *Gegenrichtung*, 14.

53. Marquardt, *Gegenrichtung*, 62.

54. It is not possible to summarize in a note Campe's thesis regarding the theory of probability and its influence on aesthetics and poetics from the

baroque to the early modern period in his monumental study *Spiel der Wahrscheinlichkeit*. With respect to the novel, Campe argues that Aristotle's comments on possibility and probability in his *Poetics* were decisive for theories of the novel in the seventeenth and eighteenth centuries, when German critics and novelists were still grappling with the basis for a genre that had no formal requirements (e.g., meter, unities of space and time). In Aristotle's comments on "probable impossibilities," they believed they found a justification for the novel as a form of knowledge unlike any other discourse, whether literary or prosaic. That the novel had to distinguish itself from all other prose discourses is itself an indication of the challenges the new genre raised for aesthetics. The novel's great strength for thinkers like Bodmer, Breitinger, and Gottsched was that it could frame a semblance as something probable (i.e., something that could occur in certain instances). In Campe's vocabulary, it turns the *Schein der Wahrheit* into a *Wahrscheinlichkeit*, a probability that, under the right conditions, could become an actuality. See Campe, *Spiel der Wahrscheinlichkeit*, 309–43.

55. Marquardt, *Gegenrichtung*, 62.

56. Marquardt, *Gegenrichtung*, 182.

57. See Kaufmann, "Romantische Aspekte," 93–109.

58. Kaufmann, "Romantische Aspekte," 98.

59. Bernhard, *Gehen*, 157. Also cited in Marquardt, *Gegenrichtung*, 14.

60. Schlegel makes a case in Atheneum Fragment 238 for a transcendental poetry that would at the same time be critical and would consequently "represent the producer along with the product [*das Produzierende mit dem Produck darstell[en]*]," in Schlegel, *Athenäums-Fragmente*, 127. Also cited in Kaufmann, "Romantische Aspekte," 99.

61. Kaufmann, "Romantische Aspekte," 102.

62. Kaufmann, "Romantische Aspekte," 104.

63. Much research has yet to be done on Bernhard's nostalgia, especially his frequent glowing descriptions of the "simple folk," like the gardeners in *Extinction*, his uncle Georg's devoted servant Jean, or even the loyal servant in *The Loser* (*Der Untergeher*) who helps Wertheimer burn his papers. Echoes of Benjamin's tribute to premodern life can be heard in Murau's remark about the gardeners: "They exuded the greatest tranquility and lived a life of harmony and routine" (*Auslöschung*, 130).

64. Benjamin, "Der Erzähler," 450.

65. Benjamin, "Der Erzähler," 449–50.

66. Schlichtmann observes that the novel's title encompasses the whole alphabet in *Das Erzählprinzip "Auslöschung,"* 27.

4. The Author

1. Zilcosky argues that this episode is characteristic of a number of modernist works in which the protagonist is no longer able to lose his way, as did the heroes of Romantic literature. Instead the modern protagonist repeatedly returns to the same spot, as if he is no longer able to venture outside himself. The idea that what defines modernism is the inability not to find but to lose oneself strikes me as a novel and striking thesis. See Zilcosky, "Lost and Found," 683.

2. Sebald, *Vertigo*, 33–34. Hereafter cited parenthetically in the text and the notes as *V*, followed by the page number. References to the German original *Schwindel. Gefühle.* will also be cited parenthetically in the text and the notes under the abbreviation sg.

3. The sickle was originally associated with Saturn, as the god of the harvest, and only in later years did it come to be associated with death, as the Grim Reaper. Although *Vertigo* was published two years before *The Rings of Saturn*, it anticipates this work in several ways. In "All'estero" the narrator's second trip to Italy falls during the "dog days" when the star Sirius is supposed to be in ascendance. Sirius represents the dog in the hunter Orion's constellation. In *The Rings of Saturn*, the narrator indicates that his journey unfolds during the "dog days": "It now seems to me that there is perhaps some justification to the old superstition that certain sicknesses of the body and of the soul tend to take root in us under the sign of the Dog Star." See Sebald, *Rings of Saturn*, 11, my translation. An analysis of the numerous references to dogs, Orion, and constellations in "All'estero" in particular, and *Vertigo* more generally, exceeds the scope of this chapter, although it is well worth pursuing, especially with reference to the question of whether Sebald's texts truly divide into different works.

4. Hell, "Angel's Enigmatic Eyes," 363.

5. See Hell, "Angel's Enigmatic Eyes," 377–80. Hell's article offers rigorous analyses of the political dimensions of Sebald's representation of historical catastrophes. My question concerns her conclusion that the narrator of "Air Wars and Literature" in particular and Sebald's work more generally avoids aestheticizing death and destruction by looking at the world with "deadened, ruined eyes . . . without pleasure." It strikes me that this conclusion comes close to a circular argument in which the use of aesthetic means to represent the horrors of war is defined as a denial of these horrors in the first place; as a result any pleasure in the representation constitutes a politically suspect gesture. Since any representation is by definition aesthetic, the "aestheticization" of death or history in literature is well nigh impossible

to avoid, unless one foregoes representing history and death, which would itself be a politically suspect project.

6. See Theisen, "Natural History," 563–81. Theisen was among the first critics to recognize Sebald's texts as allegories. In her reading of *The Rings of Saturn*, she argues that the narrator engages in practices of interpretation, which draw on the hermetic and cabbalist traditions popular in the fifteenth and sixteenth centuries.

7. Zilcosky identifies the passage in "The Uncanny" in which Freud recounts wandering in a circle in an Italian city only to return again and again to the same place as a paradigmatic example of the impossibility of getting lost in modernity, in "Lost and Found," 683. I am indebted to his essay for drawing my attention to Freud's essay and pointing out its significance for Sebald's autobiographical fiction and fictionalized travelogues.

8. Freud, "Das Unheimliche," 260, my translation.

9. Santner points to this passage to show Kafka's presence in the tale early on in *On Creaturely Life*, 117.

10. Musil, *Mann ohne Eigenschaften*, 33, my translation.

11. In Vienna the narrator talks to "jackdaws" (*V*, 42) and a single "white-headed blackbird," which could be a particular variety of this species—or, alternatively, a poetic invention designed to confuse the reader, who would search in vain for white-headed version of this species known to be black in its entirety. The reference to jackdaws ("Dohlen") is far easier to identify. As indicated previously, Kafka was well aware that his name was homonymic with the Czech *kavka*, for "jackdaw." The name of the hero of his tale "The Hunter Gracchus" is likewise based on the Italian *gracchio*, which means "jackdaw." The importance of Kafka's work in general and "The Hunter Gracchus" in particular cannot be overestimated in Sebald's text. In all four chapters, "The Hunter Gracchus" is cited more or less explicitly. With regard to the narrator's conversation with birds, it is possible that the text alludes at one and the same time to Kafka's name and Musil's story "The Blackbird," since the jackdaw is a specific variety of blackbird. It is also possible that a third figure is at play in the text: St. Francis of Assisi famously talked to sparrows and other creatures in nature. The text alludes as much to him as to Franz Kafka when referring to places like the train station "Franzensfeste" (*V*, 81) in South Tyrol and the "Franciscan nun" (*V*, 104) he sees on a train. Of note is that Grillparzer's full name was "Franz Seraphicus Grillparzer," which links him with Kafka, Francis of Assisi, and Giotto's paintings of seraphs, one of which is reproduced in "All'estero."

12. Fuchs shows in some detail how *Vertigo* in particular and Sebald's work more generally establish a web of relations between disparate events "in

order to allow an alternative, pre-rational truth to come to light through the evocation of secret correspondences" (*Schmerzenspuren*, 70). She argues that one might be inclined to align Sebald's work with an encyclopedic model of historical narrative due to its multilayered texture, but that this comparison ultimately mistakes what is at stake in his work, which is a subjectivity that comes to be through the potentially endless task of drawing connections as the labor of memory. Regarding the strange coincidences in Stendhal's and Kafka's lives, Gray notes that not only did the two writers visit Riva exactly a hundred years apart, but that they were also born a hundred years apart. He combs through a grant application Sebald submitted in 1988 in which he requested funding for the project we now know as the novel *Vertigo*. In the application Sebald identifies "Stendhal (*1783)" and "Kafka (*1883)" as the subjects of his project (60). The analysis of this one documents yields many valuable insights into the genesis of the work and the relation of biographical to autobiographical writing in Sebald's case. See Gray, *Ghostwriting*, 59–74.

13. See Barthes, "Death of the Author," 142–48. Barthes develops a similar position to the one I see at work in Sebald's text: he contends that the notion of the author as the organizing force behind a text is a rather late historical invention and one that will be short-lived, inasmuch as the proliferation of writing will make manifest that every text draws from and is constituted by other writings, not a single individual. In lieu of the term "author," he thus suggests that the person who writes be designated a "scriptor." The scriptor is merely the filter or mouthpiece for intersecting works or intertexts..

14. See Atze, "Koinzidenz und Intertextualität," 146–69, for an alternative model for understanding intertextuality in "All'estero." Atze divides the intertextual references in the chapter into three categories: texts that the narrator alludes to explicitly; texts that the reader identifies as implicit references; and texts that the reader associates with the work based on his or her own research into the people, places, and things mentioned in the chapter. While this classification is useful, I think it ignores the larger theoretical point that the work cannot be separated from any other, since, according to "All'estero," the world itself is a text, composed of intersecting pieces of writing.

15. The name "Ludwig" is one of the recurrent ciphers in the text. When the narrator arrives in Venice in 1980, he believes he sees King Ludwig II of Bavaria in a boat. He then refers to him in Italian as "Il re Lodovico" (*V*, 53). As I discuss in the next paragraph, Casanova relies on the work of Lodovico Ariosto to decide when to escape prison. In Milan the narrator stays at an inn on "Via Lodovico S" (*V*, 109). He also refers to the "power of

Ludwig [*die Macht Ludwigs*]" (*V*, 130; *SG*, 147). The recurrence of this name attests to the general structure of the return of the same in the text.

16. Banki, *Post-Katastrophische Poetik*, 61–65.

17. In his essay on Robert Walser, Sebald praises the Swiss author for the overlapping series of coincidences and correspondences in his work, which he calls "schemata of an incomprehensible order for us." See Sebald, "Le promeneur solitaire," 138.

18. The series of coincidences extends even further than I have represented. Fuchs observes that the narrator is reading a copy of Grillparzer's travelogue *Tagebuch auf der Reise nach Italien*, which he bought at a café in Vienna on the very anniversary of Casanova's escape from prison (*Schmerzensspuren*, 89–90). The anniversary falls on All Saints' Day, which is a fitting occasion for the return of so many ghosts from past centuries.

19. Schlegel, *Athenäums-Fragmente*, 125, my translation.

20. Kafka, "Der Jäger Gracchus," 285–88. Hereafter cited parenthetically in the text and in the notes in my translation as "Jäger." Scarcely an episode can be found in *Vertigo* that does not contain some allusion to Kafka's "Hunter Gracchus." In the first chapter, devoted to Henri Beyle—Stendhal's birth name—the narrator recounts that Beyle saw "two men in dark silver buttoned tunics . . . carrying a bier ashore on which, under a large, frayed, flower-patterned silk cloth lay what was evidently a human form" (*V*, 25). The passage is taken all but verbatim from Kafka's tale: "Two other men in dark tunics with silver buttons carried a bier behind the boatsman on which, under a large, flower-patterned silk cloth, a human being evidently lay" ("Jäger," 285). The same image returns in "All'estero" as the narrator recalls his abruptly ended 1980 trip to Verona: "Behind the boatmen, two figures in dark tunics with silver buttons carry a bier, upon which lies, under a large floral-patterned cover, what was clearly the body of a human being" (*V*, 164). Finally, in the last chapter the narrator recalls the death of the hunter Hans Schlag in his youth. Schlag, like Gracchus, tumbles to his death from his mountain station for inexplicable reasons. On his way home from school, the narrator chances upon a horse-drawn wagon with a sled behind it on which lay "what was plainly the body of a man under a wine-coloured horse blanket" (*V*, 246–47). For a discussion of the undead and being buried alive in one's thoughts, see Santner, *On Creaturely Life*, 116–18.

21. The resemblance between Sebald and his narrators is among the most seductive aspects of his work: it gives his texts the air of authenticity that defines their appeal and at the same time marks their literary inventiveness. A case in point for this is the woman the narrators of *The Emigrants* and *The Rings of Saturn* refer to as their lifetime partner. In both texts she is called

Clara, which was not the name of Sebald's spouse. The poetic license Sebald's texts take to generate the appearance of truth is what makes his work beguiling.

22. Hofmannsthal, *Andreas*, 257 and 239, respectively, my translation.

23. Hofmannsthal, *Andreas*, 234, my translation. Hofmannsthal's Lord Chandos is equally convinced that there are threads connecting disparate people, places, and things, but this web does not represent a hidden order that would be the truth of transient nature. Instead it is transitoriness itself that connects all things and makes any effort to find lasting meaning in them pointless.

24. Sebald frequently quotes from other authors without attributing the statements to them. Peter Filkins observes that unattributed quotes can be found throughout Sebald's work from Kafka, Thomas Browne, Proust, Celan, Adler, and Améry, among others. See Filkins, "Twisted Threads," 155.

25. Barthes's concept of the scriptor resembles what "All'estero" calls a "missing person." See Barthes, "Death of the Author," 142–48. The idea of a missing person, however, takes the concept of the scriptor further by relying on Kafka's novel *The Man Who Went Missing* (*Der Verschollene*) for its formulation. This allusion underscores that it is a series of intertextual references that constitute a text, not an individual, which even the term "scriptor" implies.

26. See Barthes, "Death of the Author," 142–48.

27. Ryan, *Novel after Theory*, 24.

28. Grimm's German dictionary defines *auftauchen* via the Latin *emergere*. A more expansive definition can be found in its entry on the root *tauchen*, which it defines as "a swift movement under the surface of a fluid body." The preposition *auf* changes the direction of this movement from a descent to an ascent.

29. This is but a brief sampling of the water imagery in the text; the image is so pervasive that it would require many pages to provide a partial inventory of all the references to water. It is worth noting, however, that the emphasis on water throughout the text aligns the narrator's travels with the wandering of the Hunter Gracchus on the waterways of the earth. Images of overflowing rivers also link several places named in the text: Vienna on the Danube, Venice on the Adriatic, and the Pyramids on the Nile.

30. Hunter Gracchus, of course, insists on the opposite. See Kafka, *Nachgelassene Schriften*, vol. 1, 378, for an earlier version in which the hunter declares, "Ich bin ja auch aus dem Binnenland. War kein Seefahrer, wollte es nicht werden, Berg und Wald waren meine Freude und jetzt–ältester Seefahrer, Jäger Gracchus Schutzgeist der Matrosen, Jäger Gracchus angebetet mit gerungenen Händen vom Schiffsjungen, der sich im Mastkorb ängstigt in der Sturmnacht."

31. Blanchot makes this point consistently throughout *The Space of Literature* and especially in the chapter "The Work's Space and Its Demand," which is my primary focus in this chapter: "The force of the writing impulse makes the world disappear. Then time loses its power of decision; nothing can really begin" (58).

32. Blanchot, *Space of Literature*, 60.

33. See Blanchot, *Space of Literature*, 61.

34. Kafka, *Tagebücher*, 663.

35. Kafka, *Tagebücher*, 838.

36. Blanchot, *Space of Literature*, 71.

37. Blanchot, *Space of Literature*, 75.

38. Blanchot, *Space of Literature*, 70.

39. Blanchot, *Space of Literature*, 75.

40. Sill, "Aus dem Jäger," 605.

41. I use Max Brod's edition of Kafka's stories in this chapter since, at the time Sebald was writing *Vertigo*, this would have been the standard edition of Kafka's work. Where necessary I make reference to the different versions of the story in Kafka's notebooks, which would have been available to Sebald in the volume *Hochzeitsvorbereitungen auf dem Lande und andere Schriften aus dem Nachlaß*, also edited by Brod and widely available in the 1970s and 1980s.

42. The statement from the early draft of Kafka's story can be found in Kafka, *Nachgelassene Schriften*, vol. 1, 311. The statement from Brod's published edition can be found in "Jäger," 288. I explain in footnote 41 my decision to use the Brod edition in the analysis of Sebald's appropriation of Kafka.

43. Blanchot, *Space of Literature*, 77.

44. Sebald, *Ringe des Saturn*, 11.

45. Sebald, *Ringe des Saturn*, 12.

46. Benveniste, "Nature of Pronouns," 217–21.

47. Kafka *Nachgelassene Schriften*, vol. 2, 56–57.

48. Jacobs, *Sebald's Vision*, xi.

49. Atze, "Koinzidenz und Intertextualität," 160.

50. The narrator sees Giotto's frescoes only on his second trip to Italy, much like Freud, who, in *The Interpretation of Dreams* reports that he was able to enter the church where Giotto's frescoes are located only during a second visit, although the path to the church keeps cropping up in his thoughts. See Freud, *Traumdeutung*, 42. Like Sebald's narrator, Freud insists on mentioning dates, as if to lay out in linear time an experience that hinted at time's circular structure.

51. An alternative etymology for the name "Gracchus" is that it derives from the Latin *graculus*, which also means "jackdaw." Additionally it is the name of a

Roman rhetorician whom Heinrich Heine mentions in his *Reisebilder*. Bianca Theisen notes that Heine is haunted by the ghost of Sempronius Gracchus while touring the Arena in Verona, and that this scene is reiterated in "All'estero," when the narrator flees from the Arena because he believes he is being followed by two men. See Theisen, "Prose of the World," 170.

52. Kafka, *Nachgelassene Schriften*, vol. 1, 383.

53. Schedel remarks that the year 1913 is "ein wiederkehrendes, rekurrentes und somit ahistorisches Moment in der Geschichtsvorstellung Sebalds," although she does not connect this observation with the narrative structure of this work. See Schedel, *Wer weiß*, 163.

54. The statement is cited in Benjamin and Scholem's correspondence. Brod is reported to have said that Kafka once told him, "Es gäbe unendlich viel Hoffnung vorhanden, nur nicht für uns." Cited in Walter Benjamin, Gershom Scholem, *Briefwechsel*, 273.

Conclusion

1. Wood argues that Heidegger is at pains to rescue the concept of a phenomenon from Cartesian metaphysics as a passive object at the disposal of an active subject. Heidegger defines a phenomenon early in *Being and Time* as "that which shows-itself-in-itself" (43), based on the roots of the term in the Greek verb *phanesthai*, which is "middle-voiced, neither active nor passive." See Wood, *Time after Time*, 43.

2. Regarding the relation between intentional objects and subjective acts in phenomenology, see §47 and §88 of the first volume of *Ideas*, where Husserl analyzes the correlation between intended objects and the intentional operations of consciousness (105–7). In §47 he states, "*Whatever physical things are*—the only physical things about which we can make statements, the only ones about the being or non-being, the being-thus or being-otherwise of which we can disagree and make rational decisions—*they are as experienceable physical things*, (106)." §88 belongs to the chapter on *noema* and *noeisis*, which are terms that Husserl introduces to designate the objective and subjective poles of lived experience and as his own variation on Descartes's *cogitatum* and *cogitationes* (*Ideas*, 213–16). The insight regarding the subjective constitution follows from the introduction of the *epoche* or bracketing of the supposition of the world's independent existence (60–62). Husserl claims that such a move is necessary to draw attention to how the world appears to us and how consciousness simultaneously intends it.

3. As discussed in chapter 2, Jakob is whisked away into the inner chambers when Lisa Benjamenta places her hands on his shoulders and tells him, "I would to show you something" (*JVG*, 98). The statement immediately

following this pronouncement reads, "We walked together. Everything lay veiled in an impenetrable darkness *before our eyes*, or at least mine, perhaps not for hers" (*JVG*, 98).

4. For Sebald's chosen literary paternity, see "Promeneur solitaire," 127–68. It is also notable that the photograph reproduced in *Vertigo* of the torso of a gentleman in a three-piece suit and a hat in his right hand is not the poet "Ernst Herbeck," as the text claims, but an edited version of a picture Carl Seelig took of Robert Walser and included in his account of years of wandering with the author, *Wanderungen mit Robert Walser*. The headless torso pictured in *Vertigo*, itself reminiscent of Rilke's "Archaic Torso of Apollo," stands in a manner that Sebald identified elsewhere with the posture of his grandfather. The link to the grandfather establishes Walser as Sebald's forebear.

5. Blanchot, "Song of the Sirens," 444. Hereafter cited parenthetically in the text as "Song," followed by the page number.

Bibliography

Adorno, Theodor W. *Aesthetic Theory*. Edited by Gretel Adorno and Rolf Tiedemann. Translated and with an introduction by Robert Hullot-Kentor. London: Bloomsbury, 1997.

Adorno, Theodor W., and Thomas Mann. *Briefwechsel, 1943–1955*. Edited by Christoph Gödde and Thomas Sprecher. Frankfurt am Main: Fischer, 2003.

Anderson, Mark M. "Fragments of a Deluge: The Theater of Thomas Bernhard's Prose." In *A Companion to the Works of Thomas Bernhard*, edited by Matthias Konzett, 119–36. Rochester: Camden House, 2002.

Aragon, Louis. *Le mentir-vrai*. Paris: Gallimard, 1980.

Arendt, Hannah. *The Human Condition*. With an introduction by Margaret Canovan. 2nd ed. Chicago: University of Chicago Press, 1998.

Aristotle. *Poetics*. Translated by S. H. Butscher. With an introduction by Francis Ferguson. New York: Hill & Wang, 1961.

Attridge, Derek. "Roland Barthes's Obtuse, Sharp Meaning and the Responsibilities of Commentary." In *Writing the Image: After Roland Barthes*, edited by Jean-Michel Rabaté, 77–89. Philadelphia: University of Pennsylvania Press, 1997.

Atze, Marcel. "Koinzidenz und Intertextualität: Der Einsatz von Prätexten in W. G. Sebalds Erzählung 'All'estero.'" In *W. G. Sebald*, edited by Franz Loquai, 146–69. Eggingen: Edition Isele, 1997.

Auerbach, Erich. *Mimesis: The Representation of Reality in Western Literature*. Translated by Willard Trask. New York: Anchor, 1957.

Banfield, Ann. *Unspeakable Sentences: Narration and Representation in the Language of Fiction*. London: Routledge, [1982] 2015.

Banki, Luisa. *Post-Katastrophische Poetik: Zu W. G. Sebald und Walter Benjamin*. Munich: Wilhelm Fink Verlag, 2016.

Bareis, J. Alexander. "The Role of Fictionality in Narrative Theory." In *Narrativity, Fictionality, and Literariness: The Narrative Turn and the Study of Literary Fiction*, edited by Lars-Åke Skalin, 155–75. Örebro SE: Örebro University Library, 2008.

Barthes, Roland. *Camera Lucida: Reflections on Photography*. Translated by Richard Howard. New York: Hill & Wang, 1981.

———. "The Death of the Author." In *Image, Music, Text*, translated by Stephen Heath, 142–48. New York: Hill & Wang, 1977.

———. *Writing Degree Zero*. Preface by Susan Sontag. Translated by Annette Lavers and Colin Smith. New York: Hill & Wang, 1968.

Beckett, Samuel. *Company*. New York: Grove, 1980.

———. *Malone Dies*. Translated by Samuel Beckett. In *Three Novels by Samuel Beckett*, 169–288. New York: Grove, 1965.

Behler, Ernst. *German Romantic Literary Theory*. Cambridge: Cambridge University Press, 1993.

Beierwaltes, Werner. *Identität und Differenz*. Frankfurt am Main: Vittorio Klostermann, 1980.

Benjamin, Walter. "Der Erzähler: Betrachtungen zum Werk Nikolai Lesskows." In *Walter Benjamin: Gesammelte Schriften*, edited by Rolf Tiedemann and Hermann Schweppenhäuser, vol. 2:2, 438–65. Frankfurt am Main: Suhrkamp, 1991.

———. "Robert Walser." In *Walter Benjamin: Gesammelte Schriften*, edited by Rolf Tiedemann and Hermann Schweppenhäuser, vol. 2:1, 324–28. Frankfurt am Main: Suhrkamp, 1991.

Benjamin, Walter, and Gershom Scholem. *Briefwechsel*. Edited by Gershom Scholem. Frankfurt am Main: Suhrkamp, 1980.

Benveniste, Emile. "The Nature of Pronouns." In *Problems in General Linguistics*, translated by Mary Elizabeth Meek, 217–21. Miami: University of Miami Press, 1971.

Bernhard, Thomas. *Alte Meister: Komödie*. Vol. 8 of *Thomas Bernhard: Werke*, edited by Martin Huber and Wendelin Schmidt-Dengler. Frankfurt am Main: Suhrkamp, 2003–15.

———. *Auslöschung: Ein Zerfall*. Edited by Hans Höller. Vol. 9 of *Thomas Bernhard: Werke*, edited by Martin Huber and Wendelin Schmidt-Dengler. Frankfurt am Main: Suhrkamp, 2005.

———. *Beton*. Vol. 5 of *Thomas Bernhard: Werke*, edited by Martin Huber and Wendelin Schmidt-Dengler. Frankfurt am Main: Suhrkamp, 2005.

———. "Gehen." Edited by Hans Höller and Manfred Mittermayer. Vol. 12 of *Thomas Bernhard: Werke*, edited by Martin Huber and Wendelin Schmidt-Dengler, 141–227. Frankfurt am Main: Suhrkamp, 2005.

———. *Holzfällen*. Vol. 7 of *Thomas Bernhard: Werke*, edited by Martin Huber and Wendelin Schmidt-Dengler. Frankfurt am Main: Suhrkamp, 2005.

———. *Korrektur*. Vol. 4 of *Thomas Bernhard: Werke*, edited by Martin Huber and Wendelin Schmidt-Dengler. Frankfurt am Main: Suhrkamp, 2005.

———. *Der Untergeher*. Vol. 6 of *Thomas Bernhard: Werke*, edited by Martin Huber and Wendelin Schmidt-Dengler. Frankfurt am Main: Suhrkamp, 2005.

Bernstein, J. M. *The Philosophy of the Novel: Lukács, Marxism, and the Dialectics of Form*. Minneapolis: University of Minnesota Press, 1984.

Blanchot, Maurice. "The Song of the Sirens: Encountering the Imaginary." Translated by Lydia Davis. In *The Station Hill Blanchot Reader: Fiction and Literary Essays*, edited by George Quasha, foreword by Christopher Fynsk, afterword by George Quasha and Charles Stein, translated by Lydia Davis, Paul Auster, and Robert Lamberton, 443–50. Barrytown NY: Station Hill, 1999.

———. *The Space of Literature*. Translated and with an introduction by Ann Smock. Lincoln: University of Nebraska Press, 1982.

Blanckenburg, Friedrich von. *Versuch über den Roman: Faksimiledruck der Originalausgabe von 1774*. Stuttgart: Metzler, [1774] 1965.

Borchmeyer, Dieter. *Dienst und Herrschaft: Ein Versuch über Robert Walser*. Tübingen: Niemeyer, 1980.

Callois, Roger. *Man, Play, and Games*. Translated by Meyer Barash. Champaign: University of Illinois Press, [1961] 2001.

———. "The Praying Mantis: From Biology to Psychoanalysis." In *The Edge of Surrealism: A Roger Caillois Reader*, edited by Claudine Frank, 69–81. Durham NC: Duke University Pres, 2003.

Campe, Rüdiger. "Form und Leben in der Theorie des Romans." In *Vita aesthetica: Szenarien ästhetischer Lebendigkeit*, edited by Armen Avanessian,Winfried Menninghaus, and Jan Völker, 193–211. Zurich: Diaphanes, 2009.

———. "Robert Walsers Institutionenroman: *Jakob von Gunten*." In *Die Macht und das Imaginäre: Eine kulturelle Verwandtschaft in der Literatur zwischen Früher Neuzeit und Moderne*, edited by Rudolf Behrens and Jörn Steigerwald, 235–50. Würzburg: Königshausen & Neumann, 2005.

———. *Das Spiel der Wahrscheinlichkeit: Literatur und Berechnung zwischen Pascal und Kleist*. Göttingen: Wallstein, 2002.

Cavarero, Adriana. "Narrative against Destruction." *New Literary History* 46, no. 1 (Winter 2015): 1–16.

———. *Relating Narrative: Storytelling and Selfhood*. Translated and with an introduction by Paul A. Kottman. London: Routledge, 2000.

Cohn, Dorrit. *The Distinction of Fiction*. Baltimore: Johns Hopkins University Press, 1999.

———. *Transparent Minds: Narrative Modes for Presenting Consciousness in Fiction*. Princeton NJ: Princeton University Press, 1978.

Coleridge, Samuel Taylor. *Biographia Literaria or Biographical Sketches of My Literary Life and Opinions*. Vol. 2. London: William Pickering, 1847.

Damerau, Burhard. *Selbstbehauptungen und Grenzen: Zu Thomas Bernhard.* Würzburg: Königshausen & Neumann, 1996.

Defoe, Daniel. *The True and Genuine Account of the Life and Actions of the Late Jonathan Wild; Not Made Up of Fiction and Fable, but Taken from His Own Mouth, and Collected from Papers of His Own Writing* (1725). Eighteenth Century Collections Online, Gale Cengage Learning, Gale Document Number CB427663371. Accessed October 28, 2018. http://find.gale.com .proxy1.library.jhu.edu/ecco/infomark.do?&source=gale&prodId=ECCO& usergroupName=balt85423&tabID=T001&docId=CB3327663372&type= multipage&contentSet=ECCOArticles&version=1.0&docLevel=FASCIMILE.

De Man, Paul. "Autobiography as De-Facement." In *The Rhetoric of Romanticism,* 67–81. New York: Columbia University Press, 1984.

Derrida, Jacques. "Cogito and the History of Madness." In *Writing and Difference,* translated with an introduction and notes by Alan Bass, 31–63. Chicago: University of Chicago Press, 1978.

Descartes, René. *Meditations on First Philosophy with Selections from the Objections and Replies.* Translated and with an introduction and notes by Michael Moriarty. Oxford: Oxford University Press, 2008.

Downing, Eric. *Artificial I's: The Self as Artwork in Ovid, Kierkegaard, and Thomas Mann.* Tübingen: Max Niemeyer Verlag, 1993.

Eyckeler, Franz. *Reflexionspoesie: Sprachskepsis, Rhetorik und Poetik in der Prosa Thomas Bernhards.* Berlin: Erich Schmidt Verlag, 1995.

Filkins, Peter. "Twisted Threads: The Entwined Narratives of W. G. Sebald and H. G. Adler." In *A Literature of Restitution: Critical Essays on W. G. Sebald,* edited by Jeannette Baxter, Valerie Henitiuk, and Ben Hutchinson, 149–65. Manchester: Manchester University Press, 2013.

Foucault, Michel. "Dream, Imagination, and Existence: An Introduction to Ludwig Binswanger's 'Dream and Existence.'" Translated by Forrest Williams. *Review of Existential Psychology and Psychiatry* 19, no. 1 (1984–85): 31–78.

Frederick, Samuel. "The Self-Destruction of the Enlightenment Novel: Voice and the Problem of Narration in Blanckenburg's *Beyträge zur Geschichte deutschen Reichs und deutscher Sitten.*" *Seminar: A Journal of German Studies* 49, no. 2 (May 2013): 148–70.

Freud, Sigmund. *Die Traumdeutung.* Vol. 2 of *Sigmund Freud: Studienausgabe,* edited by Alexander Mitscherlich, Angela Richards, and James Strachey. Frankfurt am Main: Fischer, 1972.

———. "Das Unheimliche." In *Psychologische Schriften,* 241–74. Vol. 4 of *Sigmund Freud: Studienausgabe,* edited by Alexander Mitscherlich, Angela Richards, and James Strachey. Frankfurt am Main: Fischer, 1972.

———. "Zur Einführung des Narzissmus." In *Psychologie des Unbewußten*, 37–68. Vol. 3 of *Sigmund Freud: Studienausgabe*, edited by Alexander Mitscherlich, Angela Richards, and James Strachey. Frankfurt am Main: Fischer, 1972.

Fried, Michael. "Barthes's *Punctum*." In *Photography Degree Zero: Reflections on Roland Barthes's Camera Lucida*, edited by Geoffrey Batchen, 141–69. Cambridge MA: MIT Press, 2009.

Fuchs, Anne. *Die Schmerzensspuren der Geschichte: Zur Poetik der Erinnerung in W. G. Sebalds Prosa*. Cologne: Böhlau Verlag, 2004.

Gallagher, Catherine. "The Rise of Fictionality." In *The Novel*, edited by Franco Moretti, vol. 1, 336–61. Princeton NJ: Princeton University Press, 2006.

Genette, Gérard. "Fictional Narrative, Factual Narrative." Translated by Nitsa Ben-Ari and Brian McHale. *Poetics Today* 11, no. 4 (1990): 755–74.

Gößling, Andreas. *Abendstern und Zauberstab: Studien und Interpretationen zu Robert Walsers* Der Gehülfe *und* Jakob von Gunten. Würzburg: Königshausen & Neumann, 1992.

Gray, Richard T. *Ghostwriting: W. G. Sebald's Poetics of History*. New York: Bloomsbury, 2017.

Grenz, Dagmar. *Die Romane Robert Walsers: Weltbezug und Wirklichkeitsdarstellung*. Munich: Wilhelm Fink Verlag, 1974.

Greven, Jochen. "Figuren des Widerspruchs: Zeit und Kulturkritik im Werk Robert Walsers." In *Über Robert Walser*, edited by Katharine Kerr, vol. 2, 164–93. Frankfurt am Main: Suhrkamp, 1978.

Grimm, Sieglinde. *Sprache der Existenz: Rilke, Kafka und die Rettung des Ich im Roman der klassischen Moderne*. Tübingen: A. Francke Verlag, 2003.

Hamburger, Käte. *The Logic of Literature*. Translated by Marilynn J. Rose. 2nd rev. ed. Bloomington: Indiana University Press, 1973.

———. *Thomas Mann und die Romantik: Eine problemgeschichtliche Studie*. Berlin: Junker & Dünnhaupt Verlag, 1932.

Hardenberg, Friedrich von. *Novalis: Werke*. Edited by Gerhard Schulz. 2nd rev. ed. Munich: C. H. Beck, 1981.

Harman, Mark. "Introduction: A Reluctant Modern." In *Robert Walser Rediscovered: Stories, Fairy-Tale Plays, and Critical Responses*, edited by Mark Harman, 1–14. Lebanon NH: University Press of New England, 1985.

Heftrich, Eckhard. "Der unvollendbare *Krull*—Die Krise der Selbstparodie." *Thomas-Mann-Jahrbuch* 18 (2005): 91–106.

Heidegger, Martin. "Die Frage nach der Technik." In *Vorträge und Aufsätze*, 5–36. Vol. 7 of *Martin Heidegger: Gesamtausgabe*, edited by Friedrich-Wilhelm von Hermann. Frankfurt am Main: Vittorio Klostermann, 2000.

———. "Der Ursprung des Kunstwerkes." In *Holzwege*, 1–72. Vol. 5 of *Martin Heidegger: Gesamtausgabe*, edited by Friedrich-Wilhelm von Hermann. Frankfurt am Main: Vittorio Klostermann, 2003.

Heidelberger-Leonard, Irene. "Auschwitz als Pflichtfach für Schriftsteller." In *Antiautobiografie: Thomas Bernhards Roman "Auslöschung*," edited by Irene Heidelberger-Leonard and Hans Höller, 181–96. Frankfurt am Main: Suhrkamp, 1995.

Hell, Julia. "The Angel's Enigmatic Eyes, or the Gothic Beauty of Catastrophic History in W. G. Sebald's 'Air War and Literature.'" *Criticism* 46, no. 3 (Summer 2004): 361–92.

Hiebel, Hans H. "Robert Walsers *Jakob von Gunten*: Die Zerstörung der Signifikanz im modernen Roman." In *Über Robert Walser*, edited by Katharine Kerr, vol. 2, 308–45. Frankfurt am Main: Suhrkamp, 1978.

Hobbes, Thomas. *Leviathan*. Edited and with an introduction by C. B. Macpherson. New Orleans LA: Pelican, 1968.

Hofmannsthal, Hugo von. *Andreas*. In *Erzählungen, Erfundene Gespräche und Briefe, Reisen*, 198–319. Vol. 7 of *Hugo von Hofmannsthal: Gesammelte Werke in zehn Einzelbänden*, edited by Bernd Schoeller. Frankfurt am Main: Fischer, 1979.

Honegger, Gitta. *Thomas Bernhard: The Making of an Austrian*. New Haven CT: Yale University Press, 2001.

Huizinga, Johan. *Homo Ludens: A Study of the Play-Element in Culture*. London: Routledge & Kegan Paul, 1949.

Husserl, Edmund. *Cartesian Meditations: An Introduction to Phenomenology*. Translated by Dorion Cairns. 7th ed. The Hague: Martinus Nijhoff, 1982.

———. *Cartesianische Meditationen und Pariser Vorträge*. Edited by Stephan Strasser. Vol. 1 of *Husserliana: Edmund Husserl Gesammelte Werke*. The Hague: Martinus Nijhoff, 1950.

———. *The Crisis of European Sciences and Transcendental Phenomenology: An Introduction to Phenomenological Philosophy*. Translated and with an introduction by David Carr. Evanston IL: Northwestern University Press, 1970.

———. *Ideas Pertaining to a Pure Phenomenology and to a Phenomenological Philosophy, Book I: General Introduction to a Pure Phenomenology*. Translated by F. Kersten. The Hague: Martinus Nijhoff, 1983.

———. *Die Krisis der europäischen Wissenschaften und die transzendentale Phänomenologie: Eine Einleitung in der phänomenologischen Philosophie*. Edited by Walter Biemel. Vol. 6 of *Husserliana: Edmund Husserl Gesammelte Werke*. The Hague: Martinus Nijhoff, 1954.

Iser, Wolfgang. *The Act of Reading: A Theory of Aesthetic Response*. Baltimore: Johns Hopkins University Press, 1978.

———. "The Reading Process: A Phenomenological Approach." *New Literary History* 3, no. 2 (Winter 1972): 279–99.

Jacobs, Carol. *Sebald's Vision*. New York: Columbia University Press, 2015.

James, Henry. *The Wings of the Dove*. London: Penguin, [1965] 1982.

Kafka, Franz. "Der Jäger Gracchus." In *Franz Kafka. Sämtliche Erzählungen*, edited by Paul Raabe, 285–88. Frankfurt am Main: Fischer, 1986.

———. *Nachgelassene Schriften und Fragmente*. Edited by Malcolm Pasley. 2 vols. Frankfurt am Main: Fischer, 2002.

———. *Das Schloß*. Edited by Max Brod. Frankfurt am Main: Fischer, 1968.

———. *Tagebücher*. Edited by Hans-Gerd Koch, Michael Müller, and Malcolm Pasley. Frankfurt am Main: Fischer, 2002.

Kaufmann, Sylvia. "Romantische Aspekte im Werke Thomas Bernhards." In *Thomas Bernhard: Beiträge zur Fiktion der Postmoderne*, edited by Wendelin Schmidt-Dengler, Adrian Stevens, and Fred Wagner, 93–109. Frankfurt am Main: Peter Lang, 1997.

Koskimies, Rafael. *Theorie des Romans*. Darmstadt: Wissenschaftliche Buchgesellschaft, [1935] 1966.

Kreienbrock, Jörg. *Kleiner. Feiner. Leichter. Nuancierungen zum Werk Robert Walsers*. Zurich: diaphanes, 2010.

Larmore, Charles. "The Ethics of Reading." In *The Humanities and Public Life*, edited by Peter Brooks with Hilary Jewett, 49–54. New York: Fordham University Press, 2014.

Lejeune, Philippe. *On Autobiography*. Edited and with a foreword by Paul John Eakin. Translated by Katherine Leary. Minneapolis: University of Minnesota Press, 1989.

———. *Moi aussi*. Paris: Seuil, 1986.

———. *Le pacte autobiographique*. Paris: Seuil, 1975.

Lukács, Georg. *Die Theorie des Romans: Ein geschichtsphilosophischer Versuch über die Formen der großen Epik*. 2nd ed. Munich: Deutscher Taschenbuch Verlag, 2000.

Magris, Claudio. "In den unteren Regionen: Robert Walser." In *Robert Walser*, edited by Klaus-Michael Hinz and Thomas Horst, 343–57. Frankfurt am Main: Suhrkamp, 1991.

Malkmus, Bernhard F. *The German Pícaro and Modernity: Between Underdog and Shape-Shifter*. New York: Continuum, 2011.

Mann, Thomas. *Bekenntnisse des Hochstaplers Felix Krull: Der Memoiren erster Teil*. Vol. 7 of *Thomas Mann: Gesammelte Werke in dreizehn Bänden*, edited by Peter de Mendelssohn, 2nd rev. ed. Frankfurt am Main: Fischer, 1974.

———. *Betrachtungen eines Unpolitischen.* Vol. 12 of *Thomas Mann: Gesammelte Werke in dreizehn Bänden,* edited by Peter de Mendelssohn. 2nd rev. ed. Frankfurt am Main: Fischer, 1974.

———. *Confessions of Felix Krull, Confidence Man: The Early Years.* Translated by Denver Lindley. New York: Alfred A. Knopf, 1955.

———. *Doctor Faustus: The Life of the German Composer Adrian Leverkühn as Told by a Friend.* Translated by John E. Woods. New York: Vintage, 1997.

Marquardt, Eva. *Gegenrichtung: Entwicklungstendenzen in der Erzählprosa Thomas Bernhards.* Tübingen: Max Niemeyer, 1990.

Middleton, Christopher John. "Der Herr Niemand: Anmerkungen zu Robert Walser mit einer Notiz über Walser und Kafka." Translated by Jochen Greven. In *Über Robert Walser,* edited by Katherine Kerr, vol. 3, 9–40. Frankfurt am Main: Suhrkamp, 1979.

Musil, Robert. *Der Mann ohne Eigenschaften.* Edited by Adolf Frisé. Hamburg: Rowohlt, 1952.

Naqvi, Fatima. *How We Learn Where We Live: Thomas Bernhard, Architecture, and* Bildung. Evanston IL: Northwestern University Press, 2016.

Nietzsche, Friedrich. *The Birth of Tragedy.* In *Basic Writings of Nietzsche,* translated and edited by Walter Kaufmann, introduced by Peter Gay, 1–144. New York: Modern Library, 2000.

———. *Die Geburt der Tragödie.* In *Friedrich Nietzsche: Werke in sechs Bänden,* edited by Karl Schlechta, vol. 1, 7–134. Munich: Hanser Verlag, 1980.

———. "Wahrheit und Lüge im außermoralischen Sinn." In *Friedrich Nietzsche: Werke in sechs Bänden,* edited by Karl Schlechta, vol. 5, 309–22. Munich: Hanser Verlag, 1980.

Peeters, Wim. "'Wenn kein Gebot, kein Soll herrschte in der Welt, ich würde sterben': Jakob von Gunten als Glossator." In *Gesetz. Ironie. Festschrift für Manfred Schneider,* edited by Rüdiger Campe and Michael Niehaus, 179–96. Heidelberg: Synchron, 2004.

Philippi, Klaus-Peter. "Robert Walsers *Jakob von Gunten.*" In *Der deutsche Roman im 20. Jahrhundert,* edited by Manfred Brauneck, vol. 1, 116–34. Bamberg: C. C. Buchners Verlag, 1976.

Pickford, Henry W. *Thinking with Tolstoy and Wittgenstein: Expression, Emotion, and Art.* Evanston IL: Northwestern University Press, 2016.

Pleister, Michael. "*Jakob von Gunten*: Utopie oder Resignation? Studie zu Robert Walsers Tagebuch-Roman." *Sprachkunst: Beiträge zur Literaturwissenschaft* 23, no. 1 (1992): 87–103.

Plug, Jan. *They Have All Been Healed: Reading Robert Walser.* Evanston IL: Northwestern University Press, 2016.

Rimmon-Kenan, Shlomith. *A Glance beyond Doubt: Narration, Representation, Subjectivity*. Columbus: Ohio State University Press, 1996.

Robert, Marthe. *Origins of the Novel*. Translated by Sacha Rabinowitch. Bloomington: University of Indiana Press, 1980.

Rousseau, Jean-Jacques. *The Reveries of the Solitary Walker*. Translated with notes, a preface, and an interpretive essay by Charles E. Butterworth. Indianapolis: Hackett, 1992.

Ryan, Judith. *The Novel after Theory*. New York: Columbia University Press, 2012.

Santner, Eric L. *On Creaturely Life: Rilke, Benjamin, Sebald*. Chicago: University of Chicago Press, 2006.

Saunders, Max. *Self Impression: Life-Writing, Autobiografiction, and the Forms of Modern Literature*. Oxford: Oxford University Press, 2010.

Schedel, Susanne. "Wer weiß, wie es vor Zeiten wirklich gewesen ist?" *Textbeziehungen als Mittel der Geschichtsdarstellungen bei W. G. Sebald*. Würzburg: Königshausen & Neumann, 2004.

Scheffel, Michael. "Käte Hamburgers *Logik der Dichtung*—ein 'Grundbuch' der Fiktionalitäts-und Erzähltheorie? Versuch einer Re-Lektüre." In *Käte Hamburger: Zur Aktualität einer Klassikerin*, ed. Johanna Bossinade and Angelika Schaser. Special issue, *Querelles: Jahrbuch für Frauen-und Geschlechterforschung* 8 (2003): 140–55.

Scheit, Gerhard. "Komik der Ohnmacht: Die Sehnsucht nach dem wahren Souverän und ihre Enttäuschungen bei Thomas Bernhard." In *Thomas Bernhard: Persiflage und Subversion*, edited by Mireille Tabah and Manfred Mittermayer, 147–58. Würzburg: Königshausen & Neumann, 2013.

Schlegel, Friedrich. *Athenäums-Fragmente*. Vol. 2 of *Kritische Schriften und Fragmente in 6 Bänden*, edited by Ernst Behler and Hans Eichner. Paderborn: Ferdinand Schöningh, 1988.

Schlichtmann, Silke. *Das Erzählprinzip "Auslöschung": Zum Umgang mit der Geschichte in Thomas Bernhards Roman* Auslöschung: Ein Zerfall. Trierer Studien zur Literatur 27, Frankfurt am Main: Peter Lang, 1996.

Sebald, W. G. "Le promeneur solitaire." In *Logis in einem Landhaus*, 127–68. 4th ed. Frankfurt am Main: Fischer, 2003.

——. *Die Ringe des Saturn. Eine englische Wallfahrt*. 5th ed. Frankfurt am Main: Fischer, 2002.

——. *Schwindel. Gefühle*. 5th ed. Frankfurt am Main: Fischer, 2003.

——. *Vertigo*. Translated by Michael Hulse. New York: Vintage, 2002.

Seelig, Carl. *Wanderungen mit Robert Walser*. Rev. ed. With an afterword by Elio Fröhlich and photographs by Carl Seelig. Frankfurt am Main: Suhrkamp, 1990.

Shawcross, Nancy M. *Roland Barthes on Photography: The Critical Tradition in Perspective*. Gainesville: University of Florida Press, 1997.

Siegel, Elke. *Aufträge aus dem Bleistiftgebiet: Zur Dichtung Robert Walsers*. Würzburg: Königshausen & Neumann, 2001.

Sill, Oliver. "Aus dem Jäger ist ein Schmetterling geworden: Textbeziehungen zwischen Werken von W. G. Sebald, Franz Kafka und Vladimir Nabokov." *Poetica* 29, nos. 3–4 (1997): 596–623.

Smith, Barbara Herrnstein. "Narrative Versions, Narrative Theories." In *On Narrative*, edited by W. J. T. Mitchell, 209–32. Chicago: University of Chicago Press, 1981.

Sorg, Bernhard. "Strategien der Unterwerfung im Spätwerk Thomas Bernhards." In *Rhetorik und Sprachkunst bei Thomas Bernhard*, edited by Joachim Knape and Olaf Kramer, 135–42. Würzburg: Königshausen & Neumann, 2011.

Sterne, Laurence. *The Life and Opinions of Tristram Shandy, Gentleman*. Edited by James Aiken Work. Indianapolis: Odyssey, 1940.

Theisen, Bianca. "Im Guckkasten des Kopfes: Thomas Bernhards Autobiographie." In *Politik und Medien bei Thomas Bernhard*, edited by Franziska Schößler and Ingeborg Villinger, 246–65. Würzburg: Königshausen & Neumann, 2002.

———. "A Natural History of Destruction: W. G. Sebald's *The Rings of Saturn*." *MLN* 121, no. 3 (April 2006): 563–81.

———. "Prose of the World: W. G. Sebald's Literary Travels." *Germanic Review* 79, no. 3 (Summer 2004): 163–79.

Tobias, Rochelle. "Walking Is Not Writing: Performance and Poetics in Walser's *Der Spaziergang*." In *Spazieren muß ich unbedingt. Robert Walser und die Kultur des Gehens*, edited by Annie Pfeifer and Reto Sorg, 39–49. Munich: Wilhelm Fink Verlag, 2018.

Todorov, Tzvetan. *The Fantastic: A Structural Approach to a Literary Genre*. Translated by Richard Howard with an introduction by Richard Scholes. Ithaca NY: Cornell University Press, 1975.

Utz, Peter. "Robert Walser." In *Deutsche Dichter des 20. Jahrhunderts*, edited by Hartmut Steinecke, 197–211. Berlin: Erich Schmidt, 1994.

———. "Robert Walsers *Jakob von Gunten*: Eine 'Null'-Stelle der deutschen Literatur." *Deutsche Vierteljahrsschrift für Literaturwissenschaft und Geistesgeschichte* 74 (2000): 488–512.

Walser, Robert. *Der Gehülfe*. Vol. 10 of *Robert Walser: Sämtliche Werke in Einzelausgaben*, edited by Jochen Greven. Frankfurt am Main: Suhrkamp, 1978–85.

———. *Die Geschwister Tanner*. Vol. 9 of *Robert Walser: Sämtliche Werke in Einzelausgaben*, edited by Jochen Greven. Frankfurt am Main: Suhrkamp, 1978–85.

———. *Jakob von Gunten: Ein Tagebuch*. Vol. 11 of *Robert Walser: Sämtliche Werke in Einzelausgaben*, edited by Jochen Greven. Frankfurt am Main: Suhrkamp, 1978–85.

———. *Der Spaziergang*. Vol. 5 of *Robert Walser: Sämtliche Werke in Einzelausgaben*, edited by Jochen Greven. Frankfurt am Main: Suhrkamp, 1978–85.

Watt, Ian. *The Rise of the Novel: Studies in Defoe, Richardson, and Fielding*. Berkeley: University of California Press, 1957.

Weitzman, Erica. *Irony's Antics: Walser, Kafka, Roth, and the German Comic Tradition*. Evanston IL: Northwestern University Press, 2015.

Wieland, Christoph Martin. *Geschichte des Agathon: Erste Fassung*. Edited by Fritz Martini and Hans Werner Seiffert. Stuttgart: Reclam, 2016.

Wirth, Uwe. *Die Geburt des Autors aus dem Geist der Herausgeberfunktion: Editoriale Rahmung im Roman um 1800*. Munich: Wilhelm Fink Verlag, 2008.

Wood, David. *Time after Time*. Bloomington: Indiana University Press, 2007.

Wysling, Hans. "Archivalisches Gewühl: Zur Entstehungsgeschichte der Bekenntnisse des Hochstaplers Felix Krull." In *Quellenkritische Studien zum Werk Thomas Manns*, edited by Paul Scherrer and Hans Wysling, 234–57. Vol. 1 of *Thomas-Mann-Studien*, edited by Thomas-Mann-Archiv. Tübingen: Francke Verlag, 1967.

Zilcosky, John. "Lost and Found: Disorientation, Nostalgia, and Holocaust Melodrama in Sebald's *Austerlitz*." MLN 121, no. 3 (April 2006): 679–98.

Index

Page numbers in italics indicate illustrations.

bildungsroman, 75, 84, 166n25

Binswanger, Ludwig, *Dream and Existence*, 12

birth, second, 58–59, 86

"The Blackbird" (Musil), 122, 178n11

Blanchot, Maurice, 78, 129–31, 133, 134, 140, 151–53, 182n31

Blanckenburg, Friedrich von, 155n3; *Essay on the Novel*, 2, 155n4, 155n7

Borchmeyer, Dieter, 166n25, 167n32

Brod, Max, 94, 132, 182n41, 182n54

Bühler, Karl, 70

Campe, Rüdiger, 2, 83, 155–56n7, 156n8, 168n41, 175–76n54

Casanova, Giacomo, 124, 127, 179n15, 180n18

The Castle (Kafka), 11, 131

Cavarero, Adriana, 160–61n5, 161n8

Cohn, Dorrit, 11, 70, 165n11

coincidences, 122–25, 126–27, 179n12, 179–80n15, 180n18

Coleridge, Samuel Taylor, 4, 160n1

Company (Beckett), 18

Concrete (Bernhard), 91, 157n22, 170n10, 170n13, 171n23

Confessions of Felix Krull, Confidence Man (Mann): context and precedents, 33–34; and Descartes's *Meditations*, 10; Dionysian turn in, 42–43, 47, 58, 66–67; as double fiction, 51–52; doubles in, 52–53, 56–58, 64, 66; fantasy in, 36–37, 54–56; and fortune in adversity, 37–39; illusion and spectacle in, 39–42, 45, 47, 51; and intermediary being, 53–54, 65–66; and light *vs.* dark, 36, 37, 40, 42–43; morality of, 59–60; and personae merger, 58–59, 60–61, 62–

66; suspension of disbelief in, 4–5; and unity of nature, 49–50, 61–62

consciousness: Descartes on, 11–12, 13–14, 16, 18; and doubt, 13, 15, 17–18, 158n39; intentionality of, 3, 22–23, 183n2; narration of in novels, 10–12; and subjectivity, 12, 15–16, 20–21

Correction (Bernhard), 90, 157n22, 169n4, 170n13

credibility, 4–5, 18–19

Damerau, Burghard, 97, 171n17

dark *vs.* light, 36, 37, 40, 42–43, 44

Das Leben der schwedischen Gräfin von G (Gellert), 3

death of the narrator: in *Extinction*, 92, 99–100, 104–5, 115–17; in *Vertigo*, 119, 127, 136, 144–46

Defoe, Daniel: *Robinson Crusoe*, 3, 24; *Jonathan Wild*, 4

De Man, Paul, 164n3

Derrida, Jacques, 18, 158n39

Descartes, René: critique of, 14–18, 158n32; *Discourse on Method*, 17; on evil genius, 13–14, 17–18, 19; on existence confirmed in thinking, 11–12, 13–14, 16, 18; *Meditations*, 10, 11, 12–14, 16–18, 158n38; and novel genre, 8, 157n19, 157n26

Dichtung und Wahrheit (Goethe), 34–35

Dionysian and the Apollonian, the, 26, 35, 43–51, 58, 66–67

documentary evidence, 136–39, *137*, *138*

Doktor Faustus (Mann), 34, 35

Don't Look Now (film), 139

double fiction: pseudo-memoirs as, 9; *Extinction*, 91–92; *Felix Krull*, 51–52; *Jakob von Gunten*, 72, 83–84, 87, 150; *Vertigo*, 125–26, 134–35, 150–51

Gößling, Andreas, 84, 87, 168n43
Gray, Richard T., 179n12
Greeks, understanding of the world,
    44–45, 106–8, 109
Grenz, Dagmar, 81, 166n25
Greven, Jochen, 81
Grillparzer, Franz, 121, 123, 133, 178n11
Grimm, Sieglinde, 16, 158n35
Gulliver's Travels (Swift), 3

Hamburger, Käte: critique of Hans
    Vaihinger, 164n6; on first-person
    vs. third-person narration, 12,
    69–72, 150, 164–65nn8–10, 165n14;
    The Logic of Literature, 10, 69; on
    the novel as genre, 10, 89, 156n8;
    parallels with Philippe Lejeune, 69,
    164n5
Heftrich, Eckhard, 55, 163n28
Heidegger, Martin, 35, 130, 162n16,
    174n43, 183n1
Heidelberger-Leonard, Irene, 97
Heimann, Moritz, 99
Heine, Heinrich, 182n51
Hell, Julia, 119, 177n5
Hiebel, Hans H., 166n31
hierarchy, 75–76
Hobbes, Thomas. See *Leviathan*
    (Hobbes)
Hofmannsthal, Hugo von. See *An-
    dreas* (Hofmannsthal)
Hölderlin, Friedrich, 130
Homer, 47; *The Odyssey*, 107, 118, 152
Huizinga, Johann, 31
"The Hunter Gracchus" (Kafka), 125,
    128, 131–32, 140, 142–45, 178n11,
    180n20, 181n30
Husserl, Edmund: *Cartesian Medi-
    tations*, 14; *The Crisis of European*

Sciences, 15, 16–17; critique of
    Descartes, 14–17, 158n32; on the
    epoché, 15, 21; *Ideas Pertaining to
    a Pure Phenomenology*, 15, 21, 111,
    158n34, 183n2; on intentionality of
    consciousness, 3, 183n2; on phe-
    nomenology method, 148; on tran-
    scendental phenomenology, 111, 152

illusion: and dreams, 36–37, 41–42,
    43–47, 51, 76; and fantasy, 36–37,
    54–56, 83, 85–86; and spectacle of
    the theater, 39–42, 45, 47, 51
imitation, 31–32, 35, 67, 71, 150, 155n5,
    160n2, 164n6
individuality, 32, 49, 62–63, 64–66, 76
Ingarden, Roman, 159n46
inner states, 78, 84–86
intentionality, 3, 22–23
interiority and exteriority, 107, 108–9,
    110–11
intermediary being, 53–54, 65–66
irony: Käte Hamburger on, 156n8;
    Georg Lukács on, 20, 110, 112,
    175n46; Novalis on, 72; Friedrich
    Schlegel on, 20, 110, 115
Iser, Wolfgang, 22, 159n46

Jacobs, Carol, 94, 136
Jakob von Gunten (Walser): as bil-
    dungsroman, 75, 84, 166n25; as
    double fiction, 72, 83–84, 87, 150;
    fantasy, 83, 85–86; hierarchy dy-
    namics, 75–76; law and instruc-
    tion, 78–79, 81–82; narratological
    dimensions, overview, 72–73;
    nothingness, 75, 80, 82, 88; paradox
    of service, 76–77, 79–80, 87–88;
    severing of mind and world, 148–

narrative theory, 8–9, 12, 68–72, 87

nature: and art, 44–45, 46, 50, 103; human unity in, 46, 49–50, 51, 61; photography as falsification of, 101, 103, 113

Nietzsche, Friedrich: on the Apollonian, 26, 43–47; *The Birth of Tragedy*, 26, 34, 35, 43–51; on the Dionysian, 35, 47–51, 66–67; as Thomas Mann's intellectual forebear, 34; *Genealogy of Morals*, 60; on the human being, 49, 61; on morality, 59–60; on republicanism, 76

nothingness, 75, 80, 82, 88, 105–6, 112

Novalis, 72, 111, 175n46, 175n48

novels: and Descartes's philosophy, 8, 157n19, 157n26; German, 24–25, 159–60n52; intentionality of subjectivity in, 22–23; interiority and exteriority in, 107, 108–9, 110–11; and lyric poetry, 19, 24, 43, 47–48, 50–51; narration of consciousness in, 10–12; narrative theory, 8–9, 12, 68–72, 87; realist genre, 8, 24, 152; and Romantic irony, 156n8; self-interrogation in, 155–56n7, 156n8; and tales, 152, 153; and totality, 108–10, 111–12; and tragedy, 19, 47, 48–49, 50–51, 63, 169–70n6; transcendental subjectivity in, 12, 19–21; and the true story trope, 4–5, 18–19. *See also* epic (genre)

The Odyssey (Homer), 107, 118, 152

patriarchs (biblical), 82, 87, 130

Peeters, Wim, 75

personae, 33, 58, 62–66, 155n4

phenomenology, as field and method, 3, 15–16, 147–48. *See also* Husserl, Edmund

Philippi, Klaus-Peter, 88

photography, 100–104, 113, 173–74n38

the picaro, 2

Pickford, Henry W., 162–63n22

Plato, *Symposium*, 54

Pleister, Michael, 168–69n48

Plug, Jan, 166n35

poetry. *See* lyric poetry

primal pain, 35, 45

primal unity, 45–46, 48, 50, 61–62

prosopopoeia, 22

pseudo-memoirs: *vs.* autobiographical genre, 8–9, 25; as double fiction, 9; as genre, 2–3; subjectivity in, 7–8

punctum of photographs, 102, 103–4, 173–74n38, 174n42

realist novels, 8, 24, 152

reality statement, 70–71

reason. *See* God and gods

rebirth, 58–59, 86

Reflections of a Nonpolitical Man (Mann), 24, 34, 161–62n11

repetition, 119–21, 140–42, 143, 144

republicanism, 76, 167n32

riddles, 79–80, 166n35

Rilke, Rainer Maria, 130; "Archaic Torso of Apollo," 184n4

Rimmon-Kenan, Schlomith, 22

The Rings of Saturn (Sebald), 23, 94, 122, 125, 133, 136, 177n3, 178n6, 180–81n21

The Robber (Walser), 73

Robert, Marthe, 1

Robinson Crusoe (Defoe), 3, 24

Rousseau, Jean-Jacques: *Confessions*, 24; *Reveries*, 10

Ryan, Judith, 127

Santner, Eric L., 178n9

Schedel, Susanne, 182n53

Scheit, Gerhard, 97, 171n17

Schlegel, Friedrich: on God's kingdom, 124–25; on irony, 20, 110, 115; on the novel, 25, 156n7, 165n13; on transcendental poetry, 111, 160n54, 176n60

Schlichtmann, Silke, 170n14, 171n16, 176n66

Schopenhauer, Arthur, 34, 44, 48, 162n22

Sebald, W. G., 137, 138; *The Emigrants*, 180–81n21; *The Rings of Saturn*, 23, 94, 122, 125, 133, 136, 177n3, 178n6, 180–81n21; and Robert Walser, 74, 180n17, 184n4. See also *Vertigo* (Sebald)

Seelig, Carl, 184n4

self-knowledge, 47

self-reflection process, 113–16

semblance and appearance: and disguise, 33; and doubles, 52–53, 56–58, 64, 66; and dreams, 43, 44, 45, 46; and imitation, 31–32, 35, 67, 71, 150, 155n5, 160n2, 164n6; and individuality, 32, 49; and lyric poetry, 48; and nothingness, 88; and personae merger, 58–59, 60–61, 62–66. *See also* illusion

service, paradox of, 76–77, 79–80, 87–88

Shawcross, Nancy M., 173n28

Sill, Oliver, 131

Smith, Barbara Herrnstein, 89, 91

Sorg, Bernhard, 170n15

space and time, 70–74, 78, 79, 83, 84–86

Der Spaziergang (Walser), 168n40

statement-subject, 69–72, 164–65n10

Stendhal, 122–23, 180n20

Sterne, Laurence. See *Tristram Shandy* (Sterne)

subjectivity: and intentionality, 22–23; statement-subject, 69–72, 164–65n10; transcendental, 7–8, 12, 19–21, 111, 114–15; of the world, 15–16

suspension of disbelief, 4–5, 31

Swift, Jonathan. See *Gulliver's Travels* (Swift)

tales, 152, 153

The Tanner Siblings (Walser), 73–74

theater and drama: illusion and spectacle of, 39–42, 45, 47, 51; *vs.* novels, 10, 24, 155n4

Theisen, Bianca, 119, 172n26, 178n6, 182n51

theoretical statement-subject, 164–65n10

third-person narration, 10–11, 12, 70–71, 164n8

time: circular, 119, 122, 125, 126–27, 129, 144–45; and photography, 101–2, 103, 174n42; present as past, 91, 93–94, 104–5; and space, 70–74, 78, 79, 83, 84–86; and writing process, 129–33, 134

Todorov, Tzvetan, 1

totality, 107–10, 111–12, 115–17

tragedy (genre), 19, 47, 48–49, 50–51, 63, 169–70n6

transcendental subjectivity, 7–8, 12, 19–21, 111, 114–15

transcendental unity, 106–9

Tristram Shandy (Sterne), 3, 23, 37, 162n19

truth: and credibility, 4–5, 18–19, 159n42; and God as reason, 17–18; and imitation, 31; metaphoric, 49; and paradox, 105–6, 112–13, 149–50

uniqueness and individuality, 32, 49, 62–63, 64–66
unity: and intermediary being, 53–54, 65–66; primal, 45–46, 48, 50, 61–62; transcendental, 106–9
universe. *See* the world

Vaihinger, Hans, 164n6
Vertigo (Sebald), *120*, *135*; allegorical space, 118–19, 129, 144–45; circular time, 119, 122, 125, 126–27, 129, 144–45; coincidences in, 122–25, 126–27, 178–79n12, 179–180n15, 180n18; death of the narrator, 119, 127, 136, 144–46; and documentary evidence, 136–39, *137*; as double fiction, 125–26, 134–35, 150–51; parallels with *The Rings of Saturn*, 122, 125, 133, 136, 177n3; repetition in, 119–21, 140–42, 143, 144; water imagery in, 119, 127–28, 181n29

Wagner, Richard, 34
Walser, Robert: *The Assistant*, 73, 74; *Der Spaziergang*, 168n40; *The Robber*, 73; and W. G. Sebald, 74, 180n17, 184n4; *The Tanner Siblings*,

73–74. See also *Jakob von Gunten* (Walser)
Watt, Ian, 8, 157n19
Weitzman, Erica, 75
wholeness, 107–10, 111–12, 115–17
Wieland, Christoph Martin. See *Geschichte des Agathon* (Wieland)
Wilhelm Meisters Lehrjahre (Goethe), 84, 166n25, 168n43
Wilke, Sabine, 172n26
Wilkomirski, Binjamin. See *Fragments* (Wilkomirski)
The Wings of the Dove (James), 11
Wirth, Uwe, 170n10
Wood, David, 183n1
Woodcutters (Bernhard), 91
the world: creation of meaning in, 20; Greeks understanding of, 44–45, 106–8, 109; middle, 44–45, 54; objective *vs.* subjective, 15–16, 21–22; rationality of, 16–18; secret order of, 124–25
writing process, 129–34. *See also* double fiction
Wysling, Hans, 34

Zilcosky, John, 177n1, 178n7

To order or obtain more information on these or other University of Nebraska Press titles, visit nebraskapress.unl.edu.